Alma Rubens,
Silent Snowbird

# Alma Rubens, Silent Snowbird

*Her Complete 1930 Memoir, with a New Biography and Filmography*

*by* ALMA RUBENS

*Edited by* GARY D. RHODES *and* ALEXANDER WEBB

McFarland & Company, Inc., Publishers
*Jefferson, North Carolina, and London*

LIBRARY OF CONGRESS CATALOGUING-IN-PUBLICATION DATA

Rubens, Alma, 1897–1931.
    Alma Rubens, silent snowbird : her complete 1930 memoir, with a new biography and filmography / by Alma Rubens ; edited by Gary D. Rhodes and Alexander Webb.
        p.     cm.
    Includes bibliographical references and index.

    **ISBN-13: 978-0-7864-2413-9**
    **ISBN-10: 0-7864-2413-3** (softcover : 50# alkaline paper) ∞

    1. Rubens, Alma, 1897–1931.  2. Motion picture actors and actresses—United States—Biography.  I. Rhodes, Gary Don, 1972–  II. Webb, Alexander, 1978–  III. Title.
PN2287.R778A3  2006
791.4302'8092—dc22
                                            2006010761

British Library cataloguing data are available

©2006 Gary D. Rhodes and Alexander Webb. All rights reserved

*No part of this book may be reproduced or transmitted in any form or by any means, electronic or mechanical, including photocopying or recording, or by any information storage and retrieval system, without permission in writing from the publisher.*

On the cover: Alma Rubens captured in a 1920s portrait (photographer unknown)

Manufactured in the United States of America

*McFarland & Company, Inc., Publishers*
  *Box 611, Jefferson, North Carolina 28640*
    *www.mcfarlandpub.com*

For our mothers
—G.D.R. and A.W.

# Acknowledgments

In preparation of this volume, we have been fortunate enough to work with a number of wonderful friends, colleagues, and researchers who have assisted in reconstructing Alma's life and career. These persons include Cory Bagby, Michael Copner, Geraldine Duclow, Coco Kiyonaga, Marina McDonnell, Christina McKillip, Henry Nicollela, Charlene Patterson, Michael F. Price, John Parris Springer, Karola Schwartz, Richard Sheffield, Anthony Slide, David Stenn, Nancy Waterhouse, Tom Weaver, Galen Wilkes, and John Wooley.

We would also like to acknowledge the resources of *Cult Movies* magazine, the Free Library of Philadelphia, the Margaret Herrick Library, the New York Public Library, North Texas University, the University of Central Oklahoma, and the University of Oklahoma.

The help of all of these people and organizations has been crucial to the completion of this work.

—Gary D. Rhodes and Alexander Webb

# Preface

Alma Rubens is not a name that modern filmgoers generally know. She still has her star on the Hollywood Walk of Fame, but unlike Marilyn Monroe's or James Dean's, it isn't often visited with flowers on fan pilgrimages to the movie capitol. No, Alma Rubens was a casualty of the star system, like so many others of time gone by. She and her films have faded.

To the degree she is remembered, it is much less for her individual film roles than for the tragic qualities of her own life: That she abused narcotics during the height of her Hollywood fame, that she spent time in mental institutions, and that she died so very young. It's the stuff that nightmares—not dreams—are made of.

Investigating Alma's life and career for this book meant the same kind of detective work that goes into most biographies, especially those of early film stars. Separating fan magazine fiction from reality, for example: Who did she marry and divorce? When was she actually committed for drug rehabilitation? It also meant developing a reliable filmography of her work and, in many instances, experiencing the joy of seeing her long-forgotten movies.

But our own biography and filmography serve as historically-anchored bookends for one of our greatest finds: Alma's own autobiography. A lost memoir of a silent film star, it's a time capsule of drug abuse and Hollywood in the Roaring Twenties. Embellished or not, ghost-written or not, well, those are difficult questions to answer precisely. What can be said is that the autobiography—which has never been published in book form—is one of the most fascinating pieces of literature to emerge from that period of the U.S. movie industry.

Two sides then of the same coin: The autobiography of a silent film star penned in 1930, alongside a retrospective biography written in the 21st century. We sincerely hope that this collection creates a newfound interest in Alma Rubens, so that a few more people will know who she really was when they pass over her name on the sidewalks of Hollywood.

—*Gary D. Rhodes and Alexander Webb*

# Contents

*Acknowledgments* v

*Preface* ix

**PART I. Editors' Biography** 1
    Life and Love   3
    Films and Acting   8
    Drugs and Death   25
    A Note on the Memoir   36

**PART II. *This Bright World Again***
    The Original Text   39

**PART III. Filmography** 199

*Appendix. Advertisements for Alma's Newspaper Autobiography* 227
    Notes to Part I   231
    Index   235

# PART I. Editors' Biography

> Alma Rubens *looks* like a character from the pages of an introspective novel. There is a pallor of skin, a certain depth and darkness of the eyes, hair like folded black wings. Then, too, a repose of manner, a reserve....[1]
> —*Motion Picture Magazine*, August 1920

> There is an air of nobility about Alma. Perhaps it lies in her seeming abstraction; a sense of noble detachment from the more harassing and mundane things of life; a sort of plastic serenity; a garment of glamour covering undertones of purple and passion. Or it may lie in the set of her head, poised and proud; in the remoteness of her eyes, when she is gazing into space; in the fine pallor of her skin, the firm modeling of her lips.[2]
> —*Motion Picture Classic*, October 1923

By 1918, actress Alma Rubens was a noted screen personality. By 1920, she was a major star. By 1929, she was hospitalized for drug abuse. By 1931, she was dead from its effects. Little more is generally said of Rubens, one of the first great female stars of the emergent feature film industry of the 1910s and one whose popularity continued over a fifteen year period. History is rarely kind to its casualties. Even a biographical sketch of Alma Rubens dwells as much on drugs and death as it does on her contributions to the world of film.

What more can we make of her, decades after her death? And why should we bother? Surviving films offer proof of a very talented artist and astute businesswoman. She was an actress whose onscreen subtleties often seem ahead of their time. Alma moved from genre to genre with ease, her versatility something to be very much admired. And Alma possessed that defining quality of the best silent film stars: a beauty for the ages, with the unchanging permanence of an icon. Film stock decomposes, but the impact of the face never does.

Critics and audiences regularly remarked on these qualities during Alma's career, even if we've largely forgotten them in the ensuing decades. For example, one reviewer noticed that in a particular film she was truly the "saving grace of the production."³ For another critic and another film, readers were told "her bathing suit will attract attention for its striking effect."⁴ The industry and audiences knew her for her talent and beauty, but Alma herself once said, "What does it all amount to, after all? What does [stardom] get you? A little money, easily spent. A little fame, easily forgotten. A little temporary glory. An illusion."⁵

The illusion shattered thanks to drug problems that brought scandal to the last two years of Alma's life. She had risen from poverty to the height of fame, only to be crushed by narcotics. It was a scandal particularly well-suited for the period. The candle had burned at both ends brightly, snuffed out by illicit cocaine and other drugs. There were headlines, many headlines. But even still, Alma's was certainly not the first Hollywood drug scandal. Olive Thomas and Wally Reid had garnered that kind of fame nearly a decade ahead of her. And Alma's headlines hardly ranked newspaper sales of the kind that Fatty Arbuckle or William Desmond Taylor had generated. Even Kenneth Anger's *Hollywood Babylon* (Simon and Schuster, 1975) places Alma in the same chapter with two other drug victims of the silent screen. Her scandal apparently wasn't fascinating enough to justify anything more.

This photo from the 1910s carried the following quotation when originally published in a fan magazine: "Alma Rubens is compelling, insinuating, yet always with troubled eyes seeing the futility of the future."

It is very true that Alma's problems weren't unique; the cases of actors like Juanita Hansen and Wallace Reid prove that. And her drug use offers as much or more insight into an early Hollywood star system careening out of control than it necessarily does of Alma herself. She was a casualty of narcotics and of Hollywood. The star system had claimed another victim, with the key word being "another." Hardly unique at all in those respects, one might say.

And yet there is Alma's face, that distinctive and unforgettable and completely unique face. It moves with gentle and subtle expression in her roles. It continues to gaze upon us even after the film has ended. Behind its eyes lurk joy and extreme sadness. And in front of its eyes are us, the audience. True, filmgoers have largely forgotten her, just as they have forgotten the temporary glory of most stars from the silent film era. But from old photographs and fan magazines and film footage, Alma still stares out at her audience, remembering them, with a face as unique as it ever was.

# Life and Love

At the time of Alma Rubens's death in 1931, newspapers noted how little was known about her early life.[1] She was born Alma Genevieve Reubens in San Francisco to John B. and Teresa[2] Hayes Reubens, on February 19, 1897, though some sources place the year of birth 1898 or later.[3] Alma was of French descent on her father's side, and Irish descent on her mother's side, a heritage that she mentioned during her career from time to time. She was also Catholic, and she was educated at the Sacred Heart Convent in San Francisco.

Later press accounts speak of her father's and mother's poor health and Alma's attempts to help out by earning whatever money she could. "Her earnings averaged about twelve dollars a week, not much for a family of three," one 1932 biographical story claimed. "Finally she succeeded in getting her mother in a hospital where she herself often managed to get along on the food that was left on her mother's tray."[4]

Publicity from the 1920s also often mentioned that Alma's desire to act came at an early age, and that it possibly stemmed from the relative poverty of her home life. Regardless, her opportunity arrived suddenly, when, according to one account:

> She happened to be present when a chorus girl in a musical comedy troupe [in San Francisco] was taken suddenly ill, and was asked to fill the place. Her success was immediate and she stayed with the show until Franklyn Farnum, a member of the same company ... induced her to change with him to the moving pictures.[5]

Circa 1914, Alma *did* appear on stage and make her way to Los Angeles and the studios. And given that Farnum did not play his first film role until 1914, it is possible that the quoted story is true. Alma certainly did move Los Angeles with her mother, who later recalled saying to Alma's father in San Francisco: "She's only sixteen and she needs me more than you do. ... Her papa understood, but it was hard for us both."[6] Why he remained in San Francisco rather than moving with Teresa at that time is an unanswered question; however, he at some stage apparently did move to (or at least visit) Los Angeles, as his 1916 death occurred in Los Angeles County.

A few years later, Alma married Franklyn Farnum in Los Angeles on June 14, 1918."[7] Immediately things seemed strange in that, when the press approached the couple, Farnum admitted the two had married while Alma denied it. Perhaps she made the denial because of a clause in her Triangle contract prohibiting her from marriage.[8] Regardless, the marriage soon failed.

Alma's second husband, Daniel Carson Goodman

According to Alma's claims in the divorce papers, problems began the day after the wedding in a Venice, California café when an intoxicated Farnum "cursed and swore" at Alma and "publicly slapped" her in the face.[9] Later that same day, Alma claimed he hit her again at her mother's house, dislocating her jaw. She also told the court that he hit her again on two subsequent occasions over the ensuing month, once at home and once in a hotel.[10] The union lasted for only some two months before Alma filed for divorce, which was eventually granted in December 1919.

Marriage and divorce did not dominate her thoughts, however. "I wish to goodness I could be a writer," she once said. "I wish it so much I've begun to try my hand at it...."[11] At times during her career, Alma spoke of interests other than acting, with writing always being among them:

> Fiction. Short stories. Friends of mine, critics, shall I say, tell me that my ideas are good, but my treatment can be improved upon. That's enough encouragement to begin with. I'm going to keep on trying.[12]

*Opposite:* **Alma and her mother Theresa shown at the height of Alma's career.**

As with any fan magazine accounts, it's difficult to say whether such quotations came from studio publicists or from Alma herself.

Alma's second husband Dr. Daniel Carson Goodman was himself a writer, a best-selling novelist, as well as a physician, producer, and director. The two wed on August 12, 1923 in Connecticut, but kept their marriage secret until the following year.[13] Alma had been affiliated with film projects at Goodman's own production company as early as 1920. By the time of the marriage, the two had ties to William Randolph Hearst's Cosmopolitan Pictures, at which Goodman became the studio head. In fact, Goodman was among the guests aboard Hearst's yacht when filmmaker Thomas Ince mysteriously died in 1924.

Alma's mother, Theresa Hayes Rubens

As with Alma's marriage to Farnum, problems supposedly began soon after the honeymoon. The two separated a little over four months after the wedding, with Alma filing for divorce in January 1924. To the judge, Alma alleged that on at least four occasions Goodman "cursed and swore" at her and "struck her in the face and about the body with his clenched fist."[14] On one of these occasions in August 1923, he supposedly knocked her unconscious while visiting the Adirondacks. She also claimed that Goodman hit her "across the jaw" with her own purse in their car on Christmas morning, 1923.[15]

Once the press wrote about the divorce suit, other alleged abuses came to light. Alma's mother was quoted as saying that "[Goodman] pulled [Alma's] hair and slapped her. I asked him to get out of the house because he wasn't supporting her or paying for the house anyway."[16] Alma also claimed Goodman had been verbally insulting. The *Los Angeles Times* mentioned that when "requested by the court to repeat the exact words, Miss Rubens demurred, but consented to the suggestion of her attorney, Richard Kittrelle, that she might whisper it to the court reporter, who might then read it to the judge."[17]

For his part, Goodman had initially declined to talk to the press, claiming, "...it is better under the circumstances that I say nothing."[18] Just before the trial, though, Goodman changed his mind and told the *Los Angeles Times* that he had "been very busy during the last year, and have seen Miss Rubens only occasionally. So, if Miss Rubens suffered from pugilistic complications, it must have been at the hands of some other sparring partner."[19] He also mentioned that the truth would emerge at the trial. But in the end he didn't contest the suit or her claims in court, and their parting was finalized on February 6, 1926.

In May 1925, while awaiting the final divorce decree, the press announced the next major news in Alma's life: she and her mother were heirs to a fortune in Australia. Michael Hayes, an Irish settler in Australia, had accumulated a fortune worth between $1,200,000 and $4,000,000 by the time of his death in approximately 1909. For some sixteen years heirs had been sought, with Alma and her mother numbered among them.[20] Their share was valued at around $300,000.[21]

Only months later, the press described Alma's third and final marriage, noting that at the time of her divorce from Goodman she had said, "her faith in marriage had not been shattered."[22] On January 30, 1926, she married film actor Ricardo Cortez in Riverside, California.[23] At the time, Cortez's film career was escalating higher and higher, as he appeared opposite Greta Garbo in *Torrent* (1926), her first Hollywood film. As for Alma, one press account claimed she would "retire from the screen after their marriage."[24] No retirement was possible yet, though, as she had immediate plans

**Alma and her third and final husband, actor Ricardo Cortez.**

to leave California for Idaho to act on location in a new film; the shoot meant the newlyweds' honeymoon was postponed.[25]

More than perhaps anything else, the press seized on the fact that the duo wed some days before Alma's divorce from Dr. Goodman became finalized.[26] The District Attorney for Riverside County announced an immediate investigation into the matter, telling the press that "it is an act of bigamy to marry without the final decree."[27] Cortez claimed that Alma's lawyers had said it was okay for the wedding to proceed, but they told the press that they in fact made no such statement. To solve the problem, the newlyweds decided to marry a second time, after the Goodman divorce decree was truly final. The Riverside D.A. gave his blessings and promptly dropped his investigation.[28]

The press initially considered Alma's life with Cortez a happy one, but the two separated in August 1928. A few months later, they reconciled. But the reunion was brief, with Cortez showing apparently little interest in his wife during 1929 and 1930. By September 1930, newspapers had spoken of her decision to divorce him on the grounds of desertion; she asked for alimony and $50,000 for her share of their property.[29] Several press accounts also carried Alma's story that Cortez received undue credit for helping her overcome drug addiction. "It was my own battle," Alma said. "My husband contributed very little toward helping me, most of the money coming from women friends."[30] Similar to her other marriages, the union was strained and relatively brief.

# Films and Acting

Alma fared far better in her career as a film star than she did with her marriages. The press in 1915 and in subsequent years generally claimed that her first film was a Rollin S. Sturgeon three-reeler titled *The Lorelei Madonna*, though she apparently did briefly appear in at least two earlier productions: *The Narcotic Spectre* (1914) and *The Gangsters and the Girl* (1914), both starring Charles Ray and directed by Scott Sidney.[1]

Produced in 1915 by Vitagraph and shot in the Los Angeles area, *The Lorelei Madonna* tells the story of a painter whose hope in life is to create a painting of the Madonna great enough to hang in Mission Chapel. In Tahiti, the painter visits a notorious dive where he meets "Alma," or "the Lorelei" as she is also called. Though she proves the perfect inspiration for his artwork, their love becomes strained when he tries to get her to leave Tahiti. A king, for whom The Lorelei regularly dances, becomes enraged at their affections and accidentally kills Alma with a bullet meant for the painter.[2]

Released on July 20, 1915, *The Lorelei Madonna* received strong praise from *The Moving Picture World*:

> The picture is a consecutive work of art, admirably constructed and presented in perfect settings.... The story grips, it excites an active interest in the characters and offers a really dramatic contrast in the shift from the spiritual quietude of the monastery to the tropical exuberance of Tahiti. ...Alma Reuben [sic] puts much intensity into her playing of the half-breed dancer.[3]

*The Lorelei Madonna* quickly brought Alma enough attention to be noticed by other West Coast producers.

While awaiting its release, Alma apparently appeared in a small role in the Oliver Morosco production of *Peer Gynt*, shot at Catalina Island, Imperial Valley, and the San Bernardino Mountains.[4] More importantly, Alma appeared in D.W. Griffith's monumental epic *Intolerance* (1916). In the fall of 1915, she and Ruth Darling and Margaret Mooney became the "Girls of the Marriage Market" in the Babylonian section of the film. Though *Intolerance* wouldn't be seen until the autumn of the following year, Alma's association with Griffith couldn't have hurt her next career move: a contract with the Triangle Film Corporation.

Triangle—formed by D.W. Griffith, Mack Sennett, and Thomas Ince—was incorporated in July 1915 with Thomas Aitken as its president. *The Moving Picture World* announced: "The energies of the three famous directors will be centered on the production of multiple reel photoplays in which stars from the legitimate stage will be featured."[5] Alma, after a brief appearance in a Kalem three-reeler titled *The Model's Adventure*, began appearing in a series of Triangle projects in 1916.[6]

Alma seen in Vitagraph's *The Lorelei Madonna* (1915), in which she played the title role.

"I made my screen debut with Triangle in *Reggie Mixes In*," Alma once told *Motion Picture Magazine*.[7] Released on June 1, 1916 and directed by Allan Dwan, the three-reel production featured her and Bessie Love opposite Douglas Fairbanks. Alma later claimed that Fairbanks had requested her as a costar. The trio would also appear together in the notorious Triangle film *The Mystery of the Leaping Fish* (1916), which featured Fairbanks as a drug-addled detective named "Coke Ennyday."

At the time, however, the industry trades lavished the most attention on her appearance in another Fairbanks film at Triangle, *The Half-Breed* (1916). Playing the female lead, Alma found the spotlight of attention. *Motion Picture News* wrote that she "deserves especial mention for her work."[8] But the question of precisely *who* she was remained: the cast listing and thus *Motion Picture News* dubbed her "Alma Reubens." The same would be true for Triangle's *The Children Play* (1916, which headlined Lillian Gish and included Alma in a sixth-billed role), and *Truthful Tulliver* (1917, starring William S. Hart and featuring Alma in a fourth-billed role). The exact spelling of her name would remain in flux early in her career.

Alma seen during her marriage to Daniel Carson Goodman.

Triangle soon paired her with Douglas Fairbanks again in *The Americano* (1917), in which she played the lead female role in an adventure story penned by Anita Loos and the film's director John Emerson. Released in January, Triangle again billed her as "Reubens." By the time the company released *A Woman's Awakening* (1917) in late March, she was "Reuben." By August 1917, for the dramatic film *Master of His Home* with William Desmond, she was "Ruben." A few months later, she headlined the cast of Triangle's comic western *The Firefly of Tough Luck* as "Rueben." And by November 1917, she was twice billed as "Rubens," in a small part in *The Cold Deck* (a western with Wil-

A 1920s portrait taken by photographer Edwin Bower Hesser.

Alma is pictured here seated at the table third from the left, next to Madge Bellamy and Prince Avezzanae. At right and around the table are Jorge Acosta, Ben Jackson, Maury Paul, Victor Shertzinger, Reginald Barker, Rowland V. Lee, Edmund Lowe, Marion Davies, Sol M. Wurtzel, Louella O. Parsons, and Emmett Flynn. Against the windows behind Alma are (from left to right) Jack Hill, Ricardo Cortez, E.C. Hill, and Buck Jones.

liam S. Hart and Mildred Harris) and a lead role in *The Regenerates* (a drama about drug addiction).

The spelling of her name was something that allegedly baffled even Alma. "As a matter of fact my name is not the same [spelling] as the painter's," she later told a reporter for *Photoplay*. "It's either Reubens or Ruebens—I forget which. I never could spell it. Couldn't remember where the 'e' came. So I let it go Rubens."[9]

To describe her first three years in film as a rapid ascension to fame would be somewhat accurate, but would gloss over the fact that she spent those two years alternating between small parts and lead roles. She did, after all, enter her association with Triangle as leading lady to the already well-known Douglas Fairbanks, but was still being cast in insignificant roles in other films as well. This was a period during which she was learning the film business, and films were learning the Alma Rubens business. The kinds of films in which she should appear was still a major question, as Triangle releases had shifted her from genre to genre.

By 1918, however, with her screen name crystallized as "Alma Rubens," she continued to grow in fame due to her work at Triangle. She was one of their most important leading ladies, and one who had recently scored strong reviews for films like *The Regenerates*.[10] And, at least in the eyes of the press, Triangle was perceived as a studio of major importance. As *Motion Picture News* reported at the beginning of that year, "Tri-

Alma in a sultry pose.

angle Forges Further Ahead." The article included a photograph of Alma, who "it is predicted, will corral new Triangle Triumphs."[11]

Their faith in her abilities meant that she had the lead role and top billing in every 1918 film in which she appeared: *I Love You, The Answer, False Ambition, The Painted Lily, The Love Brokers* (with Texas Guinan), *The Gown of Destiny* (based on an Earl Derr Biggers short story). She portrayed dramatic role after dramatic role. *Madame Sphinx* (also 1918) even featured Alma as an amateur detective solving a crime story.

Most importantly that year, she worked with legendary director Frank Borzage on Triangle's major production of *The Ghost Flower* (1918). The industry trades reported that the studio had created the most artistic and elaborate sets in its history to duplicate a Naples street scene for the film.[12] And

*Opposite:* **A publicity portrait taken shortly after Alma joined Triangle Films.**

*Moving Picture World* believed "Alma Rubens is an excellent type ... She has fine, expressive features, and the close-up holds no terrors for her. If anything, she gains by the nearer view. Her dramatic instinct is also true to form."[13] *Motion Picture News* more concisely proclaimed that Alma's acting in the film was the "best work of her career."[14]

Though her fame among moviegoers was firmly in place by the end of 1918, her association with Triangle was coming to an end. The studio itself dissolved due to a variety of problems ranging from the failure of *Intolerance* (1916) at the box-office to the departure of D.W. Griffith. In February 1919, Alma's final Triangle release—a drama entitled *Restless Souls*—played theater screens while she was busy setting up Winsome Stars, her own production company. The press took notice, as the new star was now in the producing business as well. "The Favorite of Millions," a Winsome advertisement called Alma, "[who] will appear in eight new and decidedly unusual photoplays."[15]

Alma as Cordelia in a 1921 Shakespearean pageant.

In April 1919, Winsome released their first film, *Diane of the Green Van*. Directed by Wallace Worsley, the film was shot partially in Los Angeles and partially on location in the Florida Everglades. In it, Alma plays a wealthy heiress who searches the country for excitement. *Moving Picture World* predicted good box-office receipts for the film, advising theater exhibitors to feature Alma's name in their advertising to help ensure profits.[16]

*A Man's Country*, the second Winsome Stars production, returned Alma to the western genre in a tale of the 1859 Gold Rush. John Lynch, formerly associated with Thomas Ince, penned the story. The cast included a third-billed Lon Chaney as "Three Card" Duncan. "Except for an occasional indulgence of heroics," wrote *Motion Picture News*, "Miss Rubens and her players are excellent."[17]

But perhaps they weren't excellent enough, as Winsome Stars seems to have disappeared from the cinematic landscape after *A Man's Country* disappeared from theaters. Instead of eight films, only two were finished and released. Within months Alma would be working for Cosmopolitan Productions, the William Randolph Hearst-owned studio that at the time was making Marion Davies films. Alma's brief foray into helming her own company ended with a lack of financial success, and as a result she's rarely been given credit for her forward-thinking plans.

Though billed third after Gaston Glass and Vera Gordon, Alma's star would glow all the brighter thanks to Cosmopolitan's *Humoresque* (1920). The film reunited her with director Frank Borzage in a scenario written by Frances Marion. The story—one of a violinist crippled by war that learns to play again thanks to love—captured the hearts of US theatergoers and became a major success that year. Alma told one movie magazine, "I think my role is giving me a chance to work from a different angle. That's another specific ambition of mine–to do something different, and I realize it's far from different to make that remark."[18]

Portrait published in the July 1919 issue of *Motion Picture* magazine.

Opening at the end of May 1920 at New York City's Criterion Theatre, *Humoresque* broke attendance records during its twelve-week stay. One notice in *Moving Picture World* announced to readers that "Alma Rubens is the featured member of the cast...."[19] Later in the decade, movie magazines would regularly point to *Humoresque* as a crucial turning point in Alma's career.[20] If she had "arrived" in the film business in 1918, she had conquered it in 1920.

Granted, *The New York Times* saw things differently. In their lengthy review of *Humoresque*, only one sentence mentions her name: "In the latter half of the narrative the heroine is Alma Rubens, and although her name is featured in the program, she has comparatively little to do."[21] Yet being

A theater marquee heralds Alma's film *The World and His Wife* (1920).

attached to such a beloved movie helped keep her career soaring, with audiences clearly thinking more of her work than some film reviewers.

Critical acclaim did come from her next 1920 Cosmopolitan film, a tragedy of jealousy and death. "Alma Rubens, whose work in *Humoresque* is entirely overshadowed by that of Vera Gordon, proves her quality in *The World and His Wife*," wrote *The New York Times*.[22] And *Moving Picture World* wrote, "When her acting ability is used to the best advantage she reaches a fine artistic level."[23] Critics also praised the Frances Marion scenario, the elaborate sets, and the use of valuable antique Spanish furniture and tapestries.[24]

For her third and final film of 1920, Alma appeared in *Thoughtless Women*, produced, directed, and written by her future husband Dr. Daniel Carson Goodman. She gave a performance "marked for its depth of feeling and understanding"[25] and showed a "lovely, dark beauty and a thoughtful evanescent charm."[26] The relatively simple story of a young woman prodded into marriage with a wealthy man by her greedy mother was crafted specifically for Alma, giving her much room for expression of character. *Motion Picture News* soon reported that the film was fast becoming an industry record breaker in the number of bookings secured for a feature film.[27]

With her strong career in place, Alma felt confident enough in 1920 to tell *Motion Picture* magazine that:

I am going, from now on, to do only the great things as I see them. I have served my apprenticeship, I think, at the lesser tasks, and I shall do nothing rather than go back to them now. Every so often in life, in work, in whatever you may be doing, you reach a certain limit, a certain definite outpost, and I have reached mine.[28]

The degree to which fan magazine quotations from this period are credible may be in question, but it does seem Alma became more particular about accepting film roles.

Not appearing in any 1921 films, Rubens returned to the screen and to Cosmopolitan in 1922. *The Valley of Silent Men* found her working once again with Frank Borzage and John Lynch. In it, she helps hide an innocent man accused of murder by the Mounties. "It's melodrama," *Photoplay* claimed, "but it is good melodrama.... A combination which agrees with most audiences."[29]

More famously, however, she appeared in a 1923 John Lynch-penned scenario called *Enemies of Women*. Its story has Alma's character fleeing Russia after her male companion has killed a Cossack in a duel. Shortly thereafter her companion discovers her with a young man that he mistakes for her lover. The companion eventually goes to fight in war, where he finds Alma's character acting as a Red Cross nurse. The two finally reconcile.

Alma pictured with actor Frank Mayo (far right).

Alma went on location in Paris, Monte Carlo, and Nice for *Enemies of Women*, working under the direction of Alan Crosland and alongside lead player Lionel Barrymore. She was ecstatic about the film shoots, returning excitedly to the US in November of 1922. The premiere of *Enemies of Women* in New York was particularly elaborate. *The New York Times* gave the following description:

> Ushered along a well-swept red carpet into the lobby of the theatre, then by girls in Russian costumes, with full skirts and flowing ribbons, one felt the atmosphere for the *Enemies of Women* was becoming more and more mysterious, especially when one's eyes met the exotic interior settings, suggesting Russianism and Futurism, all designed by Joseph Urban.
>
> Finally, about twenty minutes to nine, the Russian singers sent forth their voices to greet and please the guests of William R. Hearst, who had invited them in his own name to the theatre.[30]

The heavy promotion of the film didn't cease with the premiere. *Enemies of Women* marks one of the highest points in Alma's career; it was an acclaimed performance and one of the major Hollywood films of 1923.

But equal praise didn't greet her next Cosmopolitan film, *Under the Red Robe*. With a scenario by Bayard Veiller and direction by Alan Crosland, Alma played a third-billed role in the historical drama about a deadly duel. *The New York Times* suggested "...she is capable in her part, but again she does too much posing, instead of acting, in front of the camera."[31] And *Motion Picture Classic* claimed "Alma Rubens does not scale any emotional heights as the heroine."[32] Released in November of 1923, the film certainly undermined the heights of acclaim and success that *Enemies of Women* achieved only six months before.

Reflecting to a fan maga-

A publicity portrait

An unusual photograph of Alma enjoying a bite of candy.

zine on the changing kinds of publicity that film stars receive, Alma pronounced that:

> I would rather do without publicity than have a cheap brand of it. I think the publicity that Elsie Ferguson, Nazimova, and Mary Pickford have is ideal. It has a dignity which enhances the dignity of what they do. There is not enough thought given to the dignity of what we do in this profession. There is not enough reserve. Everything is blated [sic], in every way. Especially is this true of publicity. I do not think we are inclined to place sufficient reliance on the imaginations of others. We think we must fill every nook and cranny. In this way we do not stimulate so much as we encumber. I have very definite ideas of the strong yet quiet, the dignity and the yielding with which I should like to do all things pertaining to my work.[33]

She didn't mention more precisely what constituted the dignity of publicity she desired, but it was certainly not the kind of poor reviews given to her performance in *Under the Red Robe*.

Perhaps to help offset the bad notices, Alma appeared in another Daniel Carson Goodman film released in February 1924. Goodman wrote *Week End Husbands*, but this time left direction to E. H. Griffith. Jazz and booze cause Alma's character to come under the sus-

Alma Rubens in a "dignified" publicity portrait.

picions of her husband, with the rumor mill spreading gossip that she's been unfaithful. But even with all the partying she had remained true, and the two reunite after a brief period apart. Alma's costars included Maurice Costello, but the critics took little notice of either performer or the film as a whole.

Two new Rubens films played theater screens in May 1924, though one received much more publicity than the other. First National's *Cytherea* featured a third-billed Alma in a cast with Lewis Stone, Irene Rich, Norman Kerry, and Constance Bennett. Though for the *New York Times* the film *Cytherea* "possesses very little effective drama," it did have:

> ... some exquisite sequences of color photography, in which one enjoys the sight of the varied hues and tints of Cuban costumes and scenery. There is a delightful lot of color in one interior: one sees an officer in blue and red, women in green and pink, and possibly the most startling effect in the embroidery on the women's shawls.[34]

And if critics weren't wholly convinced by the merits of the story, some found Constance Bennett very pleasing, apparently more so than Alma.[35]

*The Rejected Woman*, Alma's other May 1924 release, is rather indicative of much of her overall output for the year. She headlines the cast in a rather undistinguished film from an undistinguished production company. *The Rejected Woman* is generally remembered today because of Rubens's costar Bela Lugosi, famed "Dracula" actor and horror film star who would reveal his own drug

Alma in an unknown role from the 1910s.

addiction to the world in the 1950s.

1924 brought a wave of Rubens's films to theaters, but they were generally unimportant. Only one film of that year could be said to have added to her reputation. Produced by Fox and released in October, *Gerald Cranston's Lady* featured Alma and James Kirkwood in a domestic drama directed by Emmett J. Flynn. Filmed on location in England, the movie offered Alma a strong female lead without the internal competition of other important female roles. It was also the key factor in nabbing Alma a five-year Fox contract.[36]

Alma shortly after returning to Fox to make *The Heart of Salome* (1927).

As her screen career moved into 1925, Alma found time to dub the movies a "funny business," claiming that:

> It seems to proceed in a series of little panics.... The trouble is, someone puts on a good costume picture and makes a fortune out of it. Then everybody else makes a mad gallop to put on more costume pictures. Naturally, most of them are rotten pictures. The result is, the public will have none of them. Then, the producers decide that they don't like costume pictures after all.[37]

And the funny business meant that while her heart was set on playing a part in any of the John Golden-Smith plays which Fox purchased in 1925 (*Lightnin,*' *The First Year*, or *The Wheel*), she didn't get the opportunity.

But Alma did appear in six films in 1925, four of which were for Fox, apparently part of her new contract with them. *The Dancers*, released in January 1925, was directed by Emmett J. Flynn and co-starred her with George O'Brien and Madge Bellamy. The *New York Times* believed that:

> By far the best performance in this picture is that of Alma Rubens, who seems ahead of everybody in her appreciation of what the situations

demand. With a curl of hair over her right eye, she makes a bewitching Argentinean dancer.

Even though not always garnering such praise, Alma's Fox releases continued throughout the rest of 1925. *She Wolves* cast her opposite Jack Mulhall, and *The Winding Stair* co-starred her with Edmund Lowe and Warner Oland.

*East Lynne*, her final Fox film of the year, would become the most successful of the group. Directed by Emmett J. Flynn and costarring Edmund Lowe and Lou Tellegen, the film was based on the famed 1861 novel by Mrs. Henry Wood. Though some reviews called the film too long and even artificial, the cast was repeatedly praised for their strong work. Alma gave "a thoroughly fine performance," according to *The Film Daily*.[38]

Alma's non-Fox films of 1925 included *A Woman's Faith*, a melodrama for Universal that costarred Percy Marmont, Jean Hersholt, and ZaSu Pitts, and *Fine Clothes*, a comedy/drama for Louis B. Mayer Productions. The latter was based on Ferenc Molnar's play *Fashions for Men*, and featured Lewis Stone and Percy Marmont. Reviews of *Fine Clothes* were strong, and the specific mentions of Alma were very positive. *Motion Picture News* claimed she "really acts,"[39] *Moving Picture World* suggested she crafted her performance "splendidly,"[40] and the *New York Times* called her "appealing and convincing."[41]

Alma's work for Fox continued throughout 1926, resulting in another three films. *The Gilded Butterfly* was a drama featuring her and Bert Lytell, while *Siberia* reunited her with Edmund Lowe and Lou Tellegen. The most interesting, however, is *Marriage License?*, a domestic drama that costarred Walter McGrail and Walter Pidgeon. Fox shot the film on the West Coast following Alma's post-*Siberia* vacation on the East Coast. Though in large part an unimportant film, it became Alma's last teaming with director Frank Borzage. During her career, Alma had been repeatedly paired with directors like Emmett Flynn or actors like Percy Marmont. However, none of her ongoing collaborations were as critically and artistically successful as the one with Borzage.

Examining Alma's career as it stood in the mid-to-late 1920s is of course a generally disheartening task, as each year that passes shows the ravages her personal life had on her professional one. Her unreliability meant, for example, that Greta Garbo replaced her as the female lead in *Torrent* (1926). To survey the films Alma did complete shows diminishing numbers: six films in 1925, three in 1926, and only one in 1927. And that one 1927 film, *The Heart of Salome*, would be her final movie for Fox. Her five-year contract, signed at the beginning of 1925, would not even be half completed.

*The Heart of Salome* is itself an interesting film, one whose production began with a "rousing welcome" at Fox after Alma "at last returned to their midst after her long period of illness."[42] Walter Pidgeon and Holmes

Alma and Jack Conway in a still from 1919's *Restless Souls*.

Herbert costarred, with Alma taking top billing. "Miss Rubens is attractive and for the most part competent," *The New York Times* noted.[43] The film came the same year that a representative of the Edward Small Agency sued Alma for over a thousand dollars. The lawsuit claimed she owed the money as a result of some work they obtained for her over two years earlier. In a written statement, Alma told the court the company had never obtained any employment for her, and her attorney was successful in his motion to get the case thrown out.[44]

Her legal success hardly translated to cinematic success, however. For 1928, Alma appeared in only one film, *The Masks of the Devil*. An MGM movie directed by Victor Sjöström and with continuity by Frances Marion, *Masks of the Devil* headlined John Gilbert. Alma played the female lead and received second billing, suggesting perhaps she maintained an ongoing appeal with audiences. But many of her scenes had to be shortened, and Frances Marion noted that on the set her "drifting speech and glassy eyes" illustrated the toll that drugs were taking.[45]

In 1929, Alma appeared in her two final films. Both were released in the summer of that year, and both featured Alma in supporting roles. Henry

King's part-talkie *She Goes to War* starred Eleanor Boardman, with Alma taking fourth billing. And for the screen's first version of *Show Boat*, produced by Universal Studios and starring Laura La Plante, Alma received fifth billing. It hadn't been since her early days with Triangle that she had been cast in such small parts. "I have constantly the feeling that what I am doing is impermanent, unimportant, and soon forgotten," Alma once said.[46] Though not necessarily true given her star on the Hollywood Walk of Fame sidewalk and moderate interest in her work among silent film specialists, Alma's movie career was forever over by 1930.

# Drugs and Death

"I am going to hold on to the things Youth says,"[1] Alma once told an interviewer, though she almost certainly didn't mean narcotics. Exactly when she started using drugs is unknown. Few people outside of family and friends would have suspected her drug use until it made a major splash in the media of 1929. If the addiction is largely the reason why Alma is remembered today, the world scarcely knew of it until the Roaring Twenties were ending.

The *New York Times* began reporting on Alma's unusual behavior during 1928 and early 1929.[2] In November 1928, for example, she was accused of intoxication, use of abusive language, and accessory to assault and battery at the scene of a Hollywood car wreck. And in January 1929, neighbors complained to the police about a "wild party" in her apartment.[3] One report even claimed she "staged 'wild brawls' and of prowling around the premises at night poking flashlights at windows in the apartment."[4] The charges were serious enough to lead to a "Peace Breach" trial, at which time Alma did not appear. The judge immediately issue a warrant for her arrest, but recalled it after hearing Alma's excuse that she had misunderstood the date of the trial.[5] She had to post a $500 while awaiting the rescheduled court appearance.

To the public, Alma's downfall would seemingly have started about this point; along with disturbing the peace, a stream of press reports made clear what had only been hinted in prior years of vague, unnamed "illnesses." The coverage also shows why Alma never physically appeared in court for the rescheduled trial date. The *New York Times* began their series of stories on January 26, 1929 with a notice entitled "Alma Rubens Put in a Sanitarium."[6] The article detailed her two escapes from an ambulance transporting her to a private, unnamed sanitarium. To flee the first time, she stabbed Dr. Emil W. Meyer with a "paper knife" and then "ran screaming down Hollywood Boulevard."[7] Recaptured once by Meyer and an assistant, she then escaped a second time only a few blocks away. Once finally delivered to the sanitarium, she was admitted under the name Genevieve Driscoll, a pseudonym drawn from her own middle name and her maternal grandmother's maiden name.[8] An aunt announced to the press that her problems stemmed from "a complete nervous collapse as a result of overstrain during the making of motion pictures."[9]

A little over two weeks later, the drug addiction story broke to the press. The leak apparently came when she was transferred in mid-February to the Hollywood Hospital for a "surgical operation."[10] By this point, federal and state agents were already completing the first phase of their criminal investigation. *The New York Times* reported that between September 21 and October 17, 1928 alone, a Dr. L. Jesse Citron issued thirty-one prescriptions for Rubens in exchange for $1,200. Along with the investigation, the State Medical Board was already discussing revocation of Citron's license.[11]

The press immediately followed up on Alma's condition, mentioning on February 17, 1929 that she had left the Hollywood Hospital and returned to her Beverly Hills home. "My daughter has promised to break the habit if it costs her life," Alma's mother Teresa announced.[12] Meanwhile, agents revealed that their investigation had expanded to seven more physicians. Citron, however, remained the name that appeared the most in the press.

Returning home did not help Alma, and by late afternoon on February 18, 1929, Alma was returned to the same "private sanitarium."[13] After only one week, *The New York Times* reported

Alma pictured after her marriage to Ricardo Cortez.

that Alma was back at home but "sinking" into a "critical condition." Private doctors held a meeting at her house on either February 24 or 25.[14] Their solution was that her mother and husband should immediately ask a judge to issue a warrant to confine Alma under official care. By February 26, 1929, at a special midnight session of court to avoid publicity, a judge complied with their request, immediately sending Rubens to the Spadra State Hospital.[15] Worst of all, perhaps, the *Times* even spoke of her stardom in the past tense.

As for Ricardo Cortez in this moment of trouble, the *Los Angeles Times* claimed that he "is constantly at his wife's bedside."[16] One story claimed that during the late twenties Cortez became involved in trying to "watch Alma" carefully, as well as her "so-called friends."[17] On one occasion, he discovered—or thought he discovered—that a physician had been selling drugs to his wife and taking her jewels, one by one, in pay-

Alma and Ricardo Cortez reunited at the Warwick Hotel in February 1930 when Alma seemed on the verge of a comeback.

ment. According to a *Good Housekeeping* article, he went "straight to the alleged scoundrel and, with his two fists, succeeded in making him disgorge."[18] Little was heard of Cortez after February 1929, however, as he and Alma became more and more estranged.

As the calendar turned to March 1929, the press continued to keep readers abreast of Alma's condition. Thomas F. Joyce, the superintendent of

Spadra, remarked on an improved and "very satisfactory" condition.[19] That same month, however, things looked worse for Dr. Citron. A federal grand jury indicted him in mid-March for violation of the Harrison Narcotics Tax Act. Evidence ranged from records of prescriptions to interview testimony from Alma's mother.[20] Citron's case would not go to trial until 1932, and though he was acquitted, he did spend some time suspended from his position at the Santa Monica Hospital.[21]

Though for health reasons Alma did not appear before the March 1929 grand jury hearings, by April 10 her situation had improved to the point that Dr. Joyce paroled her from Spadra; she returned home to her mother in a state of "marked improvement." The press announced Alma would probably convalesce in the mountains of Southern California.[22] Within two weeks, Alma attacked her private nurse and threatened suicide. Her mother called the police, whom Alma held at bay for three hours while they tried to overpower her. Later Alma's mother signed a complaint that landed Alma in the Southern California State Hospital for the Insane at Patton.[23]

By mid-May 1929, Alma was in their care.[24] The press reported that her most recent outbursts were due to ongoing drug use, which triggered a new round of investigations. After extensive press coverage of her habit and formation of a grand jury on the Citron matter, how did Alma manage to get narcotics? The newspapers reported that she had given a diamond ring to a fellow addict at Spadra, leading to some speculation that it was in trade for drugs.[25] A federal narcotics agent extensively questioned Alma at Patton. Though he refused to give details to the press of their talks, the agent made clear that Rubens gave him invaluable information on the Hollywood narcotics racket.[26]

Throughout the summer and autumn of 1929, the press spoke little about Alma and the investigations surrounding her drug use. She was still at the asylum, and while the narcotics investigation was presumably continuing, it apparently received no publicity. Little would be heard of Alma until November 1929, when Early Jensen, Director of State Institutions, announced that she would soon be released from Patton. The superintendent of Patton announced that she was "completely cured."[27]

The following month, just days before Christmas 1929, *The New York Times* announced that "Alma Rubens, once prominent on the stage and motion picture screen, has been released as cured from the state asylum at Patton...."[28] Unnamed "members of her family" claimed she had gone into seclusion at her mother's ranch, but Bruce Large, Alma's brother-in-law and resident of the ranch, denied the story.[29] The newspaper also reported on letters from Alma to unnamed friends in Los Angeles that read: "I am coming out of the hospital a new Alma Rubens. I shall devote all of

## Drugs and Death

A promotional postcard

my time to the work of going back to work on the stage and screen a better actress."³⁰

Likely Alma's first performance after her release came at the very beginning of 1930. "She appeared at a party given by the Writer's Club in the leading role of a one act playlet," where—according to a press account—she was "cheered to the echo by as hard-boiled an audience as ever assembled in Hollywood."³¹ Then, pausing in Chicago during a trip to New York City in February 1930, Alma told the press:

> I feel grand, and I have found during my long illness that this old world is a great place to live in. I've fought a hard battle and I owe my victory to the friends, many I never knew I had until I needed them so desperately.
>
> I'm so thrilled at going to New York and catching up with all the new shows. Remember, it's a year since I've been inside a theater. After the sanitarium restrictions the smallest pleasures are exciting, even my breakfast cup of coffee.³²

At the same stop, Alma also announced her forthcoming New York meeting with producer Sam Harris about appearing in one of his plays. She also spoke about a lead role she had been offered in a film, as well as an opportunity to do a vaudeville tour.³³

Broadway didn't exactly herald her arrival, but Alma soon appeared in a 17-week vaudeville act at an alleged salary of $1,500 a week. Her vaudeville movements took her to the Coliseum in New York during the second week of March, the 58th Street Theater in New York during the second week of April, and the Regent in Patterson, New Jersey in the fourth week of April.³⁴ In May, she appeared in Boston, in Brooklyn, in Providence, and then again in New York City.³⁵ A critic for *The Billboard* was at the latter performance, noting that:

> Miss Rubens, whose name has appeared often enough in the public prints of late to warrant a flier in vaude, should have made her sojourn under the frank monicker [sic] of a personal appearance rather than to have gone to the trouble of getting up this big mess about nothing.³⁶

The same critic noted that Alma's ten-minute appearance generated a good deal of applause.

After a week at New York's Fordham at the end of May, Alma next performed her act in Cincinnati in mid-June. A *Billboard* reviewer caught the show, reacting more favorably than the response given to her performance in New York. But by that time, Alma "suffered with a heavy cold, and, as a result, did only about half of her act.... A good-sized hand marked Miss Ruben's exit, and returned for a brief curtain speech, in which she voiced an apology for not being able to do all her 'stuff.'"³⁷

"Since I can remember, almost, it has been my ambition to go on the stage. While I was working in the West it did not seem feasible, but now that I'm in New York and have the opportunity—well, I confess that I have the manuscript of a play right now that I'm considering."[38] Alma spoke those words in 1920 while in New York making *Humoresque*, but her Broadway dreams never came true until she was at her lowest ebb in late 1930. After doing more vaudeville in the summer, Alma was offered the lead female role in *With Privileges*, a play by Ruth Welty. *With Privileges* was already in its fifth week at the Belmont when she took over the part from Edith Broder, though presumably Alma had been an understudy or at least rehearsing in some fashion in the

An advertisement in the January 8, 1931, issue of the *New York Daily Mirror* publicizing the serialization of Alma's autobiography.

week or more prior to walking onto the stage.[39]

The New York press certainly covered the story of the movie star–turned–drug addict–turned–Broadway lead in the days leading up to her first performance on October 13, 1930, but little publicity followed opening night. The entire play folded only days later on October 22, with no more stage offers forthcoming. On December 15, 1930, Alma left New York for the West Coast with her friend Ruth Palmer, a Broadway showgirl. It had been her mother and sister who convinced her to return to California. Friends who saw Alma off at the train depot described her as "emaciated."[40] Later one of them claimed that Alma had said that she didn't want to die on Christmas Eve "away from Mother."[41] Alma did not mention being near Cortez, as she had of course started divorce proceedings a few months earlier in September 1930; they had apparently not seen each other for months and months.[42]

Shortly after Alma had returned to California, newspapers offered the latest revelation in their ongoing coverage of Alma's problems. On January 6, 1931, the *New York Daily Mirror* headlined the story "ALMA RUBENS SEIZED ON COAST FOR DOPE." Alma had spent the prior night in a San Diego jail, where she sobbed, "I don't want my mother to know about this!" Her car had been impounded, and she faced charges of possessing 100 grams of cocaine and making plans to smuggle Mexican morphine into the US. A federal district court set her bail at $5,000.[43]

It came to light that Alma had started using drugs again during the East Coast vaudeville tour, with a New York physician writing the prescriptions. According to Ruth Palmer, Alma used drugs during their East to West Coast travel. It was a wild and screaming Palmer who attracted the attention of San Diego police. Part of her complaint alleged that on the drive back to the U.S. Alma "had Ruth's clothes almost off, then pushed her out of the car."[44] Shortly before Palmer's charges were filed, Alma's mother had told police to keep a careful watch on her daughter's movements.

Details of the charges revealed that Alma had spent three days in Agua Caliente, Mexico, in an effort to obtain drugs. She successfully purchased cocaine, which she had sewn into the lining of an evening gown for re-entry into the U.S. When booked

Alma shortly before her death.

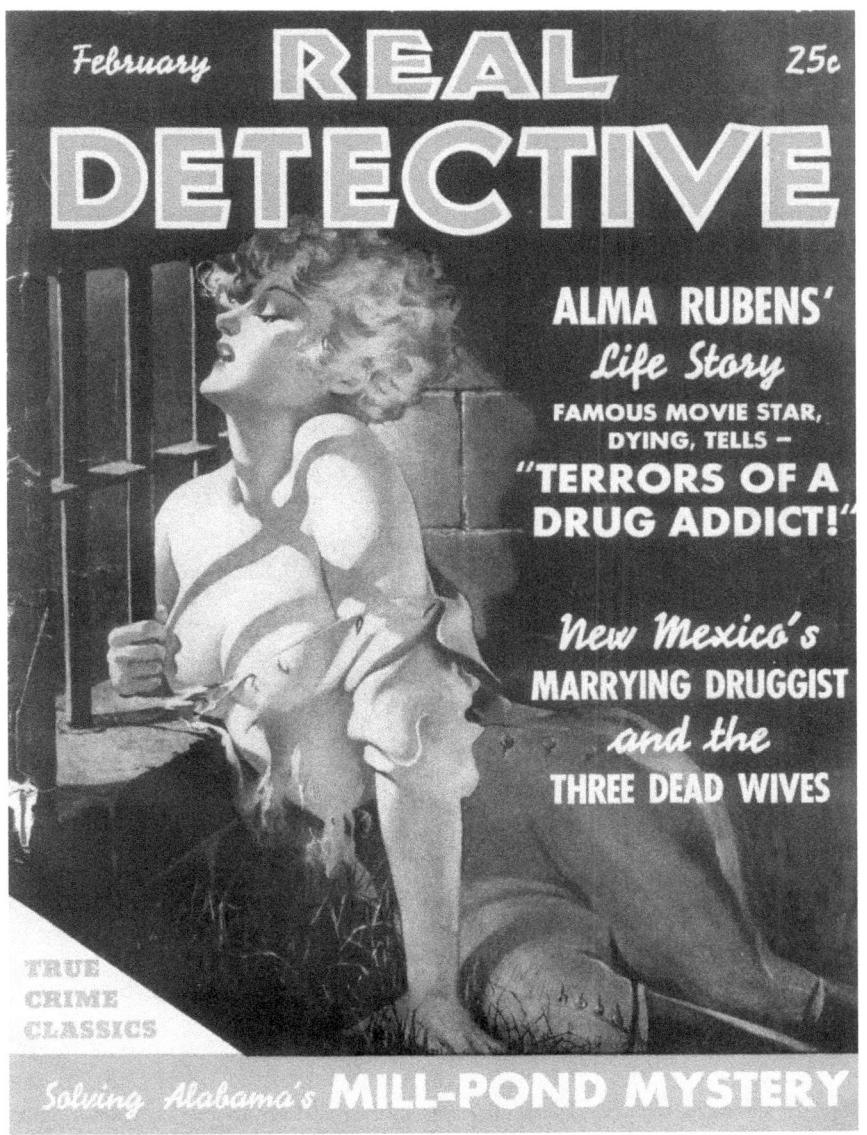

Cover of the February 1938 issue of *Real Detective* in which Alma's autobiography appeared in abbreviated form.

in San Diego, Alma was in what the *New York Daily Mirror* called a "hysterical, frantic, almost delirious" state. "I was framed," she cried. "All I've had is a little champagne!"[45] Alma accused Palmer of planting the drugs in her dress, and even accused her chauffeur of stealing an expensive brooch.

By January 7, 1931, the press had new details, mentioning that the police charges were filed against Alma and Ruth Palmer as well. Apparently the duo had been using drugs together since sharing a New York apartment right before the move back to California. They had quarreled in Los Angeles, but patched up their differences enough to make the trip to Mexico in search of more drugs. Alma's mother arranged bail money, getting Alma a rapid release. Palmer, unable to raise money, remained in jail.[46]

After giving names of drug pushers to federal agents, Alma went to Los Angeles, soon contracting a bad cold that developed into double lobar pneumonia. Her condition quickly grew worse, causing her mother to take her to the home of Dr. Charles Pflueger, on January 18, 1931. According to the *New York Herald Tribune*, the doctor was so worried about her condition that

A reflective Alma in an undated portrait.

Alma's signature byline as it appeared when her autobiography first saw print.

**Pallbearers at Alma's funeral carrying her last remains from the Little Church of Flowers in Glendale, California.**

he "feared to remove her to a hospital."[47] Alma slipped into a coma, in which she lingered for three days before dying on January 21, 1931. Her mother, her sister Hazel Large, three physicians, and two nurses were all at her bedside.[48] The death certificate cites lobar pneumonia as the official cause of death, with bronchitis listed as an added factor.[49] Pflueger told the *Los Angeles Times* that "death to Miss Rubens was peaceful. She had been irrational, but shortly before she passed away she was calm, her breathing becoming lighter and lighter until her strength entirely failed."[50] Alma was, depending on the press accounts, only 31 or 33 years old.

"Alma died fighting," her mother was quoted. "I'm proud of her."[51] At a public funeral at the Little Church of the Flowers at Forest Lawn Cemetery in Glendale on January 22, 1931, long lines of mourners appeared to pay their final respects. Police had to hold back the crowds when Ricardo Cortez arrived to kneel at Alma's casket before draping it with flowers; he had not seen her for months and had only learned of her death the day after she passed away.[52] Immediately after the funeral, the Gates, Crane, and Earl Funeral Home moved Alma's remains to Fresno to inter them the next morning in a mausoleum at Mountain View Cemetery; the interment services were conducted with only a small number of friends and family present.[53] Alma's final resting place was very near the family ranch at Mountain View Cemetery.[54] Allegedly, her mother placed the urn of her late husband John Reubens's ashes under Alma's arm for burial.[55]

Aside from the initial tributes and retrospectives in the fan magazines, Alma essentially disappeared from the public eye. A few months after her death, a federal court did look into the issue of who owned the impounded car that Alma and Ruth Palmer were driving when they were arrested in January 1931; Alma's mother appeared to announce that she owned the vehicle that in the court's eyes had been used to transport narcotics into the US from Mexico.[56] In 1939, Alma's name came up in a trial and then the press when Dr. Citron—still practicing medicine in Southern California—sued film comedian W.C. Fields for nonpayment of services rendered.[57] Later, a photo of Alma did circulate among the press in February 1942 whose caption spoke of the devastating effects of narcotics. The caption strangely added wartime propaganda that "American people were intended victims of Jap dope as a gigantic plot to break down American morals."[58] From the 1950s until the publication of Kenneth Anger's *Hollywood Babylon* (Straight Arrow, 1975), she rated even less publicity.

# A Note on the Memoir

"Poor, lonely Alma Rubens. What she does go through is frightful to contemplate let alone relate."[1] A critic once spoke those words about Alma's character in the film *Siberia* (1926), but they seem even more suited to the misfortunes that she suffered in real life, misfortunes that she wrote about at length in her long-forgotten autobiography. One fan magazine article published shortly after Alma's death spoke about her literary efforts, suggesting that,

She found time to write her experiences. Professional writers had told her once that she would have done really fine things if she had turned her talents to fiction, but this which she wrote now was not fiction. It was fact. Stark, terrible fact. She called her book, This Bright World Again. The title itself tells a story.[2]

Presumably *This Bright World Again* is the text that became serialized in the *New York Daily Mirror* in 1931 and then became published in an abbreviated form in *Real Detective* magazine in late 1938. And it is that serialized text that we can now examine after decades of being buried in the musty pages of a long-defunct newspaper.

Of course the question of verisimilitude regarding this autobiography is in need of an answer, though it's difficult to give one of any weight beyond informed speculation. We can say that there is an error or two in its pages. One gaffe is seemingly present in Chapter One, which states that Alma was born just after the turn of the century, when it seems she was born just before it. But that may well be the kind of intentional error that stars often make in order to appear younger than they are.

More importantly, the bulk of the text, laboring more on her early life and especially her drug addiction than on her career, conveys stories and details that would be difficult for anyone else to have known. Also, if Alma's mother Teresa had not endorsed the text as authentic when it first surfaced in 1931, she almost certainly would have greeted it with a lawsuit. After all, Teresa had sued Photoplay Publishing Company for $1,000,000 damages in a libel suit due to a *single* story that they published about Alma in the April 1931 of *Photoplay* magazine.[3] Teresa was still alive when the *Real Detective* publication of this autobiography occurred as well, but apparently took no legal action against it either.[4]

Our own speculation is that Alma dictated memories to an unidentified party sometime in late 1930. That would explain occasional shifts we detect in the autobiography's "voice" which go back and forth from being very much the sound of someone talking informally to an occasionally more formal and journalistic tone. A dictation/interview would also well explain the error in Chapter 11 where director Christy Cabanne is listed as Christy "Cavany," an error that seems similar to the type committed when taking notes listening to a speaker. And these notes, rather than becoming a book, became a serialized newspaper story. That the autobiography was serialized led to even further changes in voice, as subsequent newspaper printings condensed some chapters or even rewrote some sections. The edition printed herein is an amalgam of the chapters printed in the *Daily Mirror*, combined with another newspaper run where issues of the *Daily Mirror* no longer seem to exist.[5]

That the text lingers on Alma's early life and on her drug rehabilitation(s) might say something of her state of mind in late 1930 when this account was written. These pages devote some time to discussing life on the set and Alma's film successes, to be sure. And a small amount of the euphoria of drug parties is present here as well. But these topics are very subordinate to her nostalgic longing for an innocent past before her entering into the world of drugs. At the same time, of course, the space devoted to the addiction could also have been seen as desirable by a ghost writer or agent in the belief it would hold the greatest reader interest.

Ghost-written or not or somewhere in between, the text is a lost document of film history that deserves examination. The work holds extreme importance for being a period chronicle of the film industry and star system of the 1910s and 1920s. It is a major account of drug addiction and its treatment in the 1920s. It is the most exhaustive period account of any of the great scandals of early Hollywood. It is a work that speaks to the kind of information readers of the day wanted to learn about "Hollywood Babylon." And it is also the most comprehensive account of the life of Alma Rubens.

Lastly, this is a text that uses the word "snow" as slang for cocaine, with "snowbird" being a female addict. We have appropriated that phrase spoken by Alma herself for the title of this volume with the greatest of intended respect. Alma knew that she had "fallen into the clutches of the monster dope" and that it had become a major part of her legacy. As we think about her hopes at the end of Chapter 44 that someone would buy the book of her "ghastly failure of a life," we also think about her follow up statement that she can then "escape to rest and peace and home." And we also believe that film history should not, as she hoped, "forget snowbird." Silent snowbird, who knew she left a legacy of scandal, but seemed unaware that she left behind a trove of cinematic treasures that offer important insights into Hollywood culture and filmmaking of the teens and twenties.

—*Gary D. Rhodes and Alexander Webb*

# PART II.
# This Bright World Again

## The Original Text

### CHAPTER ONE

One midnight just a few weeks after the turn of the century, 'Old Doc' Washington Dodge, who survived the sinking of the Titanic and died a few years ago, was aroused from an armchair nap in the study of his home on McAllister Street, San Francisco, by a frantic pounding on the door.

A terrific gale and electrical storm was sweeping in through the Golden Gate and the rain was falling in torrents. The old man, exhausted and worn from a long vigil at the bedside of a dying patient, frowned with an air of exasperation. Then he drew his dressing robe more tightly around his portly form and shuffled to admit his nocturnal visitor.

The caller, a woman, wet, bedraggled and out of breath, was a neighbor of Theresa Hayes Reubens, long a resident of the neighborhood at No. 13 Buchanan Street.

"Hurry up, doctor," she cried hysterically. "Hurry up. Mrs. Reubens is going to have a baby!"

"Tut, tut!" the kindly old physician soothed her. "That's nothing to get excited about. Seems like all the women are doing that same thing these days, and," and he paused a moment while he peered gloomily at the belching heavens, "it seems like they always do it at midnight, too, just when a man ought to be getting some more sleep."

Wearily, he donned his great coat and arctics and followed the woman into the storm. As they entered the portals of the Reubens home, a square-built, two-story, frame structure of undescribable ugliness, there came a blinding flash and a terrific explosion, followed by a piercing scream from an upstairs room.

Almost stunned by the bolt, the doctor and his escort leaped up the stairs to the bedside of a pretty young Irish woman, who lay writhing in the agonies of childbirth.

The lightning had struck a tree just outside the one window of the drably furnished room, and had split off a huge limb, which had crashed across the legs of the unhappy victim.

Quickly the doctor cast aside the incumbrance, opened up his surgical case, fiddled around a few minutes, and then suddenly held up in his hairy hands a squirming, crimson-hued infant. He spanked it lightly, and instantly in broke into a squall of vociferous protest.

And thus, under these unusual and trying circumstances, was Alma Rubens, destined to become one of the stormy petrels of the mimic world, ushered into life.

Of course, I have no firsthand knowledge of this epochal event, except what my mother, the doctor, and Mrs. Margaret Schmidt, the neighbor, since have told me. However, I always have accepted their version of the incident—or I might more aptly term it my mother's one great tragedy—as true.

And I can also state that to this day my mother, always of a highly superstitious nature, as are so many of the Irish race, lives in mortal terror of the numeral "13," a fear founded on the trials and tribulations in her life which followed her ordeal in that rickety old house at No. 13 Buchanan Street, San Francisco.

Many persons who have followed my career on the screen and stage mistake me for a Jewess. This belief perhaps was strengthened when I married Ricardo Cortez, my third husband, the only one I ever really loved, and whom I am now trying to divorce.

Although I didn't find it out until almost a year after our marriage, "Ric," instead of being the gallant Spanish caballero which I believed him, was the son of a kosher butcher, with a shop on First Avenue, New York City. His real name is Jacob Kranz.

His origin, however, of which apparently many of my friends were aware, but of which they did nothing to apprise me, had nothing to do with our inability to get along together. The real reason for our separation will be discussed later on.

So, getting back to my theme, I must dispel the current rumors of my Jewish ancestry. As a matter of fact, I am of German-Irish descent, my father, John Bernard Reubens, having been born in Strassburg, Germany, coming to this country in the early 90's, when he was twenty-three.

My mother was born in San Francisco, of old Irish-police-officer-pioeneer stock, the entire family being most devout Catholics. My father, while never of a particularly religious bent, was an avowed Lutheran, and his difference of faith resulted in my poor mother's ostracization, so far as her family was concerned.

## Chapter One

My father was of the dreamer type, phlegmatic but possessed of a certain stoic pride, which, coupled with his extreme honesty and high ideals, ever stood in his way of becoming a business success. Bad health also hampered him during the last twenty years of his life.

I have always greatly resembled him, much to the distress of my elder sister, Hazel, and my mother, both of whom are extremely practical in a business way.

But thank heaven, they are that way, and if it wasn't for their foresight and insistence that I turn over half my earnings, when I was making the big money, to them for investment, I might now be a pauper. As it is, we have a big ranch in California and a considerable amount laid aside for the proverbial rainy day. And it has rained plenty.

My earliest recollection goes back to the time when I was about three years old. With my father, mother and sister, I was aboard a Pacific coastal steamer, en route from Alaska to my native city.

Some six months prior to my birth, my father, inspired by the tales of suddenly acquired wealth in the Klondike, had borrowed money and joined the rush to that Mecca in the late 90's and early part of this century.

Unsuccessful there, too, still he had managed to accumulate enough to send for his family when I was about five months old. But shortly after our arrival he was striken [sic] with rheumatism, a disease so painful and which became of such a chronic nature that in his later years he was able to do very little.

Eventually, when the Klondike boom has subsided, he decided he must seek a milder climate if he ever expected to get back on his feet—physically and financially.

So it happened that while en route my father developed one of his severe attacks and was for many days confined to bed aboard boat. Of course, my mother and Hazel would go to the dining room alone, leaving me, the baby, playing on the floor under my father's watchful eyes.

Up until then I never had uttered a word, a mute condition that had worried my mother almost to distraction.

My father had dozed off, and I, suddenly aware of the fact that he was off guard, toddled over to my mother's trunk, the lid of which was open, seized from within a long-cherished can of talcum powder, and proceeded to make merry.

After daubing almost everything in sight with the powder, I climaxed the proceedings by emptying the remainder on my father's shiny, black derby—the pride and joy of his existence.

He must have had a premonition of impending evil, because he awakened just as I had administered the last sad rites of rubbing it in so hard that no amount of brushing could ever make it look the same.

Father tried to leap out of the bed, but the terrible rheumatic pains which resulted from his move caused him to collapse with a groan of mingled anguish and despair.

"Baby, oh baby, baby," he moaned. "Baby, you dem [sic] little devil, leave that hat alone. By golly, I never saw such a little devil."

Just then mother and Hazel walked in and I chortled in babyish glee: "Devil, Baby dem [sic] little devil," much to their surprise and consternation. From that time on I talked fluently, and continuously, so continuously, in fact, that some of my friends—and some not so friendly—often have referred to me as a human phonograph.

Upon our arrival in San Francisco, we moved to No. 980 McAllister Street, almost next door to Dr. Dodge, who had officiated at my birth. My father, benefited somewhat by the milder climate, managed to regain his feet and became [a] distributor for a champaign in a manufacturing concern.

As soon as we became settled mother made Hazel take me with her to services in Sacred Heart Church, near by. I liked this and up until I reached the third grade, I fully intended to become a nun.

I admired their sober costumes and their stately manners appealed to me. I imitated them in every way possible, even going so far as to cut up my mother's best lace curtains to make myself a frilled surplice.

But later I developed a hatred for school; such a hatred, in fact, that nightly I prayed that it might burn down, or that we might have a devastating flood that would sweep it entirely away.

And, strange as it may seem, my prayers were answered. At least, I thought so in those days, because along came the great San Francisco earthquake, and my school building, the John Swett Grammar School, was almost completely demolished.

This did not solve my difficulties, however, because I was sent to parochial school, much against my wishes. It was while there that I felt the first great urge to become an actress.

Subsequently, I lay awake nights, trying to make up my mind whether the stage name of Rosa La France or Grace Howard would be better under which to seek my career.

I have already mentioned that I was of the idealistic, dreamer type, like my father, with an intensely inquiring and retrospective moodniness accompanied by an abnormal impulsiveness and sense of intuition. Added to these characteristics was a vivid imagination and an almost uncontrollable desire to do the forbidden.

These queer traits have, throughout my life, led me into many errors of both commission and omission, and have trapped me into many situations both ludicrous and serious.

And, in later life, I have often suspected, they have been mainly responsible for my seemingly futile fight against the deadly drug habit.

Since earliest girlhood I have had an inordinate feminine admiration for masculine courage and combativeness, which reminds me of my first great love—and my first grand hero!

## CHAPTER TWO

My loved one was a fireman attached to the station near our house on McAllister Street. I was about twelve years old at the time. I think I was drawn to him principally because of a hideous red scar that traversed his right cheek from temple to the point of his jaw, acquired, perhaps, while helping conquer the terrible conflagration which followed the earthquake.

Even now, when I recall his image in my mind, that mysterious, livid scar awes me into adoration and makes me feel quite goose-fleshy with thrills.

Anyhow, his appearance enamored me into excesses of conjecture not always strictly prudish.

I decided to marry him. He was my man! And I set out to capture him.

When in his presence the overpowering eloquence of my blazing inner flame rendered me mute, languishing and frightened. Audacious, long-legged romp that I was, the instant I would sight him I would concentrate my energies and strut past, breathlessly and self-conscious.

Then into the darkened concealment of a neighborhood telephone booth, providing I had a nickel, I would pester him with an artfully disguised voice, punctuating my arduous advances with exaggerated, deep-throated sighs, which I imagined represented the very quintessence of virginal passion.

"What d'ye say your name was?" he would growl over the wire.

"Rosa La France, the actress," I would invariably reply, affecting a high hauteur, often broken by an irresistible desire to burst into giggles. "Rosa La France. And I'm head over heels in love with you."

And, as invariably, when I had reached this point, my hero would mutter something that sounded like "lunatic" or "nuts," and hang up, much to my despair.

But I did not give up hope. Rosa La France would overcome all obstacles. True love never did run smooth. Rosa La France, in the end, would accomplish her purpose. Rosa La France. That was the name I would make famous. And that was the name my hero would acclaim when I reached the top, thus heaping coals of fire on his head for not reciprocating my love advances earlier.

So, the days and weeks and months slipped by until they approached the day of my confirmation.

As the event drew near, a harum-scarum idea, akin to genius, struck me. Its very originality, as well as its boldness, made me gasp and alternate between chills and fever of suspense and guilt lest my mother should discover my purpose.

For days I had nurtured a sullen and exasperating hurt over my inability to break down the barriers of my scar-faced hero's reserve.

I had attributed this to my appearance. My street clothes, while not slattern, were not just exactly modish, or smart. My family, while not in actual poverty, were to be classed among the respectable, and consequently inconspicuous poor; too poor to buy for me the silks and satins for which my girlish heart yearned.

Even to this day I do not fully grasp, I suppose, the sacrifices, that dreary, scrupulous, saving from out of the meagre family budget which my unflagging mother underwent to provide the gorgeous confirmation dress her never too weary fingers cut, fitted and sewed under the harsh glare of the gas jets in moments snatched from heavy household cares and precious sleep.

A new dress, hat, shoes, a pair of silk hose, or any other new piece of wearing apparel was to me, in those days, in the nature of an event. They were milestones marking periods in my development. They symbolized something pregnant with special meaning. This was especially true of this confirmation dress and also my first wedding gown which my poor mother also hand-sewed under the most heartbreaking circumstances.

To every girl, I presume, as in my own case, her confirmation dress is not only a vision, but a creation of supreme delight. It is her sacred robe of vestal purity and a symbol of the world that she has emerged forever from the era of childhood into the long-cherished plans of a full-grown woman.

The cracked mirror in my room told me that I was beautiful. I was the picture of a bride, the gown, the veil, and the flowers.

I was a bride. His bride. My triumph was at hand!

My hero could not resist me when he saw me arrayed like this.

On a pretense I sailed out of the house ahead of my sister and parents. All a quiver, my heart thumping like a pump, I fairly darted up to where my loved one stood in front of the firehouse.

Maybe he would accompany me to the church and see me transformed by a few simple words from a little girl into a woman. Maybe he would make it a double ceremony and marry me then and there.

Over and over in my mind I had repeated the words that would lead him to declare himself; declare his love for me, his vestal bride.

"Take me, my darling groom of grooms. Oh, take me while I am so beautiful, my handsome, my brave lover knight."

But, when I approached him I became tongue-tied and blushed with confusion. The words would not come. He stared at me in quizzical fashion.

Just then a fat woman, with a baby in her arms, came up and stood by his side. He whispered something to her and then they both eyed me from head to foot.

And, as I stood there, too embarrassed and sickened to flee, he burst into a lusty roar of laughter.

"Damn me, Maggie, if the little minx ain't an actress!" he chortled with glee. "Yes, sir, she's an actress, as sure as you're born."

I stood as though petrified until my mother and father came along a moment later and dragged me away. My romance was a disillusionment, my dreams of love had gone awry.

The confirmation ceremony itself is somewhat blurred in my memory. I went through it all in a daze.

All that I could think of was Rosa La France's hero was married and a father.

And he had called me a minx! Wasn't that a piece of fur?

And, an actress! Well, that part was true. At least I intended being one—and a famous one at that. He'd be sorry one of these days.

Boldly, when the priest asked my name, I replied: "Rosa La France!"

So, Rosa La France, the actress to be, I had become at last.

"By golly, Alma," my father chided me on the way home. "What made you say that? Where did you hear that name?"

"That's my stage name," I replied stubbornly. "That's the name you'll see in the electric lights over Grauman's Theatre one of these days. Just you wait and see!"

My father sadly shook his head and said no more, but mother, upon our arrival home, threatened me with dire punishment unless I relegated the idea to the scrapheap of forgotten things.

So, in the face of this bitter parental criticism and opposition, two years drifted by without any serious efforts on my part to further my stage ambitions.

From time to time, when I was able to raise the money, my chum, Nellie Kyne and I played hookey from school and attended Grauman's, a legitimate house, and the movies.

My earliest hero in the movies and my next great secret love was Arthur Johnson, that tall slim, leading man of a decade and a half ago, who was the first of the silver screen's truly great lovers.

## Chapter Three

When I "fell" for Arthur Johnson—mentally, of course—I entirely forgot about the broken heart I had acquired through my unfortunate "affair" with my scar-faced fireman. The handsome, dark-skinned leading man was to me the ultimate in the way of heroes, and nightly I kissed his picture before falling asleep with it under my pillow.

But this great love, too, quickly went the way of the other, and those later to come, without my ever having seen, in person, the John Barrymore of his day. The reason was because I fell in love with Maurice Costello, then in his heyday.

I think I loved him because he had cute dimples, just like my father's. And for days and days I mooned about, day-dreaming of the time to come when, as the actor's bride, I could sit on his knees, and poke my fingers into the pits in his face formed when he smiled.

Norma Talmadge, in those days, I looked upon as the world's greatest movie queen.

Only recently, Sid Grauman, who with his father, owned and conducted the theatre near our home, and which, to me in those days, was everything in the way of fine appurtenances that a theatre should be, were reminiscing.

"Don't you remember, Sid, the day I applied to you for a job?" I asked.

"Do I remember Rosa La France?" he chuckled. "Do I? Say, Alma, did you really take us seriously?"

"Of course, I did. When I told you that I was a quick change artist, do you know what I thought a quick change artist was? Well, I thought they changed slips of newspaper into money, and other feats of sleight-of-hand and legerdemain."

"Whatever in the world possessed you to pose as that, when you knew absolutely nothing about it?" he quizzed.

"Well, you and your father asked me what my stage specialty was and I was so floored that I couldn't think of anything else. As a matter of fact, now that the truth can be told, I never had seen a quick change artist, but had seen the designation in print somewhere and thought it sounded good."

All this, of course, occurred in San Francisco, when I was about fourteen. The Grauman Theatre was on the route I covered daily going to and from the public school which I was then attending.

On this particular day, while in passing, I had seen the Graumans, father and son, lounging against an electric light pole in front of the box office. The impulse to apply for a part in one of their shows was irresistible.

They looked me up and down in amazement, at first, then their faces became drawn—I now know—in an air of mock solemnity, as they considered my possibilities as a quick change artist, the qualities of which I had so blantantly and ignorantly described.

"How much do you think you are worth?" Grauman Senior finally asked after an exchange of knowing nods with his son.

"Ten dollars a week is the lowest I'll work for," I ventured, afraid that I might be affixing too high a figure.

"What?" They cried in unison. "Ten dollars a week! Your act must be good!"

"It certainly is," I assured them. "It is a marvelous act!" And there I stopped with the fear that they might call on me for a tryout, then and there.

They stepped to one side and debated long and earnestly in husky whispers. My heart was standing still. Maybe they were going to engage me—and at my own figure. Ten dollars a week. Heavens! Why, in no time at all I would be wealthy.

"All right, Rosa La France—I had introduced myself in my favorite name in the interim—suppose you leave your address. We'll telephone you when we're ready," Sid assured. "And, by the way, you know, we never pay less than $40 a week."

"And I'm engaged?" I finally spluttered, breathlessly.

"Certainly," he declared. "After we send for you."

I flew home fairly in a state of delirium. I had a job on the stage. I was in actuality Rosa La France. Rosa La France, the quick change artist. At forty a week. Forty dollars a week. I never had dreamed of such a magnificent sum.

When I entered the hallway of our home I was treading the pathway of the stars. My exhilarated spirits glorified its drabness into the corridors of a palace. Should I tell my mother of our unexpected good fortune? Or should I wait? I decided on the latter course.

The greater the surprise, I figured, the more infinite the joy—when the summons came. And I felt that it was coming soon. Even then, probably, the Graumans were mapping out my career.

Then, I suddenly thudded to earth. On our old-fashioned hall rack, side by side, with my father's black derby, hung a strange hat.

The sight of my father's hat there in mid-afternoon, when he usually was at his office, alone was disturbing. But this other hat, so stiff, so black, so funereal in its appearance. It spelled disaster.

For some time my father had been gradually growing worse. The pain caused by his rheumatism had dragged him down physically, yet he had doggedly persisted in continuing at work.

At the top of the stairs my mother appeared, gazing down in an agitated manner. Her haggard face left nothing to my imagination.

"What is the matter, mother?" I gasped, as I sped up to comfort her. "Is papa dead?"

"No," she said. "But he is very badly off. The doctor is with him. He may never get around again."

I knew what this meant. My father was virtually through with life. I had realized this dimly, for months. He might linger indefinitely, as he did, in great physical suffering, but his active days were over.

Even this foreknowledge, now that the inevitable had arrived, failed to serve as a buffer against the shock. My father was of the recluse scholar type, prodigal on behalf of others, always supremely indifferent to material affairs, traits which have descended to me in a somewhat lessened degree.

His income was always slender. Our efforts to make both ends meet under the best of circumstances were Spartan in the extreme. And now? Our home, pitifully modest, scrupulously neat and clean, and ruled by my austerly proud Irish mother, had always hidden our poverty from our neighbors, but now it would have to become known.

"We can rent some rooms," my mother, always ready with a practical solution of every problem, reflected, after I had gone in and kissed the suffering head of the household, "but it will be very hard for us all."

"Don't worry, mother," I reassured her mysteriously, patting her cheeks, pinching her chin and kissing her. "Everything will be all right. How does forty a week sound to you?"

"Flighty," my mother said grimly, and her eyes grew moist. "Flighty as the divvil. And it is a pity you will have to leave school. I had hoped to give you a good education, but now you will have to go to work."

"Don't worry about that," I consoled her, although I did not enlighten her as to my mysterious meaning.

Whatever instinct it was that halted my usually uncontrollable tongue that day, when my whole being cried out to comfort her, I do not know. Had I told her of my tentative engagement, her disappointment when the Graumans failed to call me would have doubled her burden.

Day by day I waited for the telephone message that never came. And, when I received no work after days and days, I finally called them, in desperation and with a quaking heart.

After many futile attempts to reach one of the Graumans, I was cut through to the elder. Usually good-natured, he must have been ill that day, because he cut me short and hung up on me before I had finished pouring out my plea for immediate work.

I was stunned. I sat around in a daze for the rest of the day. Then my vision cleared. I was a sham, a faker, and a bluffer. And the Graumans had known it from the beginning. I was a pretender and they had gotten rid of me in the easiest manner, as they would any other nuisance.

My mortification was so acute that all thoughts of the stage, for the time being, became repugnant. I began to look elsewhere for a job.

It was during this turbulent period—I was just past fourteen—that I experienced by first rude shock.

I walked blindly into a male trap.

## Chapter Four

This, my first experience with a sensual male, occurred in a store where I had found a trial job in the stock room. I was to receive $4.50 a week, but I thought that was a gold mine.

The dark knights were upon our home. Not only was my father hopelessly ill, but by this time my mother was failing and manifesting the symptoms which forewarned of the hospital and surgical operations—and expenses to come.

In spite of the income from our rented rooms, our expenses had mounted to the breaking point. Where relief from any additional financial strain was to be sought was a problem over which we all had brooded daily.

Every penny of my pitifully small wage went into the common fund. I felt my responsibility so enormously that when I received a summons to the manager's office one evening after hours I responded in a whirl of trepidation. Was I to be discharged? What had I done to be reprimanded?

"Come in, Alma," he said kindly. He stepped forward and gently closed the door. I stood soberly facing him.

"Sit there!" he directed, pointing to his secretary's vacant chair. I complied.

"How do you like it?"

"What? My job?" I inquired. "I'm crazy about it!"

"I don't mean your stock room job," he laughed. "I mean that chair. How would you like to work in here?"

I gazed at him uncertainly.

"I've been watching you," he went on. "You're not made for the stock room. I'm looking for a new secretary, somebody with looks like you."

"I'm not a stenographer. I'm not even a typist. I——." I was too greatly astonished to proceed.

He smiled and put his arm around my shoulders in a familiar manner.

"That is not so important," he said. "You can bluff at it, can't you. You know what I mean, don't you?"

And before I was aware of his intent, he held me in a tight embrace.

I scratched him, and I bit him. I fought him like a tiger. Finally, after I had fairly clawed his eyes out—blood was streaming from the scratches I had inflicted on his face and hands—he gave me a great shove that knocked me off my feet. I fell in a panting heap on the floor.

"Oh, well," he growled. "If that's the way you feel about it, you can go to —— ! I only put you in the stock room to give you a chance. You're fired! Here is your pay."

He seized a pad, scribbled a few words on it and handed it to me. I took it and stumbled away, thoroughly disillusioned and sickened by his treatment.

Years later, after I climbed to fame in the movies, through my lead in *Humoresque*, I became acquainted with his successor and just for curiosity's sake I asked him to show me my former service record.

"Discharged for being fresh," was scribbled on the card.

That same day my mother went to the hospital, leaving the house alone in my absence, taking a street car because she had insufficient funds to ride in a taxi. I was frantic when I returned and found she was gone.

I ran all the way to the institution, more than a mile from our home, and was escorted by a kind-hearted attendant to her bedside in a free ward where she had been placed for observation.

A nurse had brought her a tray of food, delicacies which had not appeared on our family table for weeks.

My mother had hidden the choice bits in a napkin under her pillow. On these, amid tears, I feasted, while she smoothed by hair and murmured reassurances.

Between bites and sobs I poured out my whole story of woe. I shall never forget my poor mother's half wild, half fatalistic expression, nor her sighfully cryptic remarks.

"It is your lot, my child," she said. "You are young, beautiful, and many men are beasts, worse than beasts. I am afraid you will have a hard time through life. And you must guard against them."

Her warning still rings in my ears. It was my lot, in more ways than one, a fact which has been more forcibly impressed upon me at each stage of my development.

But at that time I scouted my mother's fears.

"Never mind, mother," I said, stoutly determined to do my part in relieving her of worry. "I'll soon get another job and everything will be all right."

And in a way, it was. I had learned the bitter lesson of every working girl. It stunned, but it fortified me for my next assault against the world for a living.

In the ensuing weeks while my father slowly sank and my mother hovered between life and death after three major operations, I spent most of my time reading "Female Help Wanted" ads, pasted on newspaper billboards and experienced almost every degree of hope and disappointment.

Driven as I was to obtain employment, I could not settle my mind on a clear goal. The stage, which I thought I had put aside as a prospect, now and then reappeared in alluring outline, in my scanning of the restricted horizon open to young women.

The question of self-support was constantly at a clash with my inherently rhapsodic nature, the practical and the idealistic. I could not envisage myself permanently behind a counter, or at a desk, as a means of self-development, expansion and independence. I was always picturing myself in a fanciful realm for which I had absolutely no training whatsoever.

There were times when I was sure that only a stage career would satisfy my inside yearnings. Whenever I saw a poster of Pavlova, I was convinced that I was destined for the Russian ballet and to dance before the crowned heads of Europe. After reading an impassioned flight of poetry, I was enveloped in a blaze of the divine fire to leave my mark as a poetess.

On other occasions, I felt the urge to write a great and enduring love story, a romance that would stamp my name with George Eliot and George Sands in the literary hall of perpetual fame.

I was, metaphorically speaking, a star gazer, a will-o'-the-wisp hunter, a wild-goose chaser.

# Chapter Five

Just about this time there fell into my hands De Quincey's *Confessions of an English Opium Eater* and Bram Stoker's *Dracula*, books which aroused my fanciful interest through their dramatic picturization of the unreal—but which, compared to my own experiences after I became a drug addict—were not beyond my ken.

Even then, governed as I was by that almost uncontrollable impulse to do the forbidden, the bizarre, the unusual. I could mentally transport myself into the character of a dope fiend, a huge vampire bat, and as such, in my imagination, I could flit hither and yon, making deathly visitations at will, just for the sheer thrill of feeling my own power.

Is it any wonder then, with this distorted viewpoint, that I lost every job in quick succession, either because of rank or incompetence, or because my mooning and posing personality inevitably aroused the baser sex appetite of my male employers.

And, there was my meteoric experience at the ribbon counter in a San Francisco department store. I thought I was getting along fine until, suddenly without warning, the head floorwalker, accompanied by one of the proprietors, called me before a group of fellow employees for a measurement demonstration.

Now, arithmetic and its various equations were then, and still are, my chief stumbling blocks. Figures mean no more to me than the wriggly hieroglyphics on an Egyptian tomb. Struggle as I would with them, I was always wrong.

So, when my bosses came around, I was in a quandary, but I put on a brave front.

"Alma," began the chief floorwalker, "when a customer asks for three and seven-eighths yards of blue ribbon, what do you do?"

"Why, naturally," I responded, all at sea, "I measure three and seven-eighths yards and wrap it up for her."

"All right," he directed, "show Mr. Hendricks here how you do it. I am your customer. Measure me three and seven-eighths yards of this," and he handed me a bulky belt.

Airily, as though my fingers were skimming along the keyboard of a piano, I obeyed. I didn't know what I was doing, but I was doing it with great vim and vigor. Before I could complete the operation, however, the proprietor halted me with such a cry of human agony as I hope never to hear again.

"My God, John!" he groaned. "Did you see that? Did you see how she measured that? No wonder we are on the verge of bankruptcy."

He turned to the other witnesses, which by this time included several other officials of the concern, and declared: "Gentleman, the mystery is solved. No one is stealing our ribbon. It's Alma. She's measuring ribbon by the oodle, instead of by the yard. I don't believe she even knows what a yard is. She probably thinks its the place where they keep the dog penned up."

He glared at me. I stood, petrified with horror.

"Good heavens, girl! No wonder customers ask for you!"

And that was that. I was fired again. The only job I ever voluntarily quit was at a bargain shirtwaist counter where I was paid a few cents commission on every sale. The competition was so keen that after a nerve-wracking, body-bruising, throat-husking day, I earned but 50 cents, which I spent for ointment and a gargle.

Once I ran away from a job and once I was discharged because they accused me of deserting my post. The former was in a telegraph office where I was employed to fold and seal telegrams in envelopes.

My duties in the telegraph office took me to a distant section of the city at 5 o'clock in the morning, riding on the street cars among the rough element usually employed at the wharves and on construction jobs. These men never molested me.

But one raw morning I arrived at the office a little ahead of time. It was just breaking dawn. I thought I was alone in the back office, when suddenly one of the male employees appears, locking the door behind him and sliding toward me in a crawfishy manner of ominous import.

I was terrorized even before he reached out for me. Never will I forget what ensued. His fingers were long and claw-like. His face was set in a leer. He had several teeth missing in front, and the general ensemble suggested one of those moving picture Chinese monsters who used to pursue Pearl White and Juanita Hansen in the movie thrillers of long ago.

He tried to kiss me. I ducked under the table and leaped to my feet on the other side. He tried to run around and catch me, but I eluded him by dashing to the opposite side. I endeavored to keep the table between us, but he upset it and darted after me. I again eluded him by throwing a chair in his path. Then I knocked over a filing cabinet, one corner of which struck him on the foot.

Before he could recover, I threw open the window and made my exit, never to return. Even after I got outside, with men passing on their way to work, I was scared, too scared to scream.

The other job, where I was fired for deserting, led me into a still more horrible experience.

Once again I had obtained a foothold with the telephone company. During my rest period, a girl friend, who I had never dreamed was a married woman, received an urgent telephone call, requesting her to come to her home immediately. They didn't tell her what the trouble was and she was badly frightened. She begged me to accompany her, and I did so, out of sheer sympathy, seeing that she was so strangely perturbed.

The first thing we saw when we stepped into the cheaply furnished two-room apartment was a dead man, stretched out at full length on the floor. His eyes protruded and a frothy white substance dribbled from his mouth. Clots of blood appeared in his ears and nose.

It was her husband. They had quarreled that morning and he had taken poison.

This shock so completely unnerved me that it was several hours before I could get myself together sufficiently to return to my switchboard. When I did return, the chief operator curtly informed me that I was no longer employed there.

And there I was, jobless again, as usual.

## CHAPTER SIX

That was my last attempt toward a business or commercial career. I was thoroughly sick and disgusted with it all, yet I could not help but feel as though it was all my own fault, in spite of my self-pity, which I demonstrated by crying myself to sleep for several nights in succession.

I tried to analyze myself. What manner of girl was I? Was I lacking in the fundamentals of real ability, true stability? And, why was I so temperamentally misunderstood, my sense of feminine decency so thoroughly outraged?

Was I normal? The mirror into which I bared this soul-tormenting inquiry reflected nothing strange in figure or countenance. I was redolent with youth, lithe and strong, sleek and supple. I studied each feature, the firm contours of cheeks, chin and nostrils, much as a fancier appraises horseflesh.

Was it my contrasting coloring, the ivory texture of my skin, my widely separated, explanatory eyes, the wavy silkiness of my chestnut hair shot through with glinting, amber-red, the broad, low classical smoothness of my forehead, those qualities critics have since written about as "Rubenesque?"

I saw nothing unusual, no impure gleam morally destructive or immorally appealing. Was it possible that I could be a girl with a hidden scarlet nature which the male suspected? Was this why I won chances so easily only to lose them as speedily when I shrank from male aggression?

Fortunately for me, both my mother and my father had sufficiently improved in health so as to be up and about. Soon my mother had completely recovered, and, thanks God, never once since has she been ill.

Our finances, with abnormal drains, improved. I returned to school this time at the Sacred Heart Convent. There I formed a friendship with a girl, whose name I do not care to mention, but who proved to be the best pal I ever had in my life.

One day a trifling incident occurred which once more caused me to hitch my star to a comet and turn my attention toward a stage career. It was in one of those little show houses on Fillmore Street, where my chum and I saw watching a picture in which Wally Reid—God bless his soul—was the lead.

A beautiful girl flashed into the scene. My chum nudged me excitedly. "Alma," she whispered, "You're the very image of her!"

It was Blanche Sweet.

Only the most extravagant stretch of the fancy would find any resemblance between the blonde-haired Blanche and myself. Yet I was thrilled. It was an illusion which I allowed to trick and intrigue me to the absorption of everything else.

I was movie struck.

Several days later I ran across an advertisement in a morning newspaper. It was for a number of extra girls for a motion picture production by G. M. ("Bronco Billy") Anderson, then one of the important factors in the industry.

I called to see him.

"Take off your hat," he commanded brusquely, after I had waited in an outside room for more than an hour while he interviewed a dozen other girls.

"Too young and too fair," was his brief comment. "Can't use you."

My spirits sank into my shoes, but I went away with hope not entirely shattered. I know little or nothing of the art of makeup, but I reasoned with my chum that there must be some way of my darkening my complexion and simulating an older girl.

"Why not try frying powder in a pan and smear it onto your face, then go out to the beach for a day and let the sun cook it into your skin?" she suggested.

The experiment sounded promising, so we played hooky from school the next day and went through the procedure most carefully and patiently.

The sun was bright and the day extraordinarily hot. The beaches were crowded and from the moment of our arrival we were objects of varying degrees of curiosity.

Squatting backwards, using my arms as props, the sun's fierce rays beat squarely upon my up tilted face, each of my legs sprawling out stilt-wise, to brace me in position and other contortions, too numerous to mention. I must have proved a sensation to the spectators.

As the thick, greasy smears on my face began to melt and form tiny rivulets streaming from forehead to chin, passersby paused, looked, listened, then burst into uproarious laughter.

By this time the mixture had begun to trickle into my eyes and mouth, down my neck, back and front, making me decidedly uncomfortable, not to mention the terrible odor which was making me nauseous.

My chum, flopped down on the stand beside me, watching the whole ludicrous process, never cracked a smile or blinked an eyelash. God will reward her for that, if I never do.

"Is it cooking in?" occasionally I would sputter.

"Looks to me like it is cooking out," was her response, with a sigh of intense disappointment. "And how you stink! We're a regular side show, too!"

Our thinking out loud was rudely interrupted by a loud, jocular masculine voice, who demanded, between deep-throated chuckles: "What in the Sam Hill are you girls trying to do?"

"With that, I opened my eyes, braving the rivulets of the nasty mess which had almost blinded me. Around me was a boisterous mob, and through it the owner of the voice was pushing his way. He was accompanied by a pretty young woman who looked at us agape.

"Get up!" the man ordered, peremptorily.

I was frightened and leaped to my feet in an effort to make a get-away. He caught my arm and held me tightly.

"Stand still!"

With palpitating heart and on the verge of hysterics, I did so.

"What's the big idea?" he demanded.

"I'm only trying out a new kind of makeup," I stammered, mistaking him for a policeman or a deputy sheriff at least.

"A new kind of makeup!" he exploded, and for a second his eyes sought those of his female companion, who not once had stirred or made a sound.

"What do you call yourself," he went on. "A prima donna or the end girl in a female minstrel show?"

His cool, taunting voice irked me. I drew myself up on my toes and hissed right back at him, scornfully.

"I'm Rosa La France!"

"Oh!" he ejaculated, simulating surprise. "Rosa La France, eh? So you're the great, great Rosa La France, the rage of Europe, Asia, Africa and Podunk, Iowa."

He bowed deeply with an air of mock gallantry.

"Well, Rose," he said, "you can report on the stage at 9 a.m. tomorrow for rehearsals, but leave off that makeup stuff—that is, if you can scrub it off in time."

He thrust a card into my hand, and, with his companion, vanished.

I stared stupidly at the card, too surprised to utter a sound or to notice the curious crowd, which by this time had grown to proportions that could have made old P. T. Barnum envious.

"Alma!" My chum finally gushed in awe. "Do you know who that was?"

I had a hard time collecting my thoughts, but finally, after much blinking to clear my eyes of the odious makeup concoction, I saw that the card bore the names of William Rock and Maude Fulton, and a theatre on Powell Street where they had scheduled "The Girl at the Gate" for its premiere.

This production was only one of many backed, as I afterward learned, by "Bronco Billy," who just the day before had turned me down cold.

"The Girl at the Gate." I was too stupefied to move away from the rubbering throng. Yes, I was at the "gate," the golden gate of Ambition, the gateway to my chosen career.

"Is it real, or phoney," my chum, who came back to earth quicker than I did, blurted out.

Then, with that swift premonition so common among certain types of women, she answered her own question before I could think up a reply.

"It is real, Alma," she declared solemnly, and without the slightest hint of jealousy or doubt. "It is real! Your life has just begun!"

And so it had. I was Rosa La France—at last!"

## Chapter Seven

I was to get a tryout at last! I didn't sleep a wink all that night. I was up at daybreak and washed and scrubbed myself until I felt that I was as pure as a lily. The minutes dragged like hours. It seemed like the clock was standing still; that 9 o'clock would never come.

Half an hour before that time I was waiting at the stage door. A dozen times in the next hour I had seen Bronco Billy walk in and out, but he paid no more attention to me than if I had been a fire hydrant.

Finally I could stand the suspense no longer. And upon his reappearance I timidly stepped forward and handed him the card Rock had given me the previous afternoon.

"This gentleman told me to come here for a tryout," I managed to blurt out.

Bronco Billy gazed at it a moment, then looked at me as though for the first time he had realized that I was not some inanimate object.

"Oh," he said. "That's what you are waiting for, eh? I don't think you are the type, but come on back stage."

Fairly walking on the clouds, dizzy with excitement and with my heart playing leapfrog with the back of my tongue, I followed. The entire cast, some twenty-odd girls arrayed in tights were being put through their paces by one of his assistants.

They were all of the burlesque type so popular in those days. Big of limb and hip and bust and far older than myself, they presented a jaded appearance, which, with their obvious sophistication and audible wisecracks, made me feel still more self-conscious.

Dazed as I was, I could sense that they were jealous of me, that my youthful freshness and bloom made them envious, and that I would be dependent upon my own resources if I was to learn the tricks and trade of a chorus high-stepper.

I was taken in hand by an elderly matron, who led me into a dressing room and arrayed me in my first pair of tights. As I recall it, they were light green in color, with an orange middle of ruffled satin and a headpiece of drooping feathers, intended to give me the appearance of a poll parrot.

Another assistant took me in hand and directed me to watch the other girls a few minutes so I could gather some idea of the steps. Happily for me, they were easy, and with my confidence somewhat restored, I assured him that I could duplicate them.

"All right! Go ahead then," he directed, keeping time with up and down motions of his hands. "One, two," and I broke into the steps so handily that he immediately placed me in the lineup with the other girls.

We continued practicing for more than an hour, and apparently we were getting along first rate. Then the other girls were dismissed for the lunch hour and Bronco Billy himself asked if I was ready for a voice tryout.

"Oh, oh," I said to myself. "Here's where I fall flat!"

But I was game. After they had wheeled me out a dilapidated old piano they handed me a sheet of music and the pianist rattled off the prelude to "Alexander's Ragtime Band," then at the height of popularity.

In cracked tones and off key I sang the first verse and was just starting the chorus—really getting warmed up to my work, you know—when Bronco Billy gave the signal to stop, and turning to me with a rather pained expression, said:

"As a singer, you're no Jenny Lind, no Swedish nightingale, but I guess you'll do in a pinch. You got looks and you dance pretty well. You're hired. Thirty-five and you pay your own on the road. Come back at 9 tomorrow. Got to rehearse another week before we open up."

And with that he turned away. I stood rooted in my tracks, too happy, too paralyzed with joy, to move. Rosa La France was an actress at last. A real actress, with a job and everything; with a real salary, and in one more week she actually would be on the stage, ready to receive the acclaim of her public.

Finally I came to. I went back to the dressing room and changed to my street clothes, putting on one of my stockings wrong-side out in the excitement without knowing it until I got home and my mother reproached me for carelessness.

"I've got a job, mother," I squealed, as I flung open the door." "I'm on the stage. Thirty-five a week. I'm a principal in 'The Girl at the Gate'!"

I didn't know any more what a principal was than I had when I talked to the Graumans about being a quick-change artist. But my mother was duly impressed, despite my hysterics.

"Well, well, honey," she calmed me, taking me to her ample bosom and smothering me with kisses. "I'm so glad, dear. Maybe your dreams are going to come true. I hope so, dear, for your own sake."

My father, too ill to move from his bed, patted my hand and also wished me success.

Until nightfall, I walked around the house simply bubbling over with exuberance. Every few minutes I would call up a different girl friend and tell her of my good fortune. Our telephone bill that month must have been something terrible.

Then the first of my worries began: We had a woman lodger who used to be in the show business, but who had been employed in an office downtown since her husband died a few months before. She was a perfect old killjoy.

The first thing she said after I had informed her of my good luck caused me to lose another good night's sleep.

## Chapter Seven

"Why child," she said, "you haven't got any symmetricals. How do you expect to make good in the show business without them? You'll have to get some, or else you won't stick."

Now I had not the slightest idea what symmetricals were, but, as I have said before, I always have had that queer little touch of pride inherited from my father that would never allow me to admit my ignorance in the presence of others.

"Oh, that's all right," I said, in a matter-of-fact voice. "I'm going to get them in the morning. I ordered them as soon as I got the job."

Then I tore away from her as quickly as I could, determined to get me some symmetricals, whatever they were, right away quick, if not a lot sooner.

Without saying a word to my mother, I put on my hat and went downtown. I walked into a theatrical costume place which kept open evenings and went to the proprietor, a woman, with what I considered my best air of sophistication.

"I'm in the trade," I assured her, "in 'The Girl at the Gate.' I need some symmetricals and must have them at once. How much do they cost?"

"Well," she replied, apparently amazed at my cyclone manner of approach. "What kind do you want. Wool or cotton? The wool cost $15, the cotton $9. And I'll have to make them to order. I can have them for you by tomorrow night."

Not a word did she utter that might enlighten me as to their purpose. But I drew forth a dollar and gave it to her as a deposit on the cotton ones, telling her I would pay the balance when I called for them the next day. Then I started to walk out.

"How can I make them if I don't measure you," she recalled me.

I stopped and she drew out a tape measure and began measuring my calves. Even then I wasn't sure what it was all about, but I was paying my good money and asking absolutely no questions.

Nor did I know where I was going to raise the other $8.

I went home and told my mother where I had been. Always practical, she said it would be a good plan to make inquiries: to find out the use of symmetricals. We went up to our lodger's room, but she had gone out.

Well, to make a long story short, my mother managed to raise the $8, and [the] next day after rehearsal I called to get my purchase, which was already wrapped up awaiting me.

I took the bundle, paid over the cash, and ran almost all the way home. Breathlessly I went to my room and tried them on over my stockings. This operation completed, I couldn't see that my appearance had been improved in the least, but I went downstairs and showed them to my mother.

She was of the same opinion. But then, like me, she was unfamiliar with things theatrical, and said the habit of wearing symmetricals, like the wearing of the green, was a custom, no doubt, which must be rigidly adhered to.

No one mentioned symmetricals at rehearsal, so I didn't either, but I kept them in readiness should I be called upon to don them.

So the long week of rehearsal sped by.

My fellow chorus members did nothing to break the icy aloofness of their first greeting, but the leading man, Walter Catlett, since become one of the world's greatest comedians, and Zoe Barnett, the leading woman, were extremely nice to me.

Zoe especially did everything she could to help me along. I guess she took pity on my youthful greenness. Anyhow, she frequently called me to her dressing room when the day's rehearsal ended, took me with her shopping, and even accompanied me hope for dinner one evening, much to my delight.

Not even this friendship, however, served to break my pride sufficiently for me to ask her about the symmetricals, much as I was aching to do so.

Then came opening night.

## Chapter Eight

On opening night I arrived at the theatre early. I put on my costume, carefully arranging my precious symmetricals so they would appear to the best advantage. They looked sort of bulgy, but I was determined to make good. And, if one had to wear symmetricals to become a hit, Rosa La France would wear them—or bust.

The curtain went up.

Catlett and Zoe made their entrance, spoke their opening lines, and retreated, which was the signal for the chorus to appear from the wings on either side.

I was third from the end on the left hand side, opposite where Bronco Billy stood behind a curtain where he could observe everything without being seen by the audience.

Blithely I skipped into position. At last I was before the footlights. Rosa La France's premiere. Rosa La France, who was destined to electrify the world.

And then, my house of cards tumbled.

Before we were half through the number I heard a double snap and began to experience an uneasy feeling just below either knee. The bands which held my symmetricals had broken and they began to twist and slide downwards in a most horrifying manner.

The further they slid the more grotesquely they bulged.

Bronco Billy, who apparently had just noticed them for the first time, was making frantic gestures from his observation post.

Several of the other girls noticed my plight and began to titter. The audience, scenting [sic] something wrong, made a closer inspection and began to roar in laughter over my predicament. Finally Bronco Billy ordered down the curtain and I was dragged off the stage.

I fled behind one of the wings and collapsed. Rose La France had been a miserable flop. Opportunity had knocked at her door and ill luck had queered her. Perhaps she never would have another chance.

The stage manager was seeking me. "Where is that you[ng] little fool?" he inquired. "I'm going to murder her. I'll kill her in cold blood!"

I shrank even further into my huddle and a moment later, just when I was preparing to flee for my life, up came Zoe Barnett—God bless her— and knelt down beside me, putting her arms around my quaking shoulders and comforting me.

"Never mind, dear," she said. "You just didn't know any better. Cheer up. My heavens! Just listen to that audience. They're simply going wild over you. They think you did it on purpose; that it was part of your act."

I listened. The house was in an uproar. Hastily, Zoe wiped away my tears and thrust me into the arms of Bronco Billy.

"Make a bow for them, you clumsy little idiot," he commanded. "Make a bow, smile, and then get back here quick. That is, if you can without breaking your —— clumsy neck!"

Four times I had to step out alone before that hysterically laughing audience. And four times they clapped appreciation.

Rosa La France had stopped the show!

When the final curtain fell, I didn't know whether I was going to be fired or not. Bronco Billy and one of the stage managers took turns in bawling me out. With my powdered cheeks streaked with tears, I stood and accepted their abuse without protest.

And then, their tempers worn out, they assuaged my grief by giving me a speaking part, which I was to assume at the next performance. A real speaking part!

I was transported into a realm of empyrean bliss. I was in heaven. Riding on a silvery cloud, hitched to a comet.

My "lines" were these: "I'll have chocolate!"

I studied that night as I never had studied before. "I'll have chocolate. I'll have chocolate." Over and over again I repeated the magic formula. I tried various tones of voice. I recited them in the eight keys of the scale.

I gazed admiringly at myself in the mirror, watching the movements of my lips and affecting the mannerisms which I thought would befit a prima donna. And again I didn't sleep a wink.

When I would doze off, I would wake myself up with the mystic sentence: "I'll have chocolate!" Even to this day I get a thrill when I hear those words.

Two weeks I recited them nightly before the audience—my audience. Rosa La France's audience. For two whole weeks we played there in that shabby little theatre on Fillmore Street, near my home.

Then we went on the road.

Never shall I forget the thrilling sadness of my parting with my father and mother for the first time. And, they too took the departure of their "baby" much to heart.

My sister had married some three years before and was living in Fresno with her husband. While there was never any difference in the extent of my parents' love, they had always favored me because I was the "baby," a fact which Hazel deeply resented at times.

"Baby" was their pet name for me. Seldom did they call me anything else. And so when the time came for me to step out from under the parental roof they took it doubly hard.

"Baby," my father, propped up on pillows in bed, abjured in trembling tones. "Always be a good girl. No matter what happens, always be a good girl. Money and fame doesn't count. It is only here—" and he thumped his chest, "that anything matters. In the heart."

"Pick good company, Baby. If you can't make good friends, don't make any at all. Bad friends are like bad apples. They spoil all the others in the barrel."

How often in later years have I recalled that simple sermon. And, had I listened to it, probably I never would have descended into the mire of degradation and drugs that all but ruined me, mentally, morally, physically and financially. Youth is impetuous, however, and good advice, alas, is seldom heeded. And I was youth.

Naturally, I then thought that our show was the very cream of all things theatrical. Apparently, it was of the third rate variety, however, because our itinerary included all of the tank towns, Taft, Sherman, and such, small villages where the theatre owners seized upon every possible way to curtail expenses, providing tin can footlights, calico drapes, and three-piece orchestras.

From the very beginning I hated the road, probably because the other girls and men in the company, except for the two leads, considered me high hat, for no other reason than my aloofness. I didn't know any risqué jokes and couldn't bear to listen to them.

Some of the girls in the chorus doubled up, making no bones of carrying on affairs with the males of the company, and others, whom they met more or less casually.

By doing this they cut down expenses, the men invariably paying their room rent. When I first learned of this practice, I was horrified, so shocked that I came near quitting the show after my first night in a Taft hotel.

The other girls seemed to take it as a matter of course. And, now and then I would hear them whispering, sometimes with some of the men, about my prudishness.

From time to time various of the male element tried to break down the barriers of my reserve. They would engage me in conversation and then gradually lead up to a proposition. And invariably they would try to maul me, something that I never was able to stand.

I would try diplomatically to avert the dreaded climax, but it seemed to be hopeless. And, on almost every occasion our tête-à-tête would wind up by my slapping their faces, after which I would turn around and flee to my room, where I would sob out my heart for the rest of the day or night.

Time and time again in almost every town, I passed through this ordeal. The minute I would become just a little bit less aloof and try to be sociable, one of the men or another would begin making advances. They simply would not believe that I was a good girl.

So it went on for more than three weeks, until we reached Fresno, where my sister Hazel and her husband lived.

There, one of the road managers, whom I shall call "Tony," made a last frantic bid for my favors and so nearly accomplished his purpose that even now I quiver with fright when I try to recall the incident.

## Chapter Nine

"Tony's" approach was a masterpiece of subtle, male dexterity. He knew that I was out of luck so far as the others of the company were concerned because I would tolerate no lovers. He knew that I was already disgusted with the road.

The late hours and the terrible jumps had me almost frantic. Frequently we would get off the train at 5 in the morning. Not yet daylight. Four or five hours more to sleep at the most. And it seemed to me it was always raining.

Then getting settled in our hotel. Unpacking our baggage. A snack of breakfast and then we would have to hurry to the theatre to rehearse. Likely as not we would have to dress in the alley, in back of the stage. Only the principals had dressing rooms in some of those sorry, small town theatres.

If I was late to rehearsal, I would get a terrible reprimand. Some of the assistants had the vocabulary of the proverbial deep sea sailor. And how they could use it, especially on the girls.

It seemed to me that I was in tears about half the time. The other half I spent washing and powdering them away.

My father and mother had seldom scolded me, and only that I can remember was I ever spanked. That occurred one day when I was about twelve, when my mother had gone out to work some place, leaving me with my father, who was barely able to walk around.

I did something he didn't like and he rebuked me. I became fresh and made some nasty remark. He lost his temper, the only occasion upon which I ever saw this happen.

He seized me, threw me across his knee, and tapped me lightly once or twice with his open hand.

I screamed blue murder!

"Oh, you brute!" I cried. "Father. You're beating me. You're beating me. You're killing me!"

Then I fainted. With one eye open.

Father was terribly upset. Tears were rolling down his eyes. He hobbled up and down the room in the most pathetic manner. Every few turns he would stop and feel in my heart was beating. I tried to make it stand still.

"Oh, by golly, I've killed her," he moaned. "Oh, why did I do it? And I was only fooling, too. Ach! My poor, poor baby."

I stood it as long as I could. His suffering was unbearable and I was so ashamed of myself. I didn't know what to do. Cagily, I moved my arm. Then a leg. He ran up to me and I sat up.

"Baby! You're all right!" he cried gleefully. "Baby, I'm so glad. I'll never strike you again. By golly, it is a promise. I'll buy you anything you want if you won't tell mama I struck you."

This last was more than I had bargained for. I must have been a little mercenary, because I took him at his word.

"Will you buy me that gold tooth?" I quickly asked him before he could change his mind.

The tooth in question was a needed replacement for one which a quack dentist had pulled through an error. My mother had insisted on having a porcelain one put in, but I had held out for a gold one.

Anyhow, father promised me the gold tooth. He kept his word, and I did not mention the beating to my mother.

But, to get back to "Tony." He knew of my extremely sensitive nature and patiently awaited his time to take full advantage of this knowledge. His opportunity came the day we hit Fresno.

I was late at rehearsal and he gave me a terrible bawling out. I managed to stick it out, but as soon as we had finished, I dashed out to my hotel room where I cried and cried and cried, trying to make up my mind whether to quit the show or not.

## Chapter Nine

My sister didn't know that I was in town. I hadn't called her because I wanted to surprise her. I wanted to send her a couple of tickets at the last moment, so our first meeting since I had become an actress would be over the footlights.

"Tony" came up to my room. He knocked at the door and I let him in. I was frantically trying to hide the traces of my grief. I didn't want him to know that I had been crying, but try to keep back the tears, hard as I tried, was impossible, and I sobbed anew in his presence.

He put his arms around me and comforted me. He even kissed the big, salty drops right out of my eyes. It was the first bit of kindness I had met with in days and he seemed so repentant that I couldn't help but forgive him.

Before I knew it, I was sitting on his lap and he was sitting on the edge of the bed. He kissed me again and again, and I didn't make much of an effort to stop him.

Then he became intolerable.

I tried to break away then, but he held me so tightly that all I could do was squirm and wriggle, to no avail.

I threatened to scream. He dared me to!

By this time I was furious. Yet I dared make no outcry for fear I would attract attention and possibly be ejected from the hotel for having a man in my room. I thought then that this would just about the most heinous offense of which a girl could be guilty. Having a man in her room.

We wrestled and fought; fought and wrestled some more. I scratched his face. And he kept kissing me again and again. Just when I had grown so weak and exhausted that I was near collapse, he suddenly relaxed his hold and hurled me away from him. Apparently, he was utterly disgusted over my struggles. He ran out, banging the door behind him.

I laid down on the bed and cried some more. Then I packed up my suitcase, intending to go to my sister's house and tell her everything. But the old urge to make the name of Rosa La France a byword in the theatre held me, and I showed up at the theatre that night as usual.

I was one of the first to arrive. "Tony" was alone back stage. The minute he saw me, he drew himself up and growled.

"You've got some nerve, you have. Coming back here after what happened today. You're fired. And I'll have you blackballed so you'll never be able to get another job."

I pleaded with him, but he was adamant. By that time the other girls had begun to come in and I departed sorrowfully, a trembling distracted wreck of a girl too heartsick and too unstrung to know or care what happened to me.

Two hours later I was sobbing out my wild story of grief on my sister Hazel's strong shoulders. She reassured me and said she would help me get back home, 400 miles away. She said she would send her husband down to collect my pay, and thrash "Tony" if he could find him. And I was to forget all about a career on the stage and go back to school.

But such was not to be.

One of the prop men who had a room adjoining mine in the hotel had overheard our struggle. Also he had been hidden back stage and was a witness to "Tony's" actions when I came in to go to work.

I have forgotten his name, but I never shall forget his kindness. He went to Bronco Billy and told him everything. And late that night came a message for me, stating that "Tony" had been fired, and that I was to rejoin the cast in Los Angeles the next and biggest town on our circuit.

I was frantically happy again, although I did feel a bit bad about "Tony" losing his job. I suppose he thought that I was just holding back; that I was like the other girls, except that I wouldn't give in without a tussle.

Anyhow, I showed up in Los Angeles for rehearsal. And that night I was back in my old position in the chorus, proudly speaking my cherished three-word part.

And that same evening real opportunity knocked at my door.

Roland [sic] Sturgeon, Vitagraph's famed director, was in the audience. Later, I learned that William Rock had written him that I was promising material for the screen.

He watched the performance and then sent his card back stage, after the show. On it he scribbled directions for me to call the following day at the Vitagraph Studios, in Santa Monica.

## Chapter Ten

I sent in the card and Sturgeon himself, attired in puttees, knickers, cap and sweater, and with a script in his hand, came out to greet me.

"I saw you, last night," he said. "And I believe you are just the girl I have been looking for to play 'Lorelei' in *Lorelei Madonna*. I am going to begin shooting it right away. Do you want the part?"

What a foolish question. Did I want the part? I certainly did. So far as I knew *Lorelei Madonna* might have been a new kind of breakfast food that you had to eat with castor oil instead of cream, but after almost a month on the road, Rosa La France was equal to any and all emergencies.

"All right," Sturgeon said, when I had apprised him of my willingness. "Let's get going!"

One of his assistants brought out a sleazy white drape affair and threw it over my shoulders. All the talking about my part was done by Sturgeon and his helpers. I didn't say a word.

"Now," he directed, when I had been costumed to meet his approval. "Now, just like a saint. Look like Lorelei. Sweet. And tragic. A Madonna."

Maybe I was good, at least so far as my saintly appearance was concerned, or perhaps Sturgeon didn't know what Lorelei looked like either, because we got along famously. He thought my expression was perfect.

"Now, in this scene," he explained, after the camera had been set up and the lights turned on, "you come in on the stage, which is set for a Spanish cafe. When you get inside you see the sailor boy who betrayed you. He has gone all the way back to Cuba, and you have followed him, because you are about to become the mother of his child.

You walk up to him and throw your arms around his neck. He repulses you and hurls you to the floor. Then, in a fury, you dash aside your saintly costume and pull this dagger out of your stocking and stab him through the heart."

"Just a minute, Rol, just a minute," interrupted the leading man, Phil Hart. "She's too anxious. Just explain to her that she is only to pretend to stab me through the heart; that this is all in fun. She has a sort of a tragic look in her eye that makes me kinda nervous."

Everybody laughed, including myself, and the others walked off the stage to clear the way.

Everything was in readiness for my dramatic entrance. Hart was seated at the table. The camera man began to turn. It was now all up to Lorelei. Up to Rosa La France.

Gathering in the folds of my costume and wearing my most saintly expression, I blithely tripped in.

Tripped in is correct, for I stumbled over a low stool and went sprawling at the feet of my mortified sailor boy lover. The dagger flew out and stuck, quivering in the floor.

"Hey," shouted the leading man, breaking the silence which followed my spectacular performance. "I'm through with this picture unless you get that girl a rubber dagger!"

He meant it, too. And the picture was held up half an hour while Sturgeon complied with his demand.

On the second attempt everything went smoothly. Lorelei, eyes distended, arms swinging wildly all over the place, and panting, as I imagined all great dramatics panted through their tragic love scenes, carried on.

And when the dead lover lay on the floor, Lorelei picked up her flowing white robe, kicked aside the rubber dagger, resumed her saintly expression and strolled off stage, to be congratulated by the entire company, including the tragically slain but miraculously resuscitated leading man.

Rosa La France was on the way to the top!

Sturgeon was pleased. He drew me to one side and talked salary. He gave me a contract guaranteeing me five days a week "when we worked," and a salary of $3 a day. I accepted it.

Three weeks elapsed and I, much to my chagrin, learned of the joker in my contract. "When we worked," looked fine in my typewritten contract but it certainly covered a multitude of postponed meals.

I had moved into a fourth rate hotel near a theatre on Spring Street, between Eight and Ninth Avenues, Los Angeles. This dingy edifice, of the boarding house type, was frequented principally by ham actors, like myself, who were barely scraping out an existence by the skin of their teeth.

When I had spent my last dollar and had grown desperate, I solved my living expense problems by arising early in the morning, before dawn, walking around the block, and sneaking milk bottles off of isolated door steps. Another girl, who was virtually in the same boat as myself, showed me the trick.

And, throughout this period of depression, I daily wrote home, telling my parents how wonderfully my career was progressing and never mentioning the hardships and ordeals I was undergoing.

Eventually, word leaked out that Mack Sennett was about to begin shooting one and two-reel comedies in his new studio at Glendale.

Of course, I felt that I was a tragedienne, but if one must become a comedienne in order to earn three meals a day, I would drown my art if that was necessary and become a comedienne, too.

So I went to Glendale and was able to put through my paces by the great Mack Sennett in person. I had heard much of him and considered him on a parity, socially and in an executive way, so to speak, with the President of the United States.

And when he had closed our interview with the remark: "This little girl is a comer. Yes, sir. Here's a comer!" why I would have been willing to vote him greater than the President any old day.

I had always been a great admirer of Mabel Normand. When Sennett casually mentioned I was to appear in a picture with her, I felt that I was truly in fairy land. My wildest dreams had come true.

*Soldiers of Misfortune* was the title of the picture, and the leading man was named Murray, a newcomer to the screen whose first name I do not remember.

In those days every extra girl had to furnish her own costumes, usually cheap little affairs, made up in various styles, that could be used over and over again.

Sennett asked me if I had an evening dress. I didn't have one but I assured him that I had. The only one I had ever owned, one with a little piece of ermine on the collar, which I had bought with my first week's salary in "The Girl at the Gate," had been stolen from me at the hotel. Perhaps one of the girl friends I had made had traded it for a meal.

## Chapter Ten

Anyhow, it was gone and I simply had to get one by hook or crook. I was up against it and on the verge of despair when I happened to remember an evening gown which Annette Selovus, my room mate at the moment, owned. Only a day or two before, she, hard pressed by the wolf, had taken a temporary position in a department store and, consequently, had little need for it.

I broached the subject to her as soon as she arrived and obtained her permission to use it. It was a gold net affair, a little hoop at the bottom and the skirt trimmed with skunk. Truly a magnificent garment, I thought.

Arrayed in this I appeared on the Sennett lots [the] next day and, after being made up by an elderly wardrobe mistress, came into the presence of the great Normand, then at the peak of her career.

She was a peach. Star that she was, she laughed and joked with every one, from the lowliest extra girl, including myself, to the office boys, who lounged around awaiting a summons.

Often, years later, when I, too, reached stardom and we had become warm friends, Mabel and I laughed about this, our first meeting.

My role consisted of walking in front of the camera, in hautish, exaggerated "society" style, and dropping my handkerchief when directly in the middle of the stage. That concluded my part for the day and I was told to return the next.

Alas! The next day never came. Annette and I quarreled about something that night—some inconsequential thing which I don't even remember—and she wouldn't lend me her dress.

Unless I had it for the sequence I couldn't appear. So Mack Sennett lost a prospective star. I never went back, although it almost broke my heart to stay away.

Three more doleful and hungry weeks went by. I was broke, but my stubborn pride wouldn't let me write home for money. I knew that my parents couldn't afford to send me any. And I'd been writing of my sensational success, promising that I would soon be in a position, financially, to send for them.

I was in a quandary. I didn't know where to turn. And, in seeking a solution to my problems I narrowly escaped tottering over the edge of the crater of disaster.

A girl friend, Marie—that is not her real name but it will suffice—a chance acquaintance, who had magnanimously offered to share with me her twenty-dollar-a-month apartment on Orange Avenue, Hollywood—a proposal which I eagerly accepted—almost lured me into destruction.

[*Editors' note:* Some material missing at this point in extant copies of Rubens's autobiography.]

... It's easy to get along, once you get the hang of things. All the girls get wise, sooner or later."

The significance of her explanation escaped me. I was so innocent that I probably would have believed her if she had told me that she plucked dollars off of money trees. My education was to begin later on.

Regularly, I made the rounds, trying to catch on with this or that concern which I heard was casting. And, just as regularly, I would return late in the afternoons, exhausted and despondent. Occasionally, Marie would catch me crying and would comfort me.

Then, one evening, following a telephone call of somewhat mysterious import, she invited me to accompany her to a party.

You're going out with me tonight and learn all about everything," she said. "We'll have a crackerjack of a good time and we'll make some money, too. Ten dollars apiece, at least."

I thought I was ready for anything, especially if it was a chance to earn money. I had been broke so long that I would have welcomed a chance to join a gang of bank robbers.

We dolled up in our best—my best consisting of one little tailored suit, bought off a bargain counter—and started out.

To this day I don't know where we went, except that we traveled a long ways in the general direction of Berkeley. We transferred once on the trolley, I know, and then walked quite a distance.

Eventually we arrived at our destination, a stucco, two-story house with a wide veranda, that sat back from the sidewalk on a landscaped terrace. I recall that my first reaction when I saw this place was to wonder why people who lived in such a pretty home should keep all the shades tightly drawn.

I was soon to find out.

Marie rang the bell. The door opened instantly. It appeared as though the colored maid had been awaiting our arrival.

"Madame is upstairs, but the gentlemen are here," she said. "Madame said you should wait in the drawing room until she comes down and introduces you."

Even then I did not smell a rat.

We followed her over rugs so gorgeous, so luxurious and so deep, that it seemed to me like I sank in up to my ankles. There were oil paintings on the walls, richly upholstered furniture, a magnificent phonograph in one corner and a baby grand piano in the other. Overhead was a frescoed ceiling, depicting a flight of angels, while from the center was suspended the most beautiful chandelier I had ever seen.

The ensemble so enthralled me that I imagined I was in the palace of an Oriental king, an Indian potentate, or perhaps, the home of some rich movie magnate, who likely would give us jobs.

Madame "Beaucaire" swept in a moment later. She had on a beautiful evening gown, cut low in the back and trailing the floor behind her. She wore a gem-studded Spanish comb, pearl earrings, and her fingers bore at least half a dozen sparkling diamonds.

I was stricken dumb with admiration. Marie introduced me, but I don't believe I heard a word she said, or Madame's reply.

The latter excused herself and a moment later reappeared with two men. One of these was about forty-five; a tall, straight man, lean of face and deeply tanned, whom she introduced simply as "Henry."

The other, "Jimmy," was perhaps ten years older and a little inclined to stoutness. He had snow white hair, so clean and so well groomed, that little patches of the pink skin underneath shone through. He also had merry twinkling blue yes [sic], which I learned later could be transferred into wells of fury when he became provoked.

"Henry" seated himself in a wing chair and Marie promptly climbed onto his lap and began kissing him, pinching his cheeks and ruffling his hair. "Jimmy" came over and sat beside me on the divan.

Madame "Beaucaire" withdrew.

I was terribly shocked at Marie's complacency in the face of "Henry's" attentions, now becoming bolder and bolder. I seemed to shrink within myself as the premonition flashed over me that all was not well.

I knew everything was all wrong a moment later when "Jimmy," whom I later learned was a millionaire hotel magnate with enormous properties in Los Angeles, Long Beach and other resorts, tried to draw me close.

"Don't be alarmed," he reassured me, petting my hand. "I won't hurt you. You're the sweetest little girl I have seen in many and many a day. Is this your first visit here?"

"Yes. This is the first time," I answered, trying to change the subject and steer him away from petting me. "Isn't it beautiful here? You must be awfully wealthy to own a home like this. I'm going to have beautiful things, too, when I become a star."

"Oh," he said. "So you're going to be a movie star! Are you? Well, you just stick with me and you'll wear diamonds!"

He tried to draw me into his arms, but I sprang to my feet and eluded him. I looked to Marie for moral support, but she was in an embrace with "Henry," and paid absolutely no attention.

"What's the matter, little one?" my admirer quizzed, good-humoredly. "Doesn't my particular style of beauty appeal to you?"

"I never mush with a man," I declared primly, by this time almost frightened out of my wits. Dumb as I was, I had begun to grasp a faint idea of why I was there. My surprise and hurt tone of voice must have aroused Marie, for she turned away from "Henry" long enough to remark:

"Oh, I forgot to tell you. You'll have to take things easy with her for a while; 'til she learns the ropes!"

So, that was what "learning the ropes" meant. I made up my mind to flee. I backed towards the door, "Jimmy" following me, muttering what he meant, I suppose, for words of reassurance.

Back, back, I went, until I bumped into the wall. "Jimmy" had me cornered and he pressed me into his arms. Struggle as I would, I could not break loose. Then I got one hand free and I raked my nails across his pink, perfumed jowls.

He cursed. His eyes, only a moment before two merry, blue stars, contracted into pin points of fire that seemed to drill me through and through.

"So that's your game, is it?" he demanded, as he seized my free arm, pinioning it and squeezing me until I thought surely my breath would leave my body. "So that's your game! Well, we'll see. I was going to go easy with you, but now, damn you, you'll do what I want! And, I won't give you a damned cent either!"

He pressed his lips to mine. I fought him tooth and nail. Then I bit him.

Lordy, and how I bit him! Even now it makes me tingle when I recall with what delicious abandon and joy I welcomed that white-haired old roué's screech of pain.

He let out a yell that must have been heard in Long Beach, where he still owns one of the biggest hotels. He dropped me like I was a sack of hot salt and he leaped around, first on one foot and then on the other, crying in agony.

Marie leaped to her feet. "Henry" promptly did a magic disappearing act. Madame "Beaucaire" came rushing in excitedly. Several other girls in upstairs rooms began to scream. Pandemonium reigned.

And I began to laugh. Mad as I was, I couldn't help it. The sight of that white-haired old reprobate, hopping around, tickled me so that I almost laughed myself into hysterics.

Madame "Beaucaire" was aghast. Then she attacked me like a Ogress. I fought back the best I could but she virtually dragged me to the front door and kicked me down the steps. A moment later Marie came tumbling after.

We dusted ourselves off and ran half a dozen blocks before either of us said a word. She broke the ice. I shall never forget her first remark. She must have had a real sense of humor, and I never believed she was hard of heart when she took me there.

"I do believe they like us," she panted, as we stopped beneath an electric light. "Can you imagine that?"

I snickered, but made no reply. There wasn't another word spoken until we were safely back in her own little flat, on Orange Ave.

In spite of my hectic experience, I felt no animosity for Marie. I realized she had really intended to do me a favor; to show me how to get along when things were going bad. Undoubtedly, Marie was one of the most generous souls that ever lived. She'd give away her shirt.

Never again did she try to induce me to accompany her, except to the movies, although she frequently received mysterious telephone calls and went out on what, I presume, were similar engagements.

From time to time during the ensuing months I managed to catch on a day or two at a time in various studios, ekeing [sic] out enough to pay my share towards the upkeep of our apartment.

We lived near the home of William Desmond Taylor, the celebrated director, whose mysterious murder several years later, precipitated one of the greatest scandals in the history of the movies.

## Chapter Eleven

I saw William Desmond Taylor on many occasions, as well as his valet, Sands, who disappeared simultaneously with his employer's tragic death.

An ideally handsome man, Taylor used to come out of his house in his puttees and knickers, all dressed for the lots, and climb into his nifty roadster while I stood, gasping, across the street.

He was very important appearing and frequently smiled at me as though he would like to get acquainted, if I would give him a little encouragement. The Lord knows I was dying to do so, and I spent about half my time before the mirror in our flat, trying to stiffen my backbone sufficiently to carry on a flirtation with him.

I would roll my eyes with my best "come hither" look, and carry on imaginary conversations with him for a half hour at a time. I would have it all figured out; exactly what I was say to him the next time I saw him, and then, when opportunity came, and he flashed me that winning smile, I'd get cold feet. I simply was not a flirt.

Then I moved away, but through some strange coincidence, years later, after I had become a star, and had been twice married and separated from my second husband, I was again living in the very same neighborhood when the great director was murdered.

And, stranger still, Marie, with whom I have always remained friendly, happened to be visiting me in my apartment at the time.

Never shall I forget that tragic day. Like everybody else in the neighborhood, we joined the curious that gathered as near as the police would allow them, on every side of the slain director's house.

We saw Mabel Normand drive up. As I recall it, Edna Purviance, Charlie Chaplin's leading lady, was with her. My heart was torn with pity for Mabel, for I had heard that she was tremendously in love with Taylor. And she had been kind to me on that sole occasion I had been in contact with her.

So far as that goes, I felt terrible myself, for although I had never actually known him, I once was head over heels in love with him too. Mabel was inside quite some time and when she came out her face was tear-stained and her shoulders shook with body-wracking sobs.

A little later Mary Miles Minter came by.

She, too, was weeping hysterically.

A constant stream of newspaper reporters and camera men passed in and out and it was due to their patient explanations that the motley crowd outside was kept informed what was transpiring within the murder house.

There was one particular reporter who was extremely kind to Marie and I. Every time there was a "break" he would dash up and tell us of the new developments. He was a handsome youngster—I never learned his name— and I promptly forgot my love for Taylor and that I was a married woman. Ever a romanticist in my heart, I was ready to go in a big way for my handsome reporter.

But alas, this romance was of short duration, lasting but a few hours, while in the midst of telling us how the police had found Mary Miles Minter's initialed garments in the house, indicating, he said mysteriously, that she could "explain many things," he did something that caused me to turn away from him in loathing and disgust.

He spat tobacco juice on the lawn!

All my life I had been, and still am, unnerved by the sight of a man chewing tobacco, although I myself smoke cigarettes. It so sickened me that I prevailed upon Marie to leave the solution of the mystery—and apprehension of the murderer—to the police.

We returned home and I never saw my handsome reporter again.

But getting back to my story, after my exciting experience at Mme. "Beaucaires'" and the ensuing lean months, good fortune finally smiled on me once more.

Somebody told me that David Wark Griffith, then head of the Fine Art Studios, was seeking new talent. I hurried there. When I arrived the outer waiting room was crowded to capacity with men, women and girls, all of whom, apparently, had received the same tip.

For hours I stood there, on the outside of the group. My legs felt like crumbling beneath me, but I was glutton for punishment in those days, and I would have died in my tracks rather than leave before the employment manager announced that all selections were over for the day.

As I stood there, hoping against hope, Christie Cavany [sic], one of the directors, came along. He brushed by me, turned and then stopped, staring me right in the face.

"What's your name?" he demanded brusquely.

"Rosa La France!" I promptly responded.

"You ought to photo well," he said, grasping me by the arm. "Here, come along with me!"

He escorted me through—as I saw them—the golden portals into the presence of General Director Woods, who, in turn, took one look at me, and then, without comment, ushered me into the presence of the mighty Griffith, himself.

"My God!" I thought. "Here's Griffith. David Wark Griffith. How did I ever get here?"

Whereupon, as usual, when excited, I did my famous imitation of a statue in cheese.

Somehow or other I knew that Griffith was going to engage me. I had the feeling in my bones. Thump! Thump! Thump! My heart pounded rhythmically: "He'll hire you! He'll hire you!"

And hire me he did, without ever a photographic test.

But before he did he kidded me quite a bit.

"Baby," he said, using the name which my parents had always called me, "you certainly do use them big brown eyes to advantage. They remind me of a deer—a doe—just gasping out its last breath. If any one ever saw a dying doe, they'd never shoot one again. Your eyes are just like that. Just like the eyes of a dying doe."

Then he made a great ceremony about my contract, which called for $15 a week for the first three months, $20 at the end of that time, and $30 at the end of the year. This was a good contract, however, that provided under its options for my pay, regardless of whether we worked.

I felt that I was on Easy Street. I was so elated that I ran all over town, showing my contract to everybody I knew, and doubtless creating the impression that I had lost my mind.

Fifteen dollars a week for three months! Not such an enormous sum, but in those days, a guarantee that I would have to visit no more doorsteps seeking unprotected milk bottles for my daily sustenance. Yes, thanks to Griffith, my shopping hours, before dawn, were a thing of the past.

One of the first persons I met on the Fine Arts lots was Anita Loos, who later became famous as an author, playwright and scenario writer. At that time she was a general handy woman, trying to write titles, original stories, take dictation and otherwise act as office girl for John Emerson, later to become head of Actor's Equity Association, and whom she married happily, I might saw—and one of the few movie marriages that has withstood the ravages of time.

Other girls engaged about the same time, occupying the same status and who later become stars, included Mae Marsh; Mildred Harris, who later married Charlie Chaplin; Colleen Moore; Carmel Myers; Pauline Stark; and Bessie Love.

The actual star of Fine Arts was Lillian Gish, one of the sweetest girls that ever trod the face of this earth.

My first appearance in a Fine Arts picture was one in which Bessie Love was used as the lead, playing opposite Douglas Fairbanks, who had just arrived from the East. Helen Warren, also from the legitimate stage, was also in the picture.

The picture was completed in three days, after a trip to Balboa, during which the ever-agile Doug, apparently smitten by my charms, tried in every way to impress me.

As it so happened, Rosa La France died an unnatural death at this stage of my career. She was ruthlessly cast aside without mourning and without flowers.

Griffith had a habit of changing everybody's name at will. He changed one to Love Darling, another to Grace Pretty, and even Bessie Love was a name which she adopted at his suggestion.

"Your name should be Beverly Juno," he calmly informed me one day after we had returned from Balboa. "That Rosa La France sounds too affected. I don't like it. From now on you're Beverly Juno!"

I was tickled silly with the idea, although I felt that Rosa La France was getting a sordid deal. But I thought that Beverly Juno was beautiful and wrote home accordingly.

My father in the past had on many occasions, by letter, protested against my use of the name Rosa La France. And he answered: "That's just as bad as the other one. Reubens is a fine old name; one that any one should be proud of; a name that no one can despoil. It ought to be good enough for you."

I was so touched with his epistle that I showed it to Griffith. He read the letter through and thought before commenting: "It's a beautiful thought, but I think your old man is all wet. Your name is hard to spell and it ought to changed if you expect to get anywhere in the movies."

After considerable argument, friendly, of course, Griffith, ever the most democratic fellow in the world, agreed with me, the poor extra, that my real name might do if I would cut out the letter "e" in the first syllable.

So, for the purposes of the screen, I became Alma Rubens, and have stuck to it ever since.

By some freak of fate, in my next picture for Griffith, *The Half Breed*, I was chosen for the lead, opposite Fairbanks, who, apparently had liked me ever since our trip to Balboa. This, despite the fact that I had not encouraged him in the least.

We went on location, and oh, boy! Believe me, I had excitement enough with Doug, to last a lifetime.

## CHAPTER TWELVE

The first scenes were to be shot at Redwood. Allan Dwan was the director and there were fifteen in the company besides Doug and myself. The cameraman was Victor Fleming, and it was in this picture that Winifred Westover, who later married and divorced Bill Hart, crept into prominence.

Never shall I forget this, my first trip over night on location. The company was quartered in a queer little mountain shack resort in the wildest country I ever saw. No sooner had dusk settled down over us than the coyotes—I thought they were timber wolves—began their infernal yapping, which they kept up until dawn.

I lay in bed with the covers pulled over my head, afraid to breathe. For an eternity, it seemed, I lay there, my nerves tautened to the breaking point. Then—it must have been around 2 o'clock in the morning, I heard a scratchy sound at the one window of my room. I wanted to shriek, but I was so frightened that I couldn't make a sound.

There came a distinct tapping noise and I heard a husky whisper from the outside: "Alma, Alma."

I gasped with relief. Dumb as I was, I knew that no mountain lion could responsible for this so I leaped out of my bed to investigate.

It was Doug!

"Sss-ss-s-sh! Open the window and let me in," he said.

"My goodness," I whispered back. "What under the name of Heavens do you want at this time of night?"

"We've got to talk over the story," he whispered.

I threw open the window and Doug, ever the showman, made his entrance in his best Mark of Zorro style.

He wasted little time talking about the "Half Breed," offering me, instead, the opportunity to accompany him back to New York where he was to play the lead in "Manhattan Madness."

He painted a glowing picture of my future, in this event.

"Six months in New York," he explained, "and you'll be made. Your name will be in the electric lights along Broadway. You'll have jewels, gowns, a Rolls-Royce—everything. I'll make you the leading woman in every picture I play in. You'll be getting a thousand a week."

*The Half Breed* was Fine Arts' last picture. The company went broke the day after my parents—whom I had sent for on the strength of my contract—arrived in Los Angeles. I had rented a furnished flat for them on Seventh Avenue, and we had quite a celebration in honor of the event.

When I learned that Fine Arts was going out of business, I was frantic. I had used my last cent in getting my parents settled. And they had used their last penny in making the long trip from San Francisco.

I dreaded the ordeal of telling my mother. I dawdled away as much time as I could, simply to postpone meeting her. I never was any good as a liar, and even if I failed to tell her, I knew she would find out anyhow.

Then I got one of the greatest—and sweetest—surprises of my life. My mother met me at the door. She was waving a telegram.

It was from Thomas Ince, then head of Triangle, with their studio at Inceville. He wanted to know if I would play in *Truthful Tulliver* with William S. Hart.

Would I? It was manna from heaven. And I lost no time in sending him word that I would be there first thing in the morning.

It was during the filming of this picture that Hart met Winifred Westover, whom he subsequently married. She had a small part, and at the beginning he high-hatted her something terribly.

Hart complimented me on the work I had done in The Half Breed with Fairbanks, and explained to me what I would have to do in his picture. I listened intently and assured him that I could carry out the role.

Then we went on location.

I made two more pictures for Ince in which Hart played the leads.

It was during the filming of the last of these that I met Franklyn Farnum, who became the first of my three husbands; a marriage destined to last but a scant twenty-four hours.

Franklyn Farnum came to Triangle just about the time that Tex Guinan broke into the movies, trying to create a female Bill Hart. He was a handsome man and all the girls, including myself, promptly fell in love with him.

I was just at that romantic age—about eighteen—when I could fall in and out of love every twenty-four hours. I think the thing that drew me to Farnum more than anything else was his beautiful shirts. He had the most gorgeous silk shirts I ever saw. Dozens of them. He never wore the same one twice, it seemed. All monogrammed and all of the most vivid patterns.

It was also the same way with his suits. He had one for every occasion. His valet was always with him on the lots, and sometimes he would make a complete change between shots. Just for the sake of keeping his immaculate appearance.

And he had the most beautiful teeth—even, white and sparkling, and, capping the climax, as it were, was his beautiful, shiny Hupp car—a roadster, of special design. It was a thing to rave about. Dark brown, with yellow stripes, that car had me absolutely daffy. And when he finally noticed me and invited me to take a ride with him, my joy knew no bounds.

I was his for the asking, and ask me he did.

Why he asked me to marry him is something I never have been able to figure out to this day, in view of my experiences as his bride. For the purposes he wanted me, which were subsequently outlined in my annulment suit, but never published in detail, he might as well have taken me on that first day.

I was so smitten that I would joyfully have followed him to the ends of the world; would have done anything at his bidding, I suppose. But for some mysterious reason, he chose to carry on a protracted and ardent—I might say hectic—courtship.

On the occasion of our first ride he told me he loved me more dearly than anything else in the world. He said he was thirty. I afterwards found out he was forty-three.

He accompanied me home and I introduced him to my parents, my father being ill in bed—in one of his frequent relapses at the time. My mother warned me after he had gone, that he had deceived me as to his age. I wouldn't believe her.

## Chapter Thirteen

I refused to take their advice, however. I met Farnum regularly on the lots and frequently he would take me riding in his magnificent automobile.

His actual proposal of marriage came while he was engaged on a picture being filmed at Universal City. He boasted that he was getting $400 a week, a sum unheard of in those days. I was duly impressed.

He must have anticipated my acceptance, because the moment I said "yes," he reached into his waistcoat and drew out a beautiful small diamond, perhaps a carat in size. I thought it was the most gorgeous gem in existence and it made me so happy that I burst into tears.

It seems to me now, looking back over the years, that my life has been one vale of tears. I cried when I was happy and I cried when I was unhappy. I cried in between. My mother has often told me that if some way could have been found to store my tears, we never would have to spend $15,000 irrigating our ranch.

When the day's work was ended I rushed home to tell my mother and father of my good fortune. They both advised me against marriage.

I would listen to none of their entreaties, however, and, finally, mother promised to make me a wedding dress. She worked all night on that dress, a beautiful white crepe affair, with a veil and a long train. I awoke about 7 o'clock the next morning when she had completed it. Her face was drawn and haggard and her eyes bloodshot from her night of tears. But she made no protest when I informed her we were going to be married that day.

My father was too ill to attend the wedding, held in the afternoon at the Church Around the Corner, in Los Angeles. My mother and the church sexton were my witnesses. Nobody else was there.

The ceremony over, my husband drove us in his car to my home; my mother got out and went inside to get my suitcase, and we were off.

My father had refused to see Farnum, a refusal which almost broke my heart at the time, but which, in view of later events, caused me to forgive him.

Our honeymoon began in the "Ship Cafe," Santa Monica, where we went for our wedding supper. I had wanted my husband to take mother with us there, but he would have no part of her. He said we would be too conspicuous. And, as usual, I let him have his way.

Strange and sudden as this had been, I was happy. Proud of my handsome husband and head over heels in love with him, I though. We had great difficulty in getting a table, but finally the head waiter found us one almost in the middle of the room, which was crowded.

My husband ordered. I forgot what. I was too happy to care, and I don't remember having eaten a bit up to the time I was rudely shocked back to earth by his vicious remark: "What are you flirting with that man for?"

He pointed at a handsome youth, sitting with another girl at a side table. I never before had seen this man, but I later learned that it was Norman Kerry. I afterwards became acquainted with him, very friendly, in fact, and like myself, neither of us was aware of the other's presence.

My husband would not believe me, however, and insisted that we leave. Then we went to the King George Roof, atop the hotel where he had made reservations.

We had two dances and he excused himself, returning fifteen minutes later with the abrupt remark: "Well, let's go!"

There was nothing else for me to do but follow my lord and master. I would have liked a few more dances. The details of that honeymoon night I later set forth in my annulment suit. Sufficient to say that before daybreak I had fled and taken a taxicab for home.

I remember little of that ride, I was so hysterical and ill. But the sight of our own little flat was the sweetest thing I ever expect to see.

I leaped out before the cab was at a standstill and ran to the door. And as I did so, I became aware that my husband, in his brown roadster, had followed me.

Even as I rang the bell he skidded to a stop at the curb and made a dash for me. I screamed. And just before he reached for me, the door opened, my mother caught me, dragged me inside and slammed the door in his face.

## Chapter Fourteen

The next day I was too ill to get out of bed. The doctor said I must be treated for at least three weeks if I were to recover from the shock. But before that period of convalescence had passed a lawyer came and filed my suit.

And, as for my husband of less than a day, it was his end in the pictures.

A month later I was again back at work on the Triangle lots, none the worse for my sad marital experience, but, perhaps, a little wiser.

Three months afterward I met Dr. Daniel C. Goodman, then about forty, and whom I married after a long courtship.

Goodman was then head of Triangle's story department, having given up a remunerative practice in St. Louis because of his growing fame as an author.

Among those who joined Triangle at about the same time, and who later became famous, were Charles Ray, Gloria Swanson, Olive Thomas, who married Jack Pickford, became a drug addict and met a tragic death abroad, and Dorothy Dalton, now the wife of Arthur Hammerstein.

But for an unfortunate occurrence I might have been in the position occupied on the screen by Gloria Swanson. And perhaps, if I hadn't missed my golden opportunity, I might have been in Gloria's shoes today.

Of course, there is no use crying over spilled milk, but I simply must tell my greatest regretted "it might have been."

I had just been cast with William Desmond and was four days advanced on the picture when Cecil De Mille, who "discovered" Gloria, and carried her up the ladder to riches and fame, telephoned, asking that I call at his office for an interview.

I was so busy on the picture that it was not until two days later that I found time to answer the summons. And, in the meantime, he had seen and talked with Gloria with the result that he signed her up on a long contract.

Afterwards I heard from an intimate of the great director that he had been impressed with my ability and that he really had wanted me instead of Gloria, but hadn't seen fit to pursue me when I had failed to respond immediately.

Shortly after this I was introduced to Dr. Goodman, who liked me at once and invited me to accompany him to a party. He saw me home that evening and became my regular attendant.

Then he resigned from Triangle to accept a better position with Pathe in New York. And before he had been there a month I received an offer from them through Dr. Goodman to go to New York to play in "a picture of my own."

I was tickled silly. I danced and pranced around the house that evening until I almost drove my parents to distraction. My father was ill in bed, a little worse than usual, but we didn't realize how bad off he was.

Both father and mother were anxious to have me get every possible advantage, but, of curse, were reluctant to have me travel such a long distance from home. I convinced them, however, that it was necessary, and I telegraphed Dr. Goodman my acceptance.

Then began the hectic ceremony of shopping in preparation for the five-day trip. I spent almost the entire day before I was scheduled to leave down in town, making most of my purchases in the five and ten-cent stores. This was necessary because of my limited capital. Dr. Goodman had sent me my railroad ticket but nothing more, and I was afraid to wire for an advance for fear they would cancel their offer.

As I neared home I was struck with a premonition that something was wrong. I don't know how to describe the feeling, but my nerves tingled, my heart began to palpitate and I became faint.

I arrived just in time to meet our family doctor coming out. I knew he must have been to see my father and I dreaded the worst.

"How is he?" I gasped.

"Oh, he'll get along all right," reassured the doctor. "He just had an extra bad pain. It is not dangerous. So don't look so worried."

I knew that he must be wrong. I dashed up the steps to father's room. The moment that I saw him the thought struck me that he was dying. His face was pallid. His eyes seemed dimmed. Perspiration stood in little beads on his forehead. His hands clasped and unclasped nervously outside the coverlet.

My mother stood by the side of the bed. She cautioned me to remain silent; that papa was asleep. I just stood there, knowing, sensing that he was going, but in view of what the doctor had said, hoping against hope that my premonition was without foundation.

And an instant later my father awakened. When he saw me he smiled—a wan smile, a deathly smile that confirmed my suspicions.

"Alma, Baby," he called, stretching his arms to me.

I dashed to the bedside and dropped to my knees. I threw my arms around him and an instant later he was dead.

He died right there in my arms!

It was all over in an instant. I was completely crushed. My mother knelt beside me with her arms around me and we both wept until our tear wells were dry.

When the funeral was over and my dear old father buried, I resumed preparations for my trip to New York—and collapsed. My nerves were entirely shattered. It required a month's treatment before the doctor would allow me to start East.

My mother put me on the train. I had only one suitcase. One little traveling suit and one little hat. She cautioned me to beware of strange men that tried to talk to me on the way. She said I should have nothing to do with them, no matter how nice or friendly they appeared.

I had an upper berth because it was cheaper. I had never traveled before except on my one trouper's tour—nearly all short jumps. On the second day out from Los Angeles I became violently ill. Train sickness.

The man who occupied the birth under me changed with me. He talked to me like I was a little girl. He reminded me so much of my father that I paid no heed to my mother's warning, and he kept me company, entertaining me with magazines and jokes all the way to Chicago.

I had very little money and ate but two meals a day in the diner. My friend many times urged me to accompany him to dinner or lunch, but I was too prudish to accept.

Occasionally a traveling salesman—or a drummer as we always called them—would try to flirt with me. But I would not notice them. On the whole, everybody was awfully kind to me all the way.

In Chicago I had to wait four hours for my train connection. I sat the whole time on one seat in the station, my shabby little pasteboard suitcase beside me, and shivering with apprehension.

I had read stories of white slavery, and I was taking no chances.

When I arrived in New York at the Grand Central, it was snowing and blowing and the streets were dark and dreary. Dr. Goodman met me and took me to the Commodore Hotel.

After he had taken me to my room and I took off my coat, his first remark almost floored me.

"Heavens!" he said. "You can't wear an outfit like that!"

Then he laughed.

I looked myself over and finally laughed too. My little suit was a cheap little affair with black sleeves. I had them altered to make them even longer, snaky appearing things that I thought had make me look like a vampire.

I suppose I must have been thinking of Theda Bara, whom I had long admired, and felt that I could adopt a little of her personality I'd make a hit on Broadway.

Dr. Goodman's reception somewhat dampened my aspiration along that line, however. Especially when he said Pathe had given him money to buy me a completely new wardrobe.

I bought an entire outfit, modish and expensive, before we went to the Pathe offices where I was to sign a contract to play the leading role in *Thoughtless Women* with a salary of $500 a week.

Gee! I couldn't believe it. Five hundred dollars a week. For days and days I pinched myself until I was black and blue, believing I was in the midst of a pleasant dream.

My first thought after being handed my initial salary was to save so I could send for my mother. I liked Dr. Goodman a great deal. He was the first man with whom I had come in contact who was a real gentleman. I adored him for that. But, despite his kindness and his efforts to keep me happy, I longed for my mother.

Her arrival, soon after I finished my first picture in the East, was one of the happiest days in my life. She too liked Dr. Goodman. H was a quiet, studious sort of chap. He talked of things that enchanted me. And he taught me things that I really wanted to know and appreciated.

I read my first real love novel, "Virgin Soil," at his request. I was so enamored with it. I never had read anything but the cheapest trash in the past that I clamored for more. After that I devoured book after book, written by the best fiction writers, Dr. Goodman always counseling me in their selection.

Then came the great day of days, that on which I signed my first real contract as a "star." And, at a thousand a week!

## Chapter Fifteen

We had just completed the picture for Pathe, when I received an urgent message to visit the office of Zit—C. F. Zittel, publisher of Zit's Weekly—at once. I did, as I had seen "Thoughtless Women" and had liked it.

Within half an hour we agreed on a contract under which I was to receive $1000 a week for the first year, with an option of $1,500 for the second. He was acting in behalf of Cosmopolitan Pictures.

Then, as usual, the gods of chance threw a monkey wrench into the wheels of my life.

As I about to affix my signature to this most formidable pact, Zit casually asked: "I suppose you are of age?"

I dropped the pen, but my heart beat it to the floor.

I tried to say "yes" but my tongue said "no."

My feet wouldn't move. They were stuck to the floor. My mouth was open and I hadn't the power to close it. I just stood there mute, broken-hearted, utterly incapable of coping with my feelings.

Zit led me to a divan and tried to console me. "Never mind, Alma," he said. "All you'll have to do is bring your mother here. She can sign the papers and everything will be all right."

He didn't know that my mother was in California—3,000 miles away. And he wasn't aware that neither of us had enough money for her to make the trip. My first picture had taken only two weeks to make. I had spent all my money. I was at sea, but finally managed to explain the situation.

## Chapter Fifteen

Zit reached for the telephone and asked me where to call her. I told him, and when she answered at the other end of the wire, he handed the instrument to me.

"Mom, mom," was all I could say. "Momma, dear, you've got to hurry. I'm to get a thousand a week. Hurry here to sign to [sic] contract."

I don't remember what else was said, but whatever it was, everything was arranged and she was to leave at once.

I went back to my room at the Commodore, but I don't believe I slept a wink during the four days and five nights before my mother got to New York. When she arrived, I couldn't wait until she got to Zit's office. The poor woman was hustled off before she even had a chance to comb her hair. And when the contract was signed I led her back to the hotel, so excited, so exhausted, so happy, that I fell asleep in a chair.

Then began the long wait for a role. I didn't do a lick of work, except collect my salary, for the first six months I was with Cosmopolitan.

My first picture was "Humoresque," in which I was the star, supported by Gaston Glass. Never shall I forget the thrill when I first saw my name in huge electries [sic] on Broadway; recalling to my memory the prophecy I had made to my dear, sick father on the day of my confirmation and loss of my first handsome scar-faced fireman lover.

Dr. Goodman, meantime, still was attentive. I frankly told him I didn't love him. I admired him greatly, and would have cut off my right hand rather than hurt him, but I just couldn't think of marrying him.

My mother, too, adored him, and added her arguments to his, but I was adamant.

So things went along until, in my second year with Cosmopolitan I was notified without previous warning one afternoon that I, with the rest of the cast, was to sail for Europe at the end of that week.

When my mother came in we both became so excited we broke out in a nervous rash. Our arms and chests were covered with little red pimples that didn't disappear for days.

The picture was called "Enemies of Women," and most of the scenes were in Paris.

When we had completed this, mother and I made a tour that took us to Berlin, Vienna, Rome, Venice, Madrid and most of the principal cities of which we had heard so much, but which, up until I received my sailing orders, we had never hoped to be able to visit.

During my absence Dr. Goodman had been made vice-president and executive head of Cosmopolitan.

Upon our return I married Dr. Goodman. He had always been so kind, so good to me and to mother, and so sincere.

The ceremony took place in Greenwich, Conn., and we rented an apartment on West 59th St., overlooking Central Park. My mother took an apartment of her own at the San Remo Hotel.

As might have been expected in the circumstances, we were unhappy from the beginning. I found I did not love him. He was too quiet; too serious-minded. Where love is missing on one side there can be no real marital happiness.

Then came an illness, painful and nerve-wracking, though of short duration, but which proved to be the ultimate stumbling block upon which my career was wrecked.

It marked the beginning of my addiction to the use of narcotic drugs.

## Chapter Sixteen

My first shot of morphine, administered to ease my suffering, was given me by Dr. A., now one of the leading gynecologists in the country and a professor in one of our great universities.

Later, when my husband learned the exact nature of the treatment for my womanly weakness—the use of morphine—he called in another great physician, Dr. B., who said it would be a crime to operate on a girl of my tender age—and conceded that his contemporary's treatment was a most proper one.

Oh, God! If these two doctors only could have foreseen the untold suffering they so innocently caused me, they surely would have found some other method of treating my ailment.

Of course, the actual continuance of the use of morphine was the fault of myself and myself alone. I realized it eventually might lead me to becoming an addict, but I thought myself strong enough to quit it before it got a hold on me.

It is so easy to convince one's self that "this one last time won't make any difference." And, it is so hard for a young girl to suffer almost unendurable torture which had been the blight of my existence, periodically, since I reached the age of adolescence.

More and more I felt the urge to calm myself and ease my periodic pain with the soothing drops of white liquid that brought such relief.

My husband had kept remonstrating with me until, eventually, I promised to quit using the morphine. For a long time I relived my suffering with secret injections, despite his worrying, suspicious scrutiny.

Oftener and oftener it became necessary for me to resort to the treatment. The terrible pain gnawed at me daily, hourly, unless I alleviated my suffering with a "shot."

Then, for the first time (this was about a year and a half after Dr. A had given me my first injection) I realized that I was a dope addict; a term which has always and still does strike terror into my soul.

Alma Rubens was a dope fiend.

A weak, worldly girl, who hadn't sufficient will power to cast aside the treacherous needle; the insiduous [sic] liquid, responsible for my loathesome [sic] yearning.

Oh, God. No one knows how ashamed I was. No one will ever believe when I say that I spent hours, days, weeks, during that period, on my knees, praying, imploring God to save me, to give me strength to break away; and that failing, to let me die!

I had no friendly ear to listen to my troubles. I couldn't tell my husband, because our relations were already broken. After pleading heartbrokenly with me, he had removed to separate quarters in a hotel.

And, I couldn't tell my mother, because she wouldn't have understood. As I have said before, she is of an extremely practical nature. She would never fail in anything. No thing—no person—could crush her. Love me, she always has. But she has never understood me!

So, in my dilemma, after months and months of this, I decided to return to California. I thought maybe a change of atmosphere might benefit me. Maybe, in the milder climate there, the terrible longing might be overcome. I might be able to cure myself, without my mother learning of my predicament.

Upon my arrival there, I added to my woes, by falling hopelessly in love with Ricardo Cortez. Poor old Alma. What troubles!

A dope fiend. Unhappily married. Desperately in love with another man. And no one to confide in.

## Chapter Seventeen

Cortez had just been assigned a role in "Cytheria" at that time, the first picture made by First National after they had taken over Cosmopolitan Pictures. I was introduced to him by George Fitzmaurice, and, so far as I was concerned, it was a case of love at first sight.

The very day I met him I read a notice in the papers to the effect that he was engaged to marry Agnes Ayres. I grieved about that for days and days, although I continued to meet him almost daily on the set and he showed signs of reciprocating my affections.

Cortez, who, as I mentioned before, was the son of a kosher butcher with a shop on First Ave., New York, was my ideal. Tall, dark, slender and with a Greek god profile the more I saw of him the more I loved him.

Incidentally, I might mention, that, according to the story I heard more than a year after our marriage, he was given the name Cortez by J-jj-j-o-e Frr-r-r-i-s-co, that inimitable wag of the stage, who happened to become acquainted with Cortes [sic] while on the movie lots.

At that time, Cortez was a prop man, occasionally assigned to small parts, and he was complaining to Frisco, as they sat in a Los Angeles restaurant, about the difficulty he had obtaining parts because of his name, "Jacob Kranz."

Frisco, always on the alert for a chance to spring something funny, casually turned around, peered into the cigar store adjacent to their table, and counselled:

"Oh-o! Is t-t-that so? Lo-oo-o-ok at that!" and he pointed a finger at two cigar boxes reposing within. "L-loo-ok at that! A-ab-abso-lu-lutely perfect! Ri-ri-ricar-do Co-co-cortez!"

So, Ricardo Cortez, he became, the name under which I met him and which I believe his own for almost a year after our marriage. Ric was an awful prevaricator. I actually believed his long-winded story that his mother, a famous Spanish prima donna, had died when he was a small child, immediately after his father brought her to America.

I didn't learn that his mother—a quiet, intelligent, lovable old Jewish woman—was alive until the time he was suddenly called away from Hollywood to appear with Gilda Gray, in "Aloma of the South Seas," several months after he had led me to the altar.

And, when I did learn of this, it almost broke my heart. Up until that time I had trusted him implicitly.

Of course, I was deceiving him, too. Daily I was taking my morphine injections, a situation of which he had not the slightest inkling. It was a case of deceiving deceivers, I suppose. But, I am getting far ahead of my story.

As I mentioned before, I was smitten the moment I laid eyes on Ricardo Cortez, and the thought that he was engaged to Agnes Ayres preyed on my mind, day and night. I continued seeing him on the lots, however, and finally, I consented to accompany him on a party, although I had firmly made up my mind that I would have nothing further to do with him, because he was an engaged man.

Then, stories appeared in the newspapers to the effect that he and Agnes had broken, that their engagement was permanently in the discard. I never shall forget how happy I was. I believe this was the only occasion in my life that I ever reveled in somebody else's misfortune—if I might call it that. Subsequent developments, however, lead me to believe she was a lovely girl.

Ric turned out to be the most egotistical human being, I supposed, that ever lived.

Meanwhile I continued with my drugs. Day by day my need for the daily "shot" grew more aggravating. I was living in a patio—rented—at that time, and my mother had returned West.

Immediately after her arrival I had filed a suit for divorce from Dr. Goodman, and pending trial of the issue—cruelty—I felt free to go around with Ric.

He visited me almost every night, and prior to his trip East, my craving for the drugs and my heartsoreness over Ric's absence I put in a miserable two months while he was away.

Then, the day of his return, we quarreled over one of the funniest things imaginable. I had had onions—fried onions—for dinner and he raised a terrific rumpus because I dared to kiss him when he alighted from the train.

This was soon patched up. We anxiously awaited the day my divorce decree from Dr. Goodman would become final. Well, to make a long story short, we underestimated the date by one day, went to Riverside, and were married.

Upon our return to Los Angeles we were dumbfounded to see an article in the newspapers to the effect that I was guilty of bigamy.

Oh, Lord! What a night I put in! I expected every minute for the police to come in and lead me away to jail. I was terrified. So was Ric. We hastily made arrangements for separate rooms and spent our first night of wedded life apart.

And, the next day, when the required legal time was up, what a time we had in getting remarried. The pastor who had married us before thought we were crazy and wouldn't re-tie the knot.

## Chapter Eighteen

We found another one, not so fastidious, however, and we were tied all over again. And, as usual, little Alma, always to be depended upon for something different, fainted. I collapsed in a heap, unconscious, at the completion of the ceremony.

I don't know whether it was the let-down from my nervous strain, caused by the fear of arrest, or whether it was from the fact that I had not had my daily "shot." But, anyhow, I fainted in my bridegroom's arms.

Ric was extremely concerned about me and carried me out to our car. And, that night, we occupied the same room, snapping our fingers in the faces of several reporters, who deigned to break in on our happiness.

The next day we both went on location. And, upon his return, we nearly split up.

When we were married he was getting $500 weekly from Famous

Players. The first thing I did after our marriage was to goad him into seeking an increase. He did so, receiving a new contract, under which he was paid $1,000 a week for the first year, with a renewal option at $1,500.

When we both returned home, Ric had the big head so bad that I felt like crowning him. They wanted him to play the lead in "Anna Karenina," but he objected, because he didn't like the leading woman. I don't remember who she was.

He also raised the devil because, in his absence, I had had my hair bobbed.

I was quite willing to retire. He was making sufficient money to support us in regal style, and I really wanted a home; a real home, which I wanted to take care of myself, and which, if I had gotten it, might have so occupied my time that I might have forgotten about my daily "shot."

Ric would have none of this. He went out every night; going to his club here and there, and never offering to take me along. Things went along this way for months, during which my craving for the drug grew stronger and stronger.

Two humorous incidents that followed on two consecutive days, just before I had to leave for the East myself to take part in a picture, almost led us to a marital split-up. This was about a year after our marriage.

We had gone to a Spanish restaurant in Los Angeles for dinner. The elderly waiter, a Spaniard, apparently recognizing Ric, by that time becoming popular, endeavored to make a hit with him.

Up until that time I never knew, although I had begun to suspect, that Ric, despite his "nativity," knew little or no Spanish. The only Spanish words I had ever heard him utter were "adios" and "caramba."

Well, this old waiter came up the moment we had seated ourselves and greeted us with a wave of Spanish. I never made any pretense of knowing the language, and looked at Ric expectantly.

He flushed and swore at the waiter—in English—and punctuating his remarks by pounding on the table. I burst into laughter.

"Oh," I volunteered. "What's the trub? No spikka da Espanole?"

He glared at me for a moment, pushed the table away, seized his hat and ran out, leaving me sitting there feeling like—and no doubt looking like—a fool.

The very next day somebody, I don't remember who, told me the real story of his ancestry. At first I was very much upset, but later I didn't take this so seriously. Anyway, I probably was imposing on him as much—or more—by my secret use of dope, as he had imposed on me.

That same afternoon, I was sitting in the living room, entertaining several women friends at tea, when, without warning, Ric burst into the room. He was attired in a magnificent toga and wore powdered curls, for a role in "Helen of Troy."

He looked gorgeous. There was no question about that. But I simply couldn't resist the temptation to make a dirty little dig at his egoism.

"Oh," I said, in the presence of everybody. "Doesn't my little Jakie Kranz look magnificent!"

Thinking back over the time, I really believe I must have been unusually exhausted by the drugs that afternoon, although no other woman present was an addict. I followed up the insult, by adding, after I had walked up and placed my arms around his shoulders:

"Oh. You're all padded up, too. Aren't you?" Then I pointed out the huge lumps of padding on each shoulder.

Ric glared at me. You can't blame him much for that. Then he turned and rushed out, without saying a word. His face was livid and he trembled in his anger.

The other women tittered, and, much to my shame, I must confess that I enjoyed my husband's discomfiture.

## Chapter Nineteen

At this time I seriously considered seeking an annulment of my marriage. My love for Ric was dying. But, after thinking it over, I didn't dare to, because I was so afraid that it might leak out that I was using morphine.

That is the insidious thing about dope. Always one is laboring under the fear of something or other. Fear that some one will find out; fear that you will not be able to get the next day's supply; fear that your source may be shut off; a thousand fears, any one of which would be sufficient to drive a victim into insanity.

So I went East. I completed my picture, and I returned.

Ric still had not the slightest suspicion that it was dope that was making me so nervous and irritable. Not for a moment did he think I was a confirmed drug addict. Neither did my mother, who thought it was my husband's lack of interest in our married life.

Soon after my return my mother bought me a beautiful six-room house at No. 1745 Wilton Place. This was purchased with money she had saved from my salary. We insisted on going halves on it, but my mother advised against it.

Well, despite the gnawing at my vitals, I went along, buying a stick of furniture here, a piece there, all of good quality and mostly antiques, which I sent to our new home. It was all very beautiful. If it hadn't been for the shame I felt at the knowledge of my terrible addiction I could have been happy, in spite of Ric's indifference.

The second year of our married life drifted by in about the same manner. I was cold; he was indifferent. However, during this time, we took a "honeymoon" trip—"a second honeymoon," the newspapers called it—to Europe. A weird honeymoon it was!

We were not on speaking terms most of the three months this took, although we regularly posed for photographs and the public thought we were an ideally happy married couple. My life has been full of such ironies.

Throughout these first two years of our married life I had been getting my daily drug supplies from a dozen physicians, including Dr. C., with whom I later had so much trouble. He accused me of stabbing him, but it wasn't so.

It was through Dr. C., incidentally, when he could no longer safely comply with my more and more frequent demands for dope prescriptions, that I was contacted with a Federal narcotic agent of San Bernadine.

But that is getting ahead of my story. Ric and I were growing further and further apart. I didn't dare leave him and I felt he was growing suspicious of me.

Wally Reid once told me that his greatest suffering during his futile battle against the habit came through this deadly fear of being found out. Of course, I wasn't an addict at that time, but his words came back to me time and again now that I had acquired the habit.

On many occasions I was sorely tempted to go to my mother and confess. Then I would cast aside the idea because I felt that this knowledge might kill her. The Lord knows she had had a hard enough time in her earlier life without adding this.

Then came the incident through which both mother and Ric became aware of my secret.

Dr. C. was responsible.

He gave me a tube of hyocine, in mistake for morphine. I opened it and thought it was off color but went ahead and fixed myself a one-half grain "shot," with trembling hands. That was my first of the day and I was beset with deprivation pains, tearing at my body like long-fanged wolves.

Inside of five minutes I knew something was wrong. Morphine usually works quickly, but never like that. My eyes blurred and I grew dizzy. I was convinced that I was going to die.

I rushed to the bathroom, getting a pencil and a piece of paper from the dining-room table on the way. Both my mother and Ric were away at the moment. I was in the house alone. I tried to write, but I was paralyzed and couldn't make a letter.

I remember collapsing into a heap on the floor and frantically trying to crawl into my bedroom, adjoining the bathroom. Somehow, I got to my bedroom, tortured, raving, but how I got there I do not know. I lost consciousness. I seemed to float away.

Mother found me lying across the bed when she came in a little later. She called a doctor—our own family physician—and he couldn't diagnose my case. He called in other doctors and they couldn't either.

## Chapter Twenty

They thought something was wrong with my eyes. They punctured the soles of my feet with needles, on the third day of my unconsciousness, to see if my eyes would flicker.

Then, somehow or other, our family doctor thought of Dr. C., who formerly had been employed in the State Asylum at Patton—that Hell-hole which played such an important part in my life afterwards—and he immediately diagnosed the case correctly.

I was brought around to consciousness and Dr. C., never letting on that he had been regularly supplying me with drugs, informed my mother and our family doctor that he was "suspicious of my behaving like an addict."

And this, mind you, after I had given him thousands of dollars in cash—two diamond bracelets and several other valuable pieces of jewelry when my money had run out.

My mother immediately told Ric. I was frightened to death at the consequences of this, but she insisted. And while Ric did many things to make me unhappy, I must give him credit for his kindly actions when he learned that his wife was a dope fiend!

He never once mentioned it, throughout the days I lay there recuperating from the effects of that dose of hyocine, so nearly fatal.

Even our family doctor admitted that it was necessary for me to have my daily dosage of morphine during this convalescent period, and he regularly attended me, counselling [sic] me at times—and always in the presence of my mother—as to the best measures to combat the evil when I got on my feet again.

I was eager to be cured. I knew their advice was right, but, in the queer frame of mind I was in then, I resented the fact that Ric did not discuss the subject. I wanted him to ask me to go someplace for the cure.

And, strange as it may seem, his—I thought—very indifference caused me to fall in love with him all over again.

I wept in anguish for days. My mother tried to comfort me but it was futile. I fear that I had lost Ric for good, although for more than a year before that I would have welcomed his disappearance for all time.

There is no accounting for my whims and my loves, apparently. I just adored him, so tall, so handsome. Damn him, if he would just talk to me about myself and my terrible affliction!

Occasionally, he would come into my room and sit on the edge of my bed. He'd stroke one of my hands. I would go into ecstasies. He'd peck me lightly on the cheek with his lips and I'd be in heaven. I had rekindled our love. But never did he mention the dope.

Then came the time when I was able to be up and about. Our family doctor cut out my morphine injections and I was beginning to feel the terrible, gripping, deprivation pains again. I was driven frantic. On occasions I had the impulses of a maniac.

Half a dozen times I was on the verge of calling Dr. C., but each time I would hold myself back. I wanted to be cured. I hated myself. I loved my husband. I must get over the deadly habit for his sake. I was fighting hard. I would be braver. I would win!

Once my mind was made up—confused as it was, and suffering as I was—I packed a little bag, and without saying a word to anybody, I went to Hollywood Hospital.

When I walked into Hollywood Hospital I was firmly convinced that I had sufficient will power to overcome the dreadful dope habit, deep as I was in its clutches. I explained my case to the physician in charge and he seemed a most sympathetic person.

Much to my surprise I had hardly become settled in my room when in walked a nurse with a hypodermic needle in her hand.

"What's that for?" I demanded. "I don't want that. I'm trying to break myself of the habit. That's what I came here for."

"Now, don't get excited," she replied, in that coddling tone of voice generally used in coaxing children. "Just take this like a nice little girl. And you'll soon be all right."

I was furious.

"I won't take it!" I cried. "I won't take it!"

"You must," she insisted. "If you don't your heart is liable to collapse. You'll die."

"All right," I said. "Let me die then. But I won't take it. I made up my mind to break off the habit and I'm going to begin right now."

She became angry. Her mouth settled into a narrow little slit and I could see the fighting lights shimmering in her cold, steel-blue eyes.

"Oh," she exclaimed, in carefully modulated tones that bespoke of an iron will. "If that's the way you feel, we'll have to give it to you forcibly."

She called another nurse and although I fought them until I was exhausted, they finally threw me onto the bed and one of them jabbed me in the thigh with the instrument.

When I awakened I was in Compton Sanitarium. They had put knockout drops in the injection and had carried me there while I was unconscious. They didn't give me a chance.

## Chapter Twenty

In Compton, a private institution, they practiced what is known as the "cold turkey" method of dealing with addicts. That is they put a patient to bed and instead of tapering off their dope supply gradually, left them to get along the best way they could without it, no matter what their condition or degree of addiction.

This was really what I wanted to do. This was what I had firmly made up my mind to endure when I went to the Hollywood Hospital. However, the effects of the knock-out drops had so weakened me, and nauseated me, that my morale was undermined.

I craved a "shot" in the worst way.

The terrible deprivation pains were overwhelming me. My legs and arms were drawn up in a most horrible manner. Their muscles had become knotted and the cramps were driving me insane. My eyes were watering and I drooled at the mouth.

Morphine acts as a depressant. It slows the heart action. And when it is taken away from an addict suddenly, the heart action increases correspondingly and the vitality is lowered.

Such was my condition. My heart was palpitating so badly that the moment I would get my cramped limbs straightened out beneath me, I would become dizzy and collapse on the floor.

I rang for an attendant. They paid no attention to me. Finally, my suffering became so acute that I shrieked in pain at the top of my voice.

A nurse came but when I explained matters to her, she merely shook her head and said she was sorry; she couldn't do anything. The doctor had forbidden her to relieve me, she added.

This went on for three days and three nights. I suffered all the torments of hell. I died a thousand deaths!

Just when I thought I was surely going to expire, in came my mother. I recognized her and that was about all. I was absolutely a person ruled by insanity. She tried to calm me but my nerves had reached such a state that only one thing could have quieted them.

And that one thing was a drug.

She insisted on taking me home, and, as I was not formally committed, the Compton authorities allowed me to go.

We reached home shortly after 9 o'clock in the morning. We met Ric coming down the stairs.

I threw out my arms to him. "Ric. Dear Ric. Please help me," I cried.

Suffering as I was, I believe if he had been just the least bit kind at that moment, I would have died before I ever took another narcotic potion.

But he was not in that kind of a mood. He paused, looked me over coolly for an instant, then turned on his heel, remounted the stairs and slammed his own bedroom door behind him.

If it had not been for my mother, I would have fallen. I had been four days without morphine. My condition, physical and mental, was terrible, a thousand times worse than I could possibly describe.

Mother helped me to my own room.

I went straight to a little bureau drawer which I had kept locked, opened it, took out a packet of morphine and a hypodermic, fled to the bathroom. Within another minute I had injected a double dosage of the soothing narcotic in to my veins. What a relief!

While I was doing this, mother pounded on the door. She begged me not to do it. Instinctively she knew what I was doing. Then she called Ric. He did not answer her, and I was too busy to have paid heed to either.

When I had completed the operation, I calmly walked out, passed my mother into my own room, and went to bed. I slept until late in the afternoon, when once more the dope monster began gnawing at me.

I had had enough suffering for a while. I fixed another "shot," got dressed and visited Dr. C., in his office. My morphine was running low.

He professed great surprised [sic] at seeing me. As a matter of fact, he was not in the least cordial. When I explained my predicament, he said he would give me one more prescription, and that would be the end.

He said that "they" had been looking him up since I went to the hospital and he dare not have any further dealings with me.

I advanced no argument. All I wanted was the morphine. I didn't have the money to pay him, so I left a little ring as security.

When I returned home I was beset with further trouble. Either mother or Ric had trailed me to Dr. C.'s office. Later, I found out they had interrogated him when I left and he swore by all that was holy that he had turned me down flat.

Mother begged me to go to some other sanitarium. I half way promised to do so as soon as I had recovered from the shock of my first experience in such an institution.

Ric didn't come near me, although I heard him come in and slam the bedroom door behind him. A little later, he went out again and I didn't see anything more of him for several days.

The next morning, bright and early, I had a visitor. My mother admitted him. He presented a card setting forth that he was a Federal narcotic agent. This was Mr. M. He told mother he wanted to speak to me about "Dr. C." I was still asleep but she called me.

When I got dressed and came downstairs, M. told mother he thought it would be better if he talked to me alone. Coming as she did from an old line of Irish police stock, my mother, ever imbued with respect for anything that even resembled a police shield, went about her housework.

M., who said he came from San Bernardino, professed to be deeply interested in Dr. C., He asked me a lot of questions about him, none of which I truthfully answered. As badly as he had treated me, still I shielded him.

Before he had talked to me twenty minutes I knew, in some intuitive manner, that he was a friend of Dr. C., and that the doctor had sent him. And, after...

[Editors' note: Material missing in extant copies of original text.]

## Chapter Twenty-One

It might be fitting here to mention the fact that at no time, throughout the five years I have been using dope, have I ever had any real difficulty in obtaining it—that is, as long as I had the money to pay for it.

Once a person gets the reputation of being a "dope fiend," it is that way. No matter what city or village you may go to, in whatever section of the land, your reputation either travels ahead of you, or else arrives almost simultaneously.

You can break off with one doctor, and he immediately tips off another. It is the same way with peddlers, although I have seldom resorted to these vultures, except in an emergency. I was always afraid of being poisoned and God knows, the doctors are bad enough.

Up until this time the habit had never interfered with my work. Despite my suffering, physically, because of the craving for dope, and mentally, because of Ric's apparent indifference, I managed to successfully complete *Show Boat*, the last picture in which I starred.

And, up until the time when the management suddenly decided to inject dialogue into production, I don't believe any of my business associates had the slightest suspicion that I was a confirmed "hop head."

The call for my reappearance on the lots to read in the dialogue came as a great surprise. I was falling fast. I knew that I would have to go to a sanitarium, but I was holding off until my husband asked me to go. I loved him madly now. It may look silly in print, but regardless, I loved him!

My mother knew this. And she got the idea that if she'd return to the ranch at Madera, Ric might deviate from his habit of ignoring me, our of sheer sympathy. She reasoned that he had loved me when he married me, and that his affection might be restored if I were left wholly dependent upon him.

The telephone call for me to return to the lots came on the same day my mother left. I promised to appear in two days, to comply with their request.

And the same day Ric, for the first time in weekend, recognizing me directly, came in and said: "Alma, you've got to go to the hospital! You're going in the morning. You might as well make up your mind to it. Things have gone as far as they can."

Oh, if he had only been a little kind. I wanted to follow his wishes, but his manner irked me beyond measure.

I told him about the dialogue.

"I don't care," was his reply. "You're going. Tomorrow."

I begged. I pleaded with them. I promised to abide by his wishes, if he'd only let me finish my picture.

"Just think of it, Ric," I pleaded. "They've spent a million dollars making *Show Boat*. Think what will happen if they have to get a double for the dialogue. Everything may be ruined."

"Don't care," was the reply, as he turned around and strode out.

I hastened to the telephone and called my mother. She promised to return at once.

Before she got there the next morning the doorbell rang. Ric answered it. I went to the head of the stairs and who should walk in but Dr. C.!

He and my husband went into the living room and conferred for some time. I went into the bathroom, prepared myself a "shot," and then returned to bed, so nervous, and so frightened, that I was a complete wreck.

My poor picture, in which I had starred. About to be ruined. In the condition I was in, I was consumed in self pity. Since, I have realized that I didn't deserve any. But at that time felt Ric was a brute.

He came up and knocked on my door. I had locked it and didn't answer. He pounded so hard that I thought it would cave in. I got up and opened it.

"Well," he shouted. "Ain't you dressed yet? You're going away. Hear me. I told you so last night and you ought to be ready. D'you want 'em to take you like this?" He pointed to my nightgown.

"No, no, no, no," I cried. "Please no, Ric. For God's sake, just let me finish my picture and I'll do anything you want. Just let me finish that."

Suddenly he lunged at me and we grappled like a couple of frantic wrestlers.

Dr. C., downstairs, hearing the commotion, came running upstairs. I must have been a sight. He helped me onto the bed and tried to stop the blood flowing from my nose. A tooth was broken.

They sent for Dr. D., Ric's own dentist, who came in a little later. He worked on me more than an hour while Ric and Dr. C. hovered nearby, speaking in whispers.

When the dentist had completed his work, again I appealed to Ric to let me finish *Show Boat*. He was obdurate and told me to forget it. He said if I didn't go peaceably, he'd drag me out in my nightgown.

Convinced that I was beaten, I beseeched him to let me "go like a lady."

## Chapter Twenty-One

I promised to get dressed and accompany them. I wanted to be freed of the dope curse, but I didn't want to be taken as if I were a violent maniac. They agreed.

I went into my bedroom and sparred for time. Every few minutes Ric would come to the door and demand that I hurry. I was playing for time, for what reason I don't know. Nothing could help me, I was sure of that.

Finally, when I knew I could hold them off no longer, I went to my writing desk and took out a long shiny paper cutter, with the idea in mind that, if I couldn't escape, I'd kill myself before we got to a sanitarium.

I threw on a heavy fur coat and hid the dull but pointed paper knife up my sleeve. Then I flounced out and walked past them both as they stood at the top of the stairs.

They followed me downstairs and I went down the front stoop.

Dr. C. was right behind, but Ric stopped in the doorway. Then I knew that he was not coming along; that he was not even going to kiss me good-bye. He didn't care what happened to me.

Instantly, I made up my mind that I would checkmate him. I was burning inside. Forgotten was my thought of committing suicide. I would beat Ric if it was the last thing I ever did.

In the meantime, a white coated interne, or male nurse, seated in Dr. C.'s automobile, which had been parked some distance down the street, drove up and stopped in front of the door.

I turned and sped like a deer to the corner, almost bumping into a middle aged, shriveled sort of man, walking across the intersection. I apologized quickly and fell into step with him. Dr. C. was right behind.

"Help me," I whispered. "They're trying to kidnap me. Don't let them take me."

He appeared greatly surprised, as no doubt he had reason to be. Quite an unusual request, especially from a girl in broad daylight. I suppose he was too dumbfounded to reply. Anyhow, we kept walking, and, out of the corner of my eye, I could see Dr. C. signaling his companion to catch up with us with the car.

This kept up, I suppose, for a distance of about 150 feet. Then I could hear Dr. C. panting close behind me and the chugging of the automobile, alongside.

Just as he was about to seize me, I threw off my gorgeous fur coat, for which I had paid about $4,000, and tried to run. But I was too late; Dr. C. had my left wrist in his grasp.

He swung me around, and as he did so I slipped the knife down into my hand, pushed in close and struck him in the tender portion underneath his back suspenders buttons.

"Oh, oh," he screamed, loosing his hold on me. "She's stabbed me. She's stabbed me."

And, as usual, I had to laugh, frightened as I was, and in spite of my unhappy position.

Also, I ran. As fast as my legs would carry me. I reached a gasoline station, where the proprietor knew me.

I was completely out of breath.

"Why, Miss Rubens," he exclaimed. "What's the matter? What's all the trouble?"

I pointed at Dr. C. and his companion, just driving up. I hurled the knife behind the hedges adjacent to the garage.

"Those men assaulted me!" I gasped.

Biff! Biff! Bang! One, two! One, two!

And as quickly as that, both were cooling their heels in the dust.

The garage man, a big husky, had waited for no further explanation, and no sooner had they slid out of the car than he sent them whirling with well directed blows.

Just then a woman drove up in a dilapidated Ford. Even with all that excitement, I remember that it bore a Kansas license. She was a typical school-marm out on a tour.

I tried to climb in, begging her to hurry away. But I was out of luck. I suppose my disheveled looks were against me. And, while I was arguing with her a crowd was gathering and apparently, Dr. C. and his assistant had explained the situation to all.

They ran over and seized me. I wilted. I knew all was lost. I let them lift me into the car, into the seat between them, Dr. C.'s assistant being the driver. I was forced to sit with my right arm around the doctor.

Once, just as we slowed up for traffic, I saw the opportunity to have a little more fun. Stealthily, I turned the handle of the door, and out to the street fell the dear old doctor. He squawked like a kicked beggar, but I let on that it was an accident; that that I had nothing to do with it, although I was nearly bursting with laughter inside.

Then we came to ———, a private sanitarium in Glendale, where I ran into one of the most horrifying experiences that a girl possibly could survive, and retain her sanity.

While sitting in an ante-room, awaiting my official admittance, I saw one of them carry a dead woman from the cell I was to occupy!

## Chapter Twenty-Two

If I tried for a thousand years to phrase my language I would never be able to describe my feelings when I saw that dead woman being carried out. I was terrified. I could picture her as myself!

## Chapter Twenty-Two

The moment I had arrived there, I sensed something wrong. It was a dismal place. Leading up to the anteroom was a long, dark hallway, furnished in medieval style, with stern wood-cuts and etchings hung on the walls and on a pedestal in the far end, a statue of Christ on the Cross.

I sat down on a long bench. Then I became aware of someone hammering: hammering on steel as though they were nailing up bars.

My guess was right. They were. They were nailing up bars on the windows of my room—or cell, would be more descriptive—at the extreme end of the hall.

I got up and wandered down that way, trying to peek in the door, which was ajar. A nurse ran up, all excited.

"You can't go in there," she forbade. "You can't go in there. That's private."

I went back to my seat. A moment later the body was carried out. They didn't tell me it was a body. It was on a stretcher and covered with a sheet, but I saw a woman's bare foot protruding, and I knew it was a dead woman.

They had just passed the corner into an intersecting corridor, when my attention was attracted by my mother's arrival. She had driven all the way from the ranch and had got home too late to see me off and the pitiful circumstances under which I departed.

She did everything to try and comfort me.

But it was no use. I was too terrified to talk. I KNEW I was going to be placed in THAT cell, but I didn't tell her what I had seen. She broke down and began to cry.

In turn I tried to comfort her. I asked her to let me fight my own battle. I didn't mention my terrible row with Ric. I didn't tell her about the nailing up of the iron bars which I had seen.

By and by she believed that I had consented to undergo treatment, although I impressed upon her the fact that I had not been legally committed. What inner fear, or intuitive sense, led me to do this I do not know, but, happily for me, I did. Otherwise my stay there, in the end a futile one, might have been much longer.

Eventually I was booked. Dr. C. did not appear again that day until long after my mother had gone. They wouldn't let my mother go into the room with me. She kissed me good-by in the hall, after promising to write to me every day.

I tried hard to smile when she left, but steel myself as I would I burst into tears. She suspected I was keeping something from her, but I reassured her. She promised to return the next evening and to bring Ric with her.

The nurse came for me. She led me into the room, just as the institution carpenter was driving the last nail in the last bar. It was truly a cell. Dark and dreary. The only furniture was a drab-looking dresser, of imitation oak, a small rocking chair that squeaked, and the bed. There was no mirror.

The bed had not been made. There it was, the coverings torn off and heaped on the floor, the mattress turned half way over on the end, and the pillow, of the shoddiest muslin, perched on top of the upper end of the mattress like a ghostly spectre, there to warn me away.

I shuddered. The perspiration came out in little beads on my forehead, and I became violently nauseated. I could imagine that I saw that other woman's body still lying there. No! It was my body!

For hours and hours I paced the floor. Up and down. Up and down, the length of my cell. Occasionally I would try the door, but it was tightly locked.

Once in a while a nurse would come in, a big hoop of keys rattling on her arm, and try to engage me in conversation. I paid no attention to her. She'd sit down in that damned chair and rock. The squeak almost drove me crazy.

Another woman came in and fixed the bed. She did not change the mattress, although she put on fresh linen—if linen you could call it. In reality it was the same shoddy muslin as covered the pillow. Rough, unbleached.

Through the bars at the one window I could see the automobiles whizzing past on the roadway. I watched them until dark. Not thinking, not doing anything, but standing there. I was too unnerved to really understand what was going on about me.

They brought supper. I didn't touch a bite. I don't even know what was on the tray. Again the nurse came in and tried to engage me in conversation. I paid no attention.

My mind was far away. My picture, which Ric wouldn't let me finish. His treatment for me. Proof then to me that he no longer loved me. My poor mother unaware of what I had undergone. How long would I be here.

Oh, my God! For a shot!

The deadly deprivation pains began. I had had nothing for almost eleven hours. I doubled over with the cramps and the nurse brought me a drink of water. I hurled it at her, drenching her completely.

She ran out and a moment later in came Dr. C., bowing and scraping, and smiling like a cat which has just swallowed the canary.

Truly, I was a canary, just about to be gulped in one bite by an ogre.

He remained but a minute. I begged him for a "shot," but he would not listen.

And, a few minutes after he left, out went the sole light. I was left, fully dressed, and awake, without a light. I shook the door and a night attendant came. I asked him why I couldn't have one. He said it was against the rules.

I went back to the window and stood there, for hours and hours it seemed, watching the red tail lights of passing automobiles fading in the distance and trying to forget my pains.

Eventually I dropped down on the same mattress on which that other poor woman died, and dropped off into a troubled sleep with all my clothes on.

Four days and four nights later it went on like this. I was getting no dope. I was in terrible pain and could eat nothing. I could still see that dead woman in every waking moment and dream about her when I did fall asleep.

And then I broke down completely.

I suppose I became temporarily insane. When I came to I was wrapped in cold, wet blankets, my arms forcibly held so that I could not pull them off. A nurse sat beside me, rocking in that miserable, squeaky chair.

I begged her to release me, but it was not until hours later, when Dr. C. came in, that she did so. She went out, leaving me alone with him.

The moment she closed the door behind her he smirked in a knowing manner. Then he winked, as he pulled from his sleeve a hypodermic needle which he had hidden there.

I ran to him like a young child would to its father who had brought home candy. Hate him I did. But at that particular moment I idolized him. He was my savior. He—and his needle—were my gods!

He was unmoved by my plight. Before he would give me the hypodermic I had to promise him that I would pay him for the morphine. I told him I had no money, but he said that would be all right. I could give him post-dated checks for the amount and he would arrange for my release in another two weeks so that I could meet them.

In my desperate condition, I was willing to do anything; sign anything; promise anything, just to have my suffering alleviated. Later, following my release, I discovered that the checks I signed that night totaled more than $1,500.

And all he gave me was possibly $10 worth of morphine, and the needle, both of which I hid under the inner side of the semi-tubular feet of the chipped, gray-tiled bathtub, adjacent to my room.

How carefully I guarded that precious hoard through the intervening days of my incarceration there. I took half portions, weakening the compound as much as I could and get results, so that I could make it last.

My mind cleared up. I changed completely. The regular day nurse, really a most conscientious woman, was overjoyed. She thought I was being cured. And she was happy in that belief.

I was happy, too, because I had my dope!

At the end of three weeks my mother came. And, miracles of miracles, my husband came with her! My mother had called almost daily, but the hospital authorities had forbidden her seeing me, saying it would interfere with my treatments. Finally she demanded my release, and as I was not legally committed, they had to let me go.

Dr. C. had told them I was cured. My mother was in heaven. Even Ric seemed glad. He kissed me for the first time in months.

And then the first thing I did after we reached home, I confronted them both in the living room.

"You think I'm cured, don't you?" I snarled, turning towards my husband. "You're both fools. I'm still an addict. And now I'm going straight to hell!"

## Chapter Twenty-Three

Yes! That was my announcement; that I was deliberately going to start out on the road to hell! That was my answer to my husband's hopes, and to my mother's prayers. "I'm going straight to Hell!"

Mother stood there, dazed and uncertain. The most helpless expression I ever have seen on a human being, settled over her countenance, Ric, too—for a moment—seemed shocked out of his senses.

"But, Alma, darling," my mother implored in quavering tones. She threw out her arms to me, whereupon, I drew back. "Alma. My darling baby. Don't talk to me like this. Tell me. Isn't it true? Aren't you cured? Are you still using the stuff?"

"Yes," I replied coldly, wholly untouched by her piteous plea. "Yes, I'm still an addict. Just a dope fiend! That's all. A dope fiend! That's what you've both done to me!"

In my semi-delirious state of mind, I blamed them for my continued use of drugs—not myself, nor the doctors. Indirectly, of course, mainly, because Ric had sent me to the sanitarium without consulting me, without once asking me to try and help SAVE MYSELF! And, I believed that my mother had plotted with him to have me carried away in the ignominious manner which so irked me.

Well, Ric just flared at me, utterly disgusted. "Bah," he finally ejaculated, and, turning on his heel, stalked from the room. I didn't see him again for days and days.

My poor, old, forgiving mother, however, tears coursing down her blanched cheeks, came over to me, patted me on the shoulder, and led me to a chair.

"Oh, God, Alma," she pleaded, almost breaking down completely. "Alma, darling. Please don't talk like that. You mustn't. You can't. You can't talk like that!"

She paused a moment to catch her breath. I could see that her bosom was rising and falling rapidly, and she inhaled and exhaled in pitiful little jerks. Every moment I expected her to collapse. But, she went on:

"Darling. You don't realize what you are saying. You're a good girl. You're my baby. You must be cured. I'll go away with you. I'll remain up with you day and night until you ARE cured; wherever you say, wherever you want to go. But, you simply must be cured! You must!"

And, I, in my folly, laughed! I laughed at that wondrous mother of mine.

I disengaged myself from her arms, and walked out, leaving her sitting there, heartbroken and stunned, utterly powerless to combat the most heartless, selfish, and unjustifiable attack of which any daughter ever was guilty.

That is what the hydra-headed monster, dope, does to you. Once in its deadly clutches, it chokes, until EVEN LOVE is crushed out of its helpless, writhing victim.

I went to my room and locked the door. I gazed at myself in the mirror. My face was blazing. I felt not the slightest remorse for the cruel way in which I had mistreated my mother. No, I hated her. I HATED my own mother! And, I repeated aloud, to myself: "Going to Hell."

"Yes. I'm a dope fiend! And I'm going straight to hell!"

Up until now, no one, except Ric, my mother, and myself, ever has known how nearly I came to fulfilling this prophesy.

Actually, I mean—not literally—because within the next few days I came so close to the threshold of the fiery pit, that I imagined I could see Satan, just inside, waiting to rake me in.

My close call was due to an infection on my left thigh, caused, apparently, by the unclean hypodermic needle of Dr. C., given me on the occasion of his last visit before I left the sanitarium.

The infected area grew until it resembled a lump the size of an orange. This was intensely red and painful almost beyond endurance. The entire limb, except for the lump itself, was black and blue.

It had troubled me before I left the sanitarium, although not enough to cause me any great apprehension. I stood the torture for two days after I arrived home, then became so frightened that I had to tell my mother. She immediately recognized the seriousness of my plight, and sent for Dr. E., whom she had known for years.

Dr. E. was of the old-fashioned homeopathic school of physicians, who carried about with him always a big medicine case, stocked with various drugs and potions, which he himself mixed, as the occasion required.

He came in, divested himself of his coat and hat, examined the limb in his clumsy, amateurish manner, then announced that he would have to lance it. He administered a local anaesthetic, and then, prior to the actual operation, took a long, thin needle, which he stuck into the center of the infected area, to ascertain if it had frozen.

As he did so, I winced from the pain, and the needle broke off, deep inside. I fainted, but regained consciousness almost immediately, just in time to see him take out his lance. I was suffering terribly.

When he came near me with the knife in hand, I fought him off. I wouldn't let him touch me. He and mother argued with me, but to no avail. Undergoing torture, as I was, I preferred to continue in my agony, with the needle-point in the wound, rather than have him go on.

On one leg, I hopped to the bathroom, where I administered to myself a soother, the last of my morphine supply.

Next morning, I had a temperature of 103; and my mother rushed me to the hospital, where for days they had to fight to stave off the ever-threatening encroachment of the deadly gangrene.

They operated and saved my life, but they didn't find the broken needle-point. It stills remains in my leg, and I feel it occasionally, just a gentle reminder of how nearly I died.

Upon my release from the hospital, I had the greatest difficulty in purchasing either morphine or cocaine. Dr. C. wouldn't have anything more to do with me. He had my post-dated checks, and he was waiting for me to make a deposit so he could cash them.

I begged and I pleaded with him. I was willing to promise him anything, but he would not give me a single "shot."

In my dilemma, I visited a girl friend—an addict—and she sent me to Dr. P., now under indictment for his illicit trafficking in drugs, as well as for other investigations by the state medical society and by both state and county prosecutors.

Incidentally, I might mention, that the authorities were unable to prosecute several other physicians, including Dr C., because of a loophole in the California law which brought it into conflict with the Federal statute covering illicit drug sales.

When I first became acquainted with Dr. P., I thought that I had established my ideal contact. He appeared to be a thorough gentleman, and treated me like a human being, instead of like a derelict, as had so many of the other doctors with whom I had dealt.

I soon learned that my judgment was in error. He was like all the rest. His interest in me was purely a mercenary one.

He charged me $5 for my first three or four "decks" of cocaine. A week later, he raised the price to $10; then $20, and, inside of a month I was paying him $50 for a similar amount, or for a few day's [sic] supply of morphine.

From time to time I would pawn a piece of jewelry to get money to pay him. And, after the last of the jewelry was gone, I began pawning and selling my beautiful furs.

Finally, all the dealers grew suspicious and would no longer dicker for my personal habiliament [sic]. I took a $3,000 broadtail coat directly to Dr. P. and traded it to him for one week's supply of morphine.

When that gave out, I went back with another—a beautiful ermine wrap—which cost me almost $4,000. He said he didn't want it. I begged him to hold it as security for a "deck" of cocaine, but he wouldn't listen.

I was desperate. I threatened him with exposure. He laughed at me and ejected me from his office.

"Outside, you cokie," he snarled. "And stay out 'til you get some money! What you think I am? A philanthropist!"

And he with all my beautiful furs and all my jewelry, except that which I had already given to Dr. C.! I could do nothing. And, he knew it!

I couldn't tell my husband or my mother what had happened to my things, nor could I ask them for money to appease my terrible longing for a "shot."

I went home and went to bed. I was suffering agonies from the deprivation pains. Then, I remembered a colored maid that had formerly worked for me, and whom I had discharged because of laziness. Frantically, I searched for her address. I recalled that I had heard she was peddling dope.

When I found it, in an old note book, I was so happy that I cried. Seizing the ermine wrap—I knew that she had always coveted it—I ran, only half-dressed, all the way to her house.

She was greatly surprised when I, all disheveled, and gasping for breath, walked into her apartment without knocking.

"I must have some cocaine—immediately," I cried. "Here, you can have the wrap. Just get it for me quick!"

I was so desperate that I forgot all about having discharged her. Not she, however. She started to "bawl" me out, but I waved the wrap in front of her. I could see that she was weakening. Her eyes glistened and began to roll.

I knew that I had won! She wanted that wrap! And, she'd get me my dope!

I collapsed in a chair.

She went out, returning a few minutes later, with a full two week's supply of cocaine, done up in little white papers. I "sniffed" a portion of one and immediately felt better.

Although I knew she was gloating at my agony, at my humility, I took no offense. There is no offending a "cokie"; not when their supply is at stake.

The days and the weeks rolled by. Every so often, I'd trade another beautiful gown, or piece of expensive lingerie, to my former maid. And she'd give me more cocaine.

I was a nervous wreck. I knew that my family suspected what I was doing, but I didn't care.

Then, I got into an argument with Mrs. W. H. Shoelwer, of Beverly Hills, and she had me arrested for assault: It happened in front of the Tec-Art Studio, in Hollywood, after her automobile, which she was driving, struck ours, driven by our chauffeur.

The case was settled without going to trial, but the aftermath—following a terrible quarrel with mother and Ric—was, that I borrowed some money from a famous woman star and rented an apartment of my own.

And, within a month, I was again arrested; this time as a "Peeping Prissie!"

## Chapter Twenty-Four

Rita Carewe, the daughter of Edwin Carewe, the famous actor-director, and herself an aspirant for a movie crown, caused my arrest. Several others, including LeRoy Masen, an actor; Finis Fox, a scenario-writer, and Mrs. Elizabeth Uhl, owner of the apartment house in which we all lived, supported her complaint.

Where, or how, I got the "sub-title"—I call it—"Peeping Prissie," I do not know. But that is the name which all the newspapers tagged onto me, so I guess it must be all right.

I'll admit there may have been some cause for Rita's complaint—there was a rather noisy party in my apartment—but so far as I know, no one did any "peeping," especially myself.

It all came about in this way:

As I recall it, the incident took place a few days after Christmas, 1928. I was feeling extremely blue that morning when I awakened. I had many things to worry me. I hadn't heard from my mother for days. Neither she, nor Ric, had sent me a Christmas present.

For that matter I hadn't sent them any either, but, regardless of that, I was homesick. I felt hurt. I knew that my mother would welcome me if I called her, but in my hazy, narcotic, semi-stupor, I was too stubborn to make the first advance. We were still all on the "outs" because of my escapade with Mrs. Shoelwer and the ensuing family quarrel during which I left home.

My despondency was aggravated an hour later, when, in cleaning up the apartment, I picked up a Sunday newspaper magazine section, which, in great detail, printed a general resume of celebrated "dope" cases, revolving around famous addicts who had died in recent years.

It mentioned Wally Reid, Olive Thomas, and others, including poor

Julia Bruns, who was found dead in a cheaply furnished New York tenement on Christmas Eve, just two years before.

I knew Julia very well. I had met her on the occasion, when as a famous stage star, she had come to Hollywood to star in a single picture. That was in her 'hey-dey'; when her wealth was estimated at more than $8,000,000, and she was the toast of Broadway.

She was a most stunning girl; if I remember correctly, she once won a prize as the "most beautiful girl in America," and later, when I went to New York, I visited her in her palatial home on Sutton Place, near where Marjorie Rambeau also lived.

But, getting back to the party:

I was so depressed that I just moped around the apartment most of the day. Then I hit upon the idea of "throwing a party." A real "dope party."

I knew three other girls who were addicts. I had met them through my former maid, who also supplied them. I called them up, invited them, and they accepted, stating that they would bring their "boy-friends." One even volunteered to bring an extra boy for me.

In the mental state I was, any relief from the routine, from the sordid monotony of worrying over my family troubles, and over the ever-increasing difficulty of raising money to replenish my drug supply, was welcome.

I called up a caterer and ordered a supply of food. I got the address of a bootlegger from the colored maid and brought in a supply of gin. Up until that time, I had never acquired the habit of drinking; that is, except light wines, at dinner, but I had heard that all addicts liked gin.

That was my first experience at a "dope party," and, I might add, the only one I ever attended in Hollywood, except for a two-handed one a few months later, in which my companion was a Chinaman. I will tell of this later.

The girls and boys began to arrive about 8 o'clock. We all had a "sniff" or two and soon we were in the midst of a hilarious good time. We had the phonograph going; we danced, told jokes, played pranks and forgot all about our worries.

Every once in a while somebody would suggest that we all have another "sniff," or another swig of the gin, and nobody passed up the opportunity.

Not being used to drinking gin, I became ill. Soon another of the girls was likewise stricken, and she joined me in bed. Eventually, the boys, too, draped themselves over the handiest piece of furniture available and went to sleep.

Well, to make a long story short, that party went on for more than four days. Whenever one would wake up, they'd go around and arouse everybody else. We'd all have a "sniff," or a drink, and then, pretty soon, everybody would cheer up and we'd start the party all over again.

Naturally, we made a lot of noise, and on several occasions, one of the boys had to run out and replenish our supply of both dope and gin.

Along late in the evening of the fifth day, Mrs. Uhl came up and said that other tenants were complaining about so much noise. Somebody made a wise-crack—I think it was one of the boys—and she went away, greatly peeved.

A little later the cops came in. They let the others go, but took me to the station-house, where Rita Carewe and the others lodged the complaint against me. There positively was no "peeping." That's my story, and I'll stick to it.

Well, the sequel to the affair was, that I got out of the scrape; my mother took me home and things resumed their normal course.

I kept on trading my fine lingerie to my former maid for more dope, and day by day my resources dwindled, until, eventually, I had hardly any clothes, except those on my back.

Then the colored maid was arrested. The narcotic agents questioned me, but I would tell them nothing. They tried several others who had been getting their cocaine from her, but they had no better success. So they freed her.

The scare was too much for her, however. She said she was "through forever" with dope peddling, and I had to look elsewhere for my supply.

Without money, without jewelry, without clothes, and without credit, I certainly was confronted with a problem.

It has always been a great source of thanksgiving to me, that in my earlier life—when I was at the peak of my career—I formed the habit of turning over half of my earnings, no matter how large, to my mother, for investment.

Had I not done this, and had she not had practical nature, which invariably led her into making sound investments, I might now be a pauper. She always took good care to so tie up my money that I couldn't touch it without her consent.

Had this not been the case, I probably would have dissipated everything during the eleven years I have been in the coils of the drug octopus.

With the former colored maid out of business, I returned to Dr. P. He wouldn't sell me anything, although I had managed to raise $50 in cash. Then I went back to Dr. P.

He was cold at first, but when I showed him the $50 bill, he warmed right up. I left with a week's supply of cocaine. And, when that was gone I raised another $50, and got some more.

But the third time, I fooled him. I casually walked in, asked for my customary allotment, and then started to walk out without paying him. He seized me by the shoulders as I was passing through the door.

"Hold on a minute, dearie," he said. "Haven't you forgotten something?"

I tried to break away, but he held me tightly.

"I'll see you tomorrow. I forgot to bring the money with me," I lied. "I'll bring it to you sure, tomorrow."

"All right," he growled. "If that's the case, you give me back that package. I'll give you the 'you know' tomorrow, too; at the same time you give me the money."

I knew there was not the slightest chance in the world for me to raise $50 by the next day. I also knew I just HAD to have that little packet, or else I would go crazy.

I begged him to trust me, but he was granite. I tried to struggle out of his grasp, but I couldn't. I did manage, however, to drop the previous little packet down inside the front of my dress. I could feel it snuggled against my heart.

He tried to get it away from me, but I was desperate. I scratched his face and clawed at his eyes.

He struck me with his fist and I fell and feigned unconsciousness. He felt my pulse and I tried to keep my heart from beating.

Then he went to a medicine closet, only a few feet away, got some long strips of gauze and bound me to the legs of either an X-ray cabinet, or a taller, heavier medicine case.

By this time, I was so frightened I didn't know what to do. I started to plead with him again and he struck me another fierce below.

And, just then, a most amazing thing happened!

## CHAPTER TWENTY-FIVE

Just as Dr. P. was about to kick me, about to crush me—bound and helpless as I was—in rush good old Wilson Mizner, author, playwright, real estate operator, all-around good fellow, and long a friend of the family, to my rescue!

He had driven out to the ranch at Madera, and finding my mother absent, he had gone on to our home in Santa Monica. My mother, always worried and depressed during my absences, had told him that she suspected I was visiting Dr. P., in search of more dope.

I do not to this day know how she learned of him, but it is a lucky thing for me that she did.

Anyhow, Mizner took in the situation at a glance. There I was, bound to the leg of the cabinet. Dr. P. was towering over me, his foot already drawn back to kick.

With one leap, Mizner was upon him. He floored the doctor with one blow. He picked him up by the collar and knocked him down again. He did the same thing, over and over, until that arrogant "shyster," was a cringing, bloody wreck.

Then, he unbound me, carried me to the street and hailed a taxicab. He took me to the hospital, where it was found my injuries were not serious, and then drove me home. All this later came out in court.

By the time I reached home, I had forgotten all about my injuries. I was happy, because I had that precious little packet of dope in my bosom.

The following day I went to the ranch, where I remained almost a month, trying to straighten out. I was willing, eager, to get away from the drugs, but the craving was too great.

I simply had to have it!

Soon afterwards, I had a recurrence of the old trouble with my hip. It was causing me great pain. The infection had returned and it was swollen beyond belief.

My mother called Dr. Emil Meyers, who after a hasty examination telephoned for an ambulance. I was frightened almost to death. I had the idea he was taking me to the psychopathic ward. I had been without drugs for a whole day, and I was in a highly nervous state.

I don't remember much about that trip, but from what I later learned, I made two desperate bids for freedom, twice breaking away from Dr. Meyers and his assistant, and hiding in the adjacent woods.

Once, according to his story, I stabbed him with a paper knife, which I had hidden on my person before we left the house. The last time I broke away it took the two doctors, and several policemen they called more than three hours to find me.

At the hospital, they lanced the infected area, but within a few days I was a wild woman because of my need for drugs, and the authorities directed my mother to take me home before it was completely healed.

There, I again made a contact with a colored woman, who sold me a packet of cocaine. This put me on my feet again, but I was virtually a nervous wreck. The mental and physical suffering I had undergone, because of the scantiness of my drug supply, had taken its toll.

Not only myself, but my family were on the verge of despair.

Then, much to our relief, came good news.

A very wealthy and influential man, who long had taken a great interest in my career, learned of my downfall. He interceded with Governor Young to place me in the State Hospital for Drug Addicts, at Spadra.

Governor Young made a special ruling in my favor. I was the first woman ever sent there for treatment, the institution, theretofore, having been solely devoted to the treatment of men.

## Chapter Twenty-Five

I personally applied for commitment. I wanted to be cured, and, by this time, I had forgotten all about my expressed intention of setting out on the road to perdition. Ric and mother accompanied me to Superior Court Judge McCohn's chambers.

He was lovely to me, sympathetic and helpful, in every aspect. He signed the writ and we returned home and packed my bags.

I was in a most cheerful mood. I was fairly swimming in a pool of delight; so happy that Ric was speaking to me again, and so happy that at last I was to have a real opportunity to be cured of the dreadful drug habit.

My elation was not to continue long, however. Before I had been at Spadra a week, I realized that if ever I was to become well again, it would have to be in a different environment. The necessarily rigid routine terribly depressed me.

Dr. Thomas Joyce, formerly in charge of the hospital on Welfare Island, New York City, was in charge. He was a strict disciplinarian, a fact which I never held against him. However, I learned that his position was a most untenable one, his superiors bearing down on him to exercise unusual measures in treating me.

Anyhow, I ran into many difficulties, little things that didn't mean much on their face, but, which to me, in my highly unsettled state of mind, and undergoing the physical torture from the ever-present deprivation pains, as I was, meant everything to me.

I was allowed no freedom. And very little exercise. There were two female nurses regularly assigned to my care. A day and a night nurse. I was never allowed out of their sight.

Before long, I actually hated them. Not because they—at that time—were unkind, but simply because I grew tired of looking at them. Perhaps they felt the same way about me. I shouldn't be surprised if they did.

I realized I could no [sic] nothing about the matter, however, so I tried to cultivate them. I tried to ingratiate myself with them in the hopes of being able to obtain little favors.

In a measure, I was successful. One of them drank!

And, she gave me my first drink of whiskey.

During all the years I had been in the movies, working with movie actors, traveling around with them, attending their parties, I never had drunk, except now and then, perhaps a little champagne, or light wine. And then, never to excess! That is, with the exception of my own little gin party just after Christmas.

It might be well to mention here while I think of it, that so far as my personal knowledge is concerned, there is comparatively little drinking, or carousing in Hollywood. The movie people simply do not have time for it. They work too hard!

Orgies in Hollywood are the exception rather than the rule, despite efforts of certain interests to disseminate such reports.

It was not until after I was "cured" at Patton, and went to New York that I really learned what "orgies" were.

There, in the bright lights of Broadway, as well as in the sheltered areas of the "400," in Park and 5th Aves., I really learned what the word meant. But, more of that anon.

Getting back to Spadra, and to my stay there, I found that one of my women nurses was susceptible to bribery. She couldn't get dope for me, but she could—and did—get me plenty of whiskey.

Then, she'd drink most of it herself.

Things drifted along from bad to worse. Some of the male patients would see me out walking with my nurse, and would send me poppies, great big red poppies, which grew in great abundance on the institution grounds.

Of course, I'd smile at them. Then it would be written in the institution record that I was incorrigible; that I flirted with the men.

Everyone once in so often, one of the officials would come around and tell me what [a] terrible time he was having on my account. He said that one of his superiors was "riding" him, and that he'd give a thousand dollars, out of his own pocket, if he could be assured he'd never see my face again.

This didn't help me in the least. It made me feel miserable and I would have left that instant if they would have let me. But they wouldn't.

No! They'd all become martyrs and wear long faces for the rest of their lives, but they simply couldn't get along without constantly reminding me about it.

Then they let me go an entire week without a cathartic. Strong cathartics are absolutely necessary for one addicted to the use of drugs.

When I became ill, the doctor and both nurses alibied themselves by expressing great surprise, and, with arched eyebrows, demanding:

"Why? Why didn't you remind me of it?" It must have been a stock phrase.

Every once in a while mother would come to see me, and on each occasion, I'd beg a little money, for "luxuries." If she didn't visit me, she'd write almost every day, usually enclosing a dollar or so, never once suspecting that I was using it to buy whiskey.

Eventually, my imbibing-pal-nurse's appetite for drink grew beyond my slender purse's capacity.

I'd pay for it. She'd drink most of it!

And, then we'd quarrel because there was none left. Each would accuse the other of taking more than a fair share.

One day the quarrel developed into a real fight and it was with great joy, before she and another nurse subdued me, that I managed to yank out a few of her locks.

She reported the occurrence and there was an investigation. I didn't tell on her and finally it was decided that I must have bribed a delivery boy to bring me the whiskey.

They had found the empty bottle outside the window of my room, exactly where SHE had thrown it, after draining it to the last drop.

And, as punishment, I was placed in solitary confinement.

## Chapter Twenty-Six

Placed in solitary confinement after this last unhappy episode, my life became unbearable. Without dope, without the extra-strong rye whiskey which, for a time—and in a small measure—had temporarily filled my crying need for drugs, my suffering grew more and more intense. I was constantly on pins and needles. I felt that I was losing my mind.

My thoughts turned to suicide; my plans for escape. I lay awake day and night, scheming and plotting means of gaining my liberty.

By-and-by, I found the opportunity to write a letter to the influential man who had arranged for my treatment at Spadra, and I managed to smuggle it out. I explained my circumstances to him and implored him in the strongest language I knew, to seek my release.

A week later, I was fairly frantic, so great was my need for a soothing "shot." It was not forthcoming. I tore my hair; scratched my face. I bit my lips until the blood streamed from the corners of my mouth.

One of the nurses called a doctor. I told him I had a terrible toothache that was driving me crazy. In the back of my mind was the scheme to get out of that solitary cell, then trust to Providence for further means to effect my escape.

The plan worked! The doctor directed my nurse to escort me downtown—to a dentist. There was a drugstore on the ground floor of the dentist's office. On the pretext that I wished to purchase an astringent, I entered, she remaining outside where she could keep me under observation.

I asked for a patent medicine wine tonic, one with a high alcoholic content, which one of the men patients at Spadra had recommended for use as an emergency substitute for whiskey.

Upstairs, in the dentist's office, I went to the ladies' room, where I drained the bottle to its last drop. It was wonderfully potent, so potent, in fact, that within a few minutes I didn't give a hoot if that dentist pulled all my teeth.

And, I suppose that if the pain had been so excruciating, he would have done that very thing. As it was, he extracted a perfectly sound tooth, a back molar, which had never troubled me in the least.

I promptly let out a screech and went into a tantrum, resulting in being carried downstairs, placed in an automobile with the nurse astride me and taken to the hospital.

There they gave me a sleeping potion, and, when I awakened I was in a most beautiful cottage near the shore, at Pomona. My benefactor had had it especially furnished for me, and for my treatment, immediately after receipt of my letter.

The only blot on my horizon was the presence of my nurse, who had been "loaned" by the Spadra authorities to supervise my treatments.

Incongruous, as it may seem, I almost forgot my "deprivation" symptoms, so absorbed was I, day and night, in thinking up some measure to get rid of her.

I doubt very much, however, that even if she hadn't been present, whether I could have been cured at that time. Of necessity, so I have been told, a dope addict must be harshly treated; and my benefactor had given orders that I was to be shown every kindness.

In my distorted mind grew the obsession that my nurse was responsible for all my unhappiness. I believe I would have killed her if I hadn't feared her tremendous physical strength. She could pick me up and carry me like a baby.

I did discover, though, that neither she nor the other nurse cared for music. Even playing the phonograph annoyed them extremely.

Consequently, I played it 24 hours a day.

Day in and day out, I played it. The same old tunes, with the shutter wide open, never changing the needle, resulting in the most discordant squeaking and grinding it would be possible to imagine.

I gloated in my triumph!

And, they knew it, although they never said a word. They didn't dare to, but, if I had been in possession of all my faculties, I couldn't help knowing that by making enemies I was adding to my troubles.

Eventually, this "atmosphere of music" so palled upon the nerves of my nurse that she went out for a walk. She brought a bottle home with her—and I stole it!

I drank so much of this liquor that I "passed out like a light."

When I recovered consciousness, I was in bed, with all my clothes on and a doctor bending over me—Dr. F.—the owner of one of the "smartest" sanitariums in the State.

Two women, neither of whom I had ever seen before, stood near him. They looked liked [sic] robots, mechanical women, with faces of ice.

"Why, hello, dear," spoke the doctor. "How are you feeling?"

Awakened out of my stupor, I was dazed. Through my mind flitted the child's story of the terrible ogre who threatened little "Jack, the Giant Killer" hero. This was the ogre, in person.

He had a red toupe!

And I, was "Jack the Giant Killer!"

"I'm fine, thank you," I answered, nonchalantly reaching up and plucking off his flaming head piece. I twirled it in my fingers and tossed it to the floor.

"Ha! Ha!" I snickered. "So, you're that terrible ogre. Eh?"

He sputtered and he spewed. He fussed and he cussed. And, the two automatons broke into a grin.

That made him furious!

"You're no lady!" he hissed. If ever daggerish looks killed a person I would have been pierced through and through.

"Well. You are!" I snickered contemptuously, struggling to my feet. "You're a perfect old lady, with a false wig and everything."

He went wild. He stamped up and down the room.

"Take her!" he yelled. "Put this on her! I'll show her what discipline is. I'll show her a thing or two!"

And into the straitjacket, I went!

That was the way I was taken to ———, one of the finest sanitariums in California, where most of the wealthy insane are sent for treatment—in a straitjacket.

On the ride over there I had made up my mind to become tractable. As a matter of fact I DID want to be cured and go home to my family. I realized that my temperamental outbursts had not helped matters; that, in the long run, they always proved boomerangs!

And, upon my arrival, I began to think that my stay there might be a pleasant one; that is, pleasant as possible, under the circumstances under which I had been whisked away from Pomona.

I was placed in a beautiful three-room suite, tastily and comfortably furnished. It ought to have been. Afterwards I learned that it cost $1,000 a month.

But, my good resolutions were short-lived! Hardly had I finished making them when things began to happen that caused me to change my mind.

The first thing to upset me was the presence of my former nurse. They had decided to retain her because she "handled me so well."

I leaped from the bed to my feet when she strutted into the room. Right behind her came Dr. F., his flaming red toupe duly anchored in place and smiling once more in that effeminate manner so characteristic of him.

"Well, Alma, darling," chirruped the nurse, in honeyed tones. "How do you think you'll like it here? Isn't this a beautiful place?"

"It would be if you were in Halifax," I retorted. "Or even further away—in hell!"

"Here—here—here," interrupted the doctor, dropping his waxen-image smile. "I'll have none of that. What you need, young lady, is discipline. We'll put you in the barred section if you continue in your present mood."

He walked over and stood facing me. I glared at him!

"Do I get any cigarettes?" I demanded, sharply. To me this was an all-important issue.

"Cigarettes?" he smirked. "Cigarettes? Young lady, we are not only going to cure you of the drug habit, but of smoking as well. We shall cure you both physically and morally!"

"Then I'll escape," I warned him. "I'm willing to be cured of the dope habit. I'll undergo any treatment, no matter how severe. But I must have my cigarettes. I don't want to be cured of smoking!"

"That is a matter for us to determine," he gloated. "You are here—not because you want to be—because you were placed here. And, so far as your threat to escape is concerned, just try it. It has been tried many times, and no one, absolutely no one, has ever been successful."

With that, he turned and walked out. The moment that he closed the door behind him, my ex-drinking-pal-nurse stuck out her tongue at me in a grimace of disdain.

Right then and there, I made up my mind to escape—or die in the attempt. And, leave it to little Alma, I did! And, in what a spectacular manner!

## Chapter Twenty-Seven

When that nurse stuck out her tongue at me it made me boiling mad inside. She knew it, too, and her expression changed instantly to one of benign innocence. This acting made me doubly furious, but I checked my emotions. I would be too foxy for her, I thought, recalling a favorite saying of my mother: "You can catch more flies with sugar than you can with vinegar."

I suggested that we take a little walk, knowing that the exercise would help me master my feelings. I also had in the back of my head the thought that perhaps I might find opportunity to break away from her, once I was outside those four walls.

My mind was firmly made up to escape. Nothing could have changed it. But I was doomed to disappointment, for the time being, at least.

"I wouldn't take a walk with you if your life depended on it," she declared. "Now we know how WE stand! Don't we?"

Her arrogance was too much for my shattered nerves, already tautened to the breaking point.

"You——!" I screamed at the top of my voice and flew at her throat. And, instantly, the door swung open and in came two other nurses—the two robots—followed by a doctor. All four seized me and threw me on the bed.

Apparently they had been stationed outside my door, listening to my nurse baiting me, and waiting for this very thing to happen.

Then I saw through their game. They wanted to put me in a barred cell, but they wanted to establish first that I was violently insane. They wanted me to make a scene so they could have a "legitimate" excuse to carry out their intentions.

I vowed—mentally, of course—to outwit them. I ceased to struggle and, when they released their hold on me, I dropped back in bed without saying another word.

After a moment they all walked to the door, whispered a second, and then the doctor and his double equation in mechanics, stalked out single file, leaving me in the tender care of my Nemesis.

She spoke not another word. Neither did I. And, eventually, suffering the terrible deprivation pains as I was, I dropped off to sleep from sheer nervous and mental exhaustion.

When I awakened it was morning. An attendant was standing beside my bed, a tray in her hands. On it was a glass full of orange juice, dainty toast, some marmalade and coffee. I devoured it like a famished animal.

Then I began pacing the floor. Up and down. Across and back. Every once in so often I would pause in front of the window and gaze out into the glorious sunshine; the sunshine that meant freedom, that means everything that was worth living.

Much to my surprise I saw mother drive up in our car. The chauffeur stopped directly in front of the entrance—possibly fifty feet away from my window—and she got out.

Like a flash, I thought of a way to escape!

I ran into the bathroom and twisted off the steel rack placed there to hold wash rags. Then I bent the bars back and fourth [sic], back and forth, until I broke one off. Then I twisted it free at the other end. I had in my hands a steel tube, perhaps five inches long. I placed it inside the waist of my dress.

An instant later an attendant opened my door and notified me that my mother was waiting in the visitors' room. I walked out, following her down the long hall.

Six other nurses, or attendants, stood in a group outside and just a little to the left of the open front door.

I followed the other attendant into my mother's presence. She kissed and hugged me, and asked me how I liked it there. I told her that everything was fine; that I felt sure they'd be able to cure me.

Not once did I mention the terrible things that had happened to me elsewhere. Instead, I kept a wary eye on the group of nurses standing in the hall. Finally, after a lifetime, it seemed to me, three of them left, leaving three standing there. I was afraid to wait any longer.

Through the open window I could see Fred, our chauffeur, dozing in the front seat. "Now, or never, is my time," I thought. Turning to mother, I asked her for a dollar; "to give to a nurse," I explained.

She fumbled in her pocketbook a moment, and then produced one.

"Wait just a minute, mother. I'll be right back," I said.

I stepped outside, sidled past the three nurses by the door, and was out on the sidewalk and into the rear seat of our car before anyone noticed my maneuver.

Pulling the steel tube from my bosom, I placed the end against the back of Fred's neck. He thought it was a pistol barrel.

"Don't turn around, or make an outcry," I threatened him. "If you do, I'll blow off the top of your head. Throw in your gears and drive like hell till I tell you to stop!"

"But, please, Miss Rubens," he begged. "Please don't make me do this. You'll get me into trouble. I'll lose my job."

My answer was to press the steel tube still harder against his neck.

"Drive on like I told you," I snarled. "This is your last chance. Get going. And drive fast."

And, as we vanished in a whirl of dust, I could see my mother, on the sidewalk, surrounded by a dozen doctors and nurses, excitedly pointing after our speeding automobile.

## Chapter Twenty-Eight

After driving perhaps half an hour Fred finally mustered up sufficient nerve to turn around and look at me. When he saw that my "pistol" was nothing but a broken piece of steel tubing, he slowed up and said he was going to turn around and take me back.

I dared him to. I said I would jump out of the car and break my neck—commit suicide—if he did. I guess he was afraid to take the chance of my keeping my word, because he kept on. Occasionally I gave him directions, until we reached the postoffice [sic] in Pasadena.

There we were held up by a traffic jam and I got out. He tried to stop me but I sped away like a deer. I walked around the block, then went into a drug store and called the sanitarium. My mother was still there. They brought her to the telephone and I assured her I was all right.

"Where are you, darling?" she asked. "At the postoffice [sic] in Pasadena," I replied. Then I hung up. I ran outside, hailed a taxicab and directed him to drive me to our home in Santa Monica. I knew that inside of five minutes all the policemen in Pasadena would be at the postoffice [sic], looking for me.

When I got home I kept the taxicab waiting outside at the curb. I went in, hurriedly threw a few clothes into a bag and started to run out. Then I was forced to stop a moment because of an unusually severe deprivation cramp in my stomach.

I sat down on the edge of the bed to rest. Then the thought struck me of a number I might call, where I could get a "shot." I had only the one dollar in cash, but I had on my wedding ring. It was studded with small diamonds and had cost $500.

I made the telephone call, and in doing so I did something inadvertently that led to my re-capture more than 24 hours later. As I waited for central to connect me, I idly jotted down the number I was calling on the little pad attached to the telephone.

When the pain eased up, I seized my bag, ran downstairs, and slipped out the back way, leaving my taxicab parked in front of the house. Later, I learned he was still "watchfully waiting" when my mother returned home late that evening.

I climbed over the hedges in the rear, crossed an alley and went through a neighbor's lot to the next street. Then I walked to the street car line, climbed aboard and was on my way.

Well, to make a long story short, when the police, urged on by my mother and Ric, found me the next morning, I was sound asleep in a cot in a cheap little rooming house down in the Chinese and Negro section near the railroad in Los Angeles.

And, asleep on the floor beside the cot, was my "boy friend," Henry Tape, a Chinaman. I had become acquainted with Tape, also known to the police as Henry "Foo," at Spadra. He had been discharged a few days before I was taken to Pomona. He had a long record as a peddler and an addict.

Henry and I had had quite an "opium-smoking party," before the police located me. The tell-tale jottings of my subconscious mind on the telephone pad at home had led them on.

The opium, while it temporarily relieved my deprivation pains, had made me deathly sick, and Henry had put me to bed. Afterwards he, too, had "hit the pipe," and we were both "sleeping it off" when the police, accompanied by mother and Ric, crashed the door.

I was taken home, but poor Henry was arrested, not only for possession and sale of narcotics, but for stealing my wedding ring. He had it on when they awakened us. I don't remember whether I gave it to him, or whether he took it off my finger after I fell asleep, but anyhow I was unharmed.

Then, within the next few days, came the events that led up to my commitment to Patton, the California State Asylum for the Insane, where the temperature reaches 118 degrees at noonday and one always freezes at night.

There I witnessed atrocities, calumnies heaped by the law upon the poor, unfortunate crazy people, the flotsam and jetsam of society, that would stir the imagination of another De Quincey, another Stoker, another Edgar Allen Poe!

## Chapter Twenty-Nine

On the evening before I was started on my way to Patton Asylum for the Insane—I had had a certain uneasy feeling that presaged impending unhappiness. Always of an extremely sensitive nature, I knew instinctively that some secret move was under way, but I couldn't exactly figure out how it affected me.

Earlier in the afternoon Dorothy Davenport—Wally Reid's widow—had called. I had noticed that she had tried to draw a parallel between my own case and that pitifully weak and futile fight of her husband against the relentless dope monster in the months preceding his death.

I had met Wally when I was only a beginning in the movies, and he, in turn, had introduced me to Dorothy. We had, thereafter, upon many occasions, exchanged visits, both before and after I had risen to stardom.

My presentiment was aggravated upon her departure. She kissed me with unusual fervor, a long, lingering embrace, as though she was saying good-bye forever; as though she never again expected to see me. And as she stepped down off the stoop, she hesitated a moment, as though there was something she wanted to say but was afraid.

She turned and went on, however. I went inside and sat down to think it over. I was in a terrible plight. I was penniless. I had disposed of my jewelry, my luxurious sables, my beautiful ermine wrap, my exquisite lingerie—everything I possessed—in my battle against overwhelming odds to keep myself supplied with drugs.

I realized that these conditions could not go forever, that the end was close at hand. On many occasions, after my frequent escapades, both my mother and Ric had threatened me with Patton; that is, not exactly threatened, but had hinted at it vaguely.

"So help me, God, Alma, you're going to wind up in Patton," had become a stock phrase in our household. It had been ding-donged into my ears, night and day, for so long, that I had become accustomed to it. To me, it was the old cry of "wolf, wolf," and it didn't mean anything. Never for a moment had I seriously considered that either Ric or my mother would ever consent to my removal there, no matter what the provocation. Patton had a hard name but up until this particular evening I had always felt secure.

But Dorothy's visit had unnerved me. Her actions had me guessing, and I began to wonder whether, after all, my family might not resort to this step as a final gesture in their efforts to have me cured.

Long in the night I lay awake, ever pondering, ever trying to peer into the future and the final outcome of the problem confronting us all.

Eventually I fell into a troubled sleep, from which I awoke with the feeling that someone was peeking in my bedroom window. It was broad daylight and I leaped to my feet.

Hastily throwing a dressing gown over my shoulders, I ran to the window, just in time to see two—to me it seemed—ruffianly figures, darting into a hiding place behind a bush in our yard.

I was frightened stiff! I didn't know what to do.

But I didn't have long to wonder. A doctor who was an old friend knocked at my bedroom door and asked how I was feeling. I told him "fine;" to sit down in the living room and that I would get dressed and come out.

I did so and he conversed on a varied line of subjects. Never before had I known him to remain such a long time. There was a peculiar little glint of sadness or worry in his eyes that I had never seen there before. He couldn't meet my gaze. The moment I would catch his eye he'd turn away.

I thought of the two men hiding in the yard, but did not mention my fears.

But over and over, recurred to my mind, the thought of Patton. The tall grandfather clock in the corner struck nine. Nine times over it repeated— that is in my mind—the dreaded word "Patton." I was ghastly afraid, but I wouldn't let on; not until he said something definite.

The doctor moved restlessly about the room. Finally, he heaved an almost inaudible sigh, went to his medicine case and took out a bottle. He withdrew the cork, got a glass, and poured out a drink of the light-brown liquid.

"Here, Alma," he said. "Take a drink of this. It is very fine old Bourbon."

That confirmed my suspicions; that and the fact that neither Ric, nor my mother, had shown up. Usually, they were up far ahead of me. I knew that that liquor was drugged. Some inner prompting made me refuse.

"I don't want it," I said. "I don't care for liquor at all."

I could see a disappointed look creep over his face. Then I was sure it was drugged; sure that those two men in the yard were there to take me to Patton.

The doctor walked over to the window. I saw him beckon to someone outside. He turned around to me and asked permission to use the telephone, which was kept in a little booth in the hall, some distance away from my bedroom door.

The moment he left the room I ran to the front door—a Dutch-style door divided in two, cross-wise. The upper half was open. The two men stood there looking in.

"What do you want?" I screamed. "You can't come in."

"Take it easy, lady," one of them said. "Take it easy. We came to take you to the hospital and you mustn't excite yourself."

They tried to open the lower half of the door, but it was tightly locked. As one of them turned sideways, I saw a huge lump bulging in one of his pockets.

Instantly, I knew what that was, too. It was a straitjacket. They had come for me with a straitjacket.

I fled into my room. I locked the door and tightly closed the shutters. The doctor had made a futile attempt to catch me as I ran past him.

He pounded on the panels.

"Open it, Alma," he shouted. "I tell you to open that door. I won't hurt you. I'll promise you I won't. I'm here for your own good, Alma. Open that door!"

I ran into my private bathroom and locked the door of that. A moment later I heard something give way and I knew that the doctor, and perhaps the two men, were inside my bedroom. I braced the back of a little bathroom chair under the door knob.

Then my eyes fell on a sharp butcher knife, lying on the bath room clothes-horse. How it got there, I have no idea. But, there it was! I seized it.

## CHAPTER THIRTY

"I have a knife here," I shrieked to the doctor, who was trying to force the door. "If you break down that door, I'll slash my throat; my wrists. I'll kill myself sure."

He knew that I was desperate. He feared that I might, in my hysteria, carry out my threat. He left the room and I heard him return to the telephone.

I just sat there and waited; I don't know what for, but I just sat there.

Some time later I heard another voice at the door. It was an old family friend. I loved him dearly.

"Ah," I sighed, with a feeling of sweetest relief. "Here is someone I can talk to. Someone I can trust!"

"Alma," he called. "Let me come inside and talk to you, dear."

"I will, if you'll promise not to let them take me away, " I cried. I was so glad, so happy, that at last here was someone who would sympathize with me, one that would protect me. "I'll let you in if you'll promise you won't let them take me to Patton."

"Why, the very idea," he reassured me. "The very idea. Who said anything about taking you to Patton. They told me you had a big knife and were threatening to kill yourself. If you have, put it down. You know that I wouldn't let anyone hurt you."

I hid the knife in the closet behind me. I was ashamed of myself. I trusted him implicitly. I went to the door, drew aside the chair and unlocked it.

My friend stepped into the room. His face was haggard and drawn and he must have been undergoing the tortures of hell. Right behind him were two strange men. They had handcuffs and a restraining belt in their hands.

All this I took in in an instant. I tried to reach the closet, where I had hidden the knife. But they were too quick for me. I had lost my battle. I knew it. It was no use prolonging the ordeal. I submitted without further protest.

They led me downstairs, our friendly old family doctor behind them. Down in the living room I turned half way around and called to my friends, trying my best to smile:

"Don't worry so much, dear. You thought you were doing everything for the best. I forgive you. Come and kiss me goodbye."

I don't believe I ever saw such an unhappy look on a man's face in my life. I'm sure he was enduring agonies a thousand times worse than my own; a thousand times harder to bear than my own terrible deprivation pains; my heartbreak and the mental hurt from his deceit.

So, clad only in a flimsy housedress, handcuffed and tightly bound in the restraining belt, I kissed him and was led away to an ambulance, which a moment later started off, siren shrieking, on the way to the psychopathic ward, where I was locked in a padded cell.

No one had told me I was destined for Patton, but I knew it. I knew that it was but a question of hours until I reached there to stay for God only knew how long.

The next morning, without waking to feed me or to relieve the excruciating pains from my long hours without drugs, I was loaded into the front seat of an automobile, with the driver on one side and a strapping nurse on the other, on my way to Patton!

And, before I reached there, while yet on that nerve-wracking, seemingly endless drive, I was insulted.

Broken, physically and mentally, and only about half-dressed, I started out on that tortuous ride to the "California Crazy House." I had a blanket draped over my thin house-dress and the satin mules I had worn when taken from my home the previous morning had been replaced with a badly worn pair of shoes, apparently left behind by some other poor unfortunate who had occupied that psychopathic ward cell ahead of me.

I had no powder for my face. They hadn't even given me a chance to wash it. My hair was uncombed and matted into a tangled mess. When I asked the husky Amazon assigned as my nurse for a hairpin, she refused, with the soul-soothing remark:

"Never mind hairpins. You won't need no hairpins where you're going."

"Where are we going; where are you taking me?" I then asked, looking first at the nurse and then at the driver.

The Amazon merely smiled; the driver turned away. But I was just as sure as if they had told me that I was on the way to Patton.

While he did not answer my question, still I could feel that he, at least, in some small measure, felt sorry for me. I was ravenously hungry. I had had nothing to eat for 24 hours and I told him so.

"I'll get you something," he promised. "Soon as we reach the first soft-drink stand, I'll stop and get you something to eat."

He did so, buying some apples and cigarettes, which he divided with me.

I ate my share of the fruit, making it last as long as I could. My hunger was still unsatisfied, so I began smoking the cigarettes, one after another. Eventually, I became drowsy.

Then I awoke with a start!

The nurse was snoring in the rear seat. And the driver, the man who had pitied me, who had actually stopped and spent his own hard-earned pennies to fill my aching void, was trying to comfort me by putting his arm around me.

I was highly insulted at the time. But after a few months at Patton, such an adventure would have struck me as exceedingly mild. Not only a male attendant, but a doctor, actually offered to trade me a 5-cent bag of candy and ONE cigarette—they were forbidden there—FOR MY BODY!

The automobile rolled along over the smooth road. Orange groves, picturesque bungalows, flowers on every side. The blue California sky shone down on this typically California landscape. The birds flitted overhead, and once in a while I heard a meadowlark give vent to his tuneful lilt.

The birds and the bees, all the wild things; the flowers, the trees, the people I saw along the roadside, everybody was happy, except me.

And, I—Alma Rubens, the pampered toast of a million screen fans—was on my way to the "crazy house."

Miles, ahead of us occasionally, I could glimpse a huge pile of gray stone buildings. When the road sloped downward I lost sight of them for a time, but each time when we'd mount another rise, there they'd be, ever a little bit nearer, a little plainer in outline, than they had been before.

"Is that Patton" I again asked the driver. He only smiled, and looked away, BUT I KNEW.

An hour passed. I was on the verge of fainting. Hunger. Thirst. Weariness from the tiresome drive. Heartsickness. Shame... All were dragging me down, mentally and physically; and, above all, that terrifying, gnawing, aching, indescribable yearning within—for just one more "shot" of dope before I was locked up.

We entered the driveway and drew up in front of the main administration building. I sat with the driver while the nurse went inside.

A long procession of queer-looking people came into view, emerging from a small woods onto a pathway leading to the main group of buildings. Could these be insane persons?

Up until then I had always pictured insane people as most of us do: violent, screaming, tearing at their hair, raving! But these! They couldn't be insane!

It seemed to be like a drab parade of lost souls.

Silently and wearily, and hopelessly, they were returning from their morning of hard labor in the fields, their hoes, rakes, and shovels slung across their shoulders.

Just so many cattle. Nothing human about them, except their figures. Human cattle, prodded by harsh-voiced attendants mounted on horseback; too subdued, too baffled, to know what it was all about.

Never shall I forget that, my first view of the unhappy patients that inhabit Patton—the City of the Living Dead—the graveyard of almost five thousand animated ghosts.

One of the asylum officials came out and aroused me from my sordid reverie. He took me by the arm, helped me from the car, and escorted me into the reception room, where he left me alone.

The moment he stepped out again I heard the heavy door clang shut behind him. I heard the key grate in the lock. I imagined I could feel a stale, icy breeze, whipping soundlessly overhead. In the dark corners of the room I could also see shapeless, slithering objects, sometimes gliding, sometimes darting, here and there.

There are no bars visible from the outside of Patton, but now that I was inside I could see that every window was heavily barred, every door was doubly locked. There was no escape from there. I was trapped!

Depressed beyond belief, I examined my surroundings more carefully. I got up and walked around. There was a rag carpet, worn and tattered, almost, but not quite, covering the warped, waxed floor. A combination writing-desk and book-case of heavy, golden oak, stood in one corner; an oak stand of a different grain, held an imitation china lamp, on the shade of which was painted the picture of a fisherman's cottage.

The chairs were of fumed oak, nicked in many places either by the knives of dawdling attendants or by wear. Safe to say, that the patients were not responsible for this; they were kept too busy.

My heart had sunked into my torn, runover shoes, if such a thing is possible. Of course, I know that it isn't, but that's the only way I can describe it. I kept telling myself that it all was a grotesque nightmare; a practical joke sprung to frighten me into a cure of the drug habit.

Surely, I thought, my family couldn't have sent me into this sordid environment. But I was in Patton, nevertheless.

All hope perished in that moment of realization. But, I bore up. Mentally, I vowed to be brave. Whatever happened, no one would ever be able to see how I had suffered. I would not let them break my spirit. I might die, but I'd never shed a tear!

## Chapter Thirty-One

My mid-day nightmare was broken by the entrance of a woman—a short, cocky woman with thin lips, cruel eyes, and a hard, almost mannish voice. She rattled a huge bunch of keys, strung on a huge steel ring. Ah! those keys. Those ever-present, rattling, heavy brass keys that play such an important bit in life at Patton.

"So you're Alma Rubens!" she rasped, as she walked over and faced me. "So you're Alma Rubens, the movie star! How in the world did you get here?"

I gulped! Her voice stabbed me as would have a dagger had it been thrust into my heart. I was paralyzed with fear. She reminded me so much of that other nurse, who had made life so hard for me in Spadra, the Pomona cottage, and the last private sanitarium from which I had escaped I could not reply.

She unbuckled the heavy belt which bound my arms against my body. She was very rough, but the relief at the release of my hands was such that I made no protest. My body felt as though it had been freed from a vise.

She grasped me by one arm and led me outside into a long, narrow passageway, or corridor.

I asked her where she was taking me.

"Never mind. Come along!" she answered in no uncertain tones of command. "Never mind where you're going. Just do as you're told. You'll find out soon enough and that will be plenty of time for you to begin worrying."

I meekly followed her.

Through half a dozen wards, we passed, keys turning in locks both before and behind us, until I was fairly frantic from the rattling, banging, grating sounds.

Occasionally, I could hear cacklings and gibberings from unseen occupants of the various cells we passed. Once I saw a haggard face, peering through the slot high in the door of a cell. That redoubled my terror.

Suddenly our journey was halted, temporarily, by a shriek, a high, wailing, despairing, soul-ripping crescendo, that soared to the highest note of the scale, wavered, and then ceased as suddenly as it had begun.

I collapsed in a heap on the floor. My custodian, however, stepped to the door of an adjacent cell and cried:

"Shut up, you so-and-so! Or you'll know what you'll get!"

Then she went on.

I managed to regain my feet and stumbled after her.

That piercing shriek by that poor insane woman and the cruel manner in which she was silenced, had completely unnerved me. My limbs were shaking, my lips were quivering, and I could feel the cold sweat starting from every pore in my body. Fearing that every step would be my last. I kept on my feet, however, tottering, stumbling on after my hard-visaged, harsh-voiced guide, through half a dozen other long, cell-lined rooms until we reached our destination—the receiving ward.

"So that's Alma Rubens," other coarse-featured attendants would mutter to my chaperon each time we'd pause to unlock and relock the various doors. "So that's Alma Rubens—the movie star. Just look at her now. Don't look so pretty now, does she? Ain't it a pity?"

Upon each occasion the grim, narrow-lipped woman escorting me, would confirm my identity with a nod or a grin, and, sometimes, a remark, such as: "Yes; that's her. They say she's a 'hophead' now."

Just that way, casual like. I might as well have been some wild animal so far as they were concerned, a beast of the fields, without a brain, without feelings.

And I, too crumpled and bruised in body and soul to protest or to care, didn't give a sign to denote that I had heard. I just stumbled on, hoping and praying that my legs would hold up under me until we arrived at wherever she was taking me.

When we reached the receiving ward the woman unceremoniously shoved me toward a scale in the corner. She snatched the blanket from my shoulders, and then, for the first time, noticed that I was still clutching in one hand the pitiful half dozen cigarettes remaining in the package the chauffeur had purchased at that wayside stand. She took those, too.

When I stepped from the scale they were gone; had vanished into the capacious pocket in the Dutch apron of her uniform.

"Where are my cigarettes?" I asked.

"Never mind," she replied. "You won't need cigarettes here."

"Oh. Can't I smoke?" I ventured.

"You heard me!" she snapped.

Next, I was taken into a huge bathroom, more like a laundry room. The tub was a brown, metal, badly chipped affair. God only knows how many other patients had used it that day. And it obviously had not been cleaned.

Yet, I was made to undress and she motioned for me to climb in. She turned on the water, not even luke-warm, and seizing me by the shoulders, forced me into it.

Before I could voice a protest, she had seized a can of brown-looking soft soap and had poured it over my head.

"Please," I cried. "Let me wash my own hair. You're hurting me."

Her answer was a snort.

## Chapter Thirty-Two

The soap was in my eyes and ears and mouth. It burned like fire. But my suffering was already so great that a few more little burns, or aches, or pains, didn't matter, and soon the ordeal was over.

I was bathed and combed and given my "Crazy House" attire.

It was a single garment made out of old, unbleached, white-muslin flour sacks. You could still see the lettering on the sides, although it had been washed until these had become quite faded. The dress itself resembled a sack, open at the bottom, holes to stick the arms through, and a straw-string around the top, which, when tied, completed the dressing operation. I was allowed no shoes, no stockings.

Then she took me to my room. She called it a room, but it really was a cell. It was just big enough for an iron hospital bed and contained absolutely no other article of furniture.

She gave me a shove. I fell across the bed, and she went out, slamming the door and rattling her keys as she locked it. I got up and looked over my surroundings. By standing on my tiptoes I could bring my eyes to the level with the barred opening high up in the heavy oaken door.

Outside I could see a cluster of white caps, which represented a gathering of the attendants, all discussing my arrival in husky whispers.

I guess I was the first "movie star" they had ever seen in person. And, thinking it over, I must have been a sight.

What, with the ordeal I had been through, the long, dusty drive, the bath which left me stickier than I was before I got in the tub, the outfit I wore, and my emaciated appearance caused by the dreadful deprivation cramps—yes, I must have been a picture no artist could paint. No wonder they congregated outside my cell and gossiped until they were chased away by their superior.

I went to the other end of the room in which, thank God, there was a window. Barred, of course, but nevertheless a window. And I could look outside and see God's beautiful sunshine. Trees, too, tough they were some distance away, and, across a lawn, a little cluster of white, green-shuttered houses where the doctors lived with their families.

As I stood there, thinking of my beautiful home, my ruined career, my mother, my husband—whom I still adored in spite of all his unsympathetic treatment—and the terrible physical ordeal through which I had just gone, there came to me the words of a verse of Oscar Wilde's immortal poem: "Ballad of Reading Gaol."

> "But I never saw a man who looked
> So wistfully at the day
> I never saw a man who looked
> With such a wistful eye
> Upon the little tent of blue
> Which prisoners call the sky
> And at every drifting cloud that went
> With sails of silver by."

Truly, I was in the same position as that other poor prisoner. Except that he knew his days of suffering were limited, that soon he was free to face his doom on the gallows, while I was a prisoner for no telling how long, to be shunted around like a wild animal with little prospect of sweet death to ease my suffering.

Then, my thoughts returned to my friends, and yet another verse of the same beautiful ballad:

> "Yet each man kills the thing he loves,
> By each let this be heard.
> Some do it with a bitter look,
> Some with a flattering word.
> The coward does it with a kiss,
> The brave man with a sword."

A wave of self-pity swept over me. I staggered to the bed and tried to go to sleep. But I couldn't.

I was famished. Except for that little bit of fruit the driver had given me that morning, I had had nothing since the night before. The extent of my suffering from the lack of drugs is impossible to describe. My nerves were a million imps, stabbing me, scratching me, biting me, and sneering at my anguish.

I shrieked at the top of my voice, even as had that other poor woman whose cell I had passed on the way to the receiving ward a few minutes—or was it hours—before. But no one came.

The attendants at Patton are used to shrieks at all times of the day or night, and one more, or one less, screaming patient in their care, means nothing to their deadly routine.

I screamed again, then fell into a fitful sobbing.

## Chapter Thirty-Three

Eventually, I must have dozed, because I was startled some time later by a heavy hand on my shoulder. Two attendants, their crisply starched uniforms rustling as they touched the bed, ordered me to "get up."

I did so.

"We're taking you to the doctor," one of them observed. "Come on."

"I'm too sick," I answered. "Can't the doctor come here?"

"What? Of all the nerve," was their rejoinder. "Where do you think you are? Home?"

I tried to follow them but I fell to my knees. They half-carried, half-dragged me into the doctor's office.

The medico was standing with his back to the door when I entered. He was a tall man with iron-gray hair. Somehow, or other, the sight of his shock of curly, iron-gray hair gave me hope. Surely here was an educated man, a refined man, a gentleman, to whom I could talk and who would at least give me a little sympathy.

I was mistaken, however. I knew it the minute he turned around.

He was the ordinary institution doctor, remaining in such a position simply because he had not the ability or ambition to keep afloat in the stream of outside competition. A man satisfied with a meager salary, contented to drift along from day to day, and with no interest in his work, except to put in the hours required of him by his superiors.

There are, of course, some fine, conscientious, humanitarian physicians and scientists in the state institutions—some, no doubt, in Patton, but this doctor was not one of them. I may as well have been a bag of straw, so far as his sympathies were concerned.

He asked me the usual stereotyped questions and put me through the usual routine examination all addicts and insane persons must undergo in such an institution.

## Chapter Thirty-Three

"What is this?" was his final question. He thrust a bottle of camphor under my nose. I was weak and swaying on my feet.

"Camphor," I managed to whisper.

"Okay!" said the doctor. "No signs of insanity. She's a 'cokie.' Lock her up."

And they dragged me back and carried out his instructions.

Not until the next morning did they bring me anything to eat.

And, when they did, it was a plateful of white Mexican beans, swimming in the grease of the near-rancid piece of fat pork in which they had been cooked. Such a breakfast! And I, deathly sick, mentally and physically. I was supposed to eat that—and like it!

Hungry as I was, the very sight of that unpalatable mess, served on a greasy, gray, aluminum tray, on which was a gray, cracked bowl, a gray pewter spoon—patients were not allowed forks—and a gray chunk of bread, completely killed my appetite.

Gray was the prevailing color at Patton. The walls were supposed to be white-washed, but they, too, were gray. Gray walls, gray furnishings, gray clothing, gray food, and drab-gray existence for the near 5,000 souls incarcerated there. That's Patton.

My first breakfast was typical of the place. At least once a day we'd get beans. Sometimes they'd be for breakfast; sometimes at one or the other two meals. But never a day without beans; white Mexican beans, swimming in grease.

Occasionally our diet was varied. We'd get the same grayish bowl, half-filled with grayish-blue milk, some grayish cornmeal porridge, and always that grayish, muddy coffee that tasted like dirty dishwater smells.

Of course, I couldn't eat that first breakfast. It nauseated me. But they forced me to. But, my stomach was victorious in the end. The food simply wouldn't stay down, much to the chagrin of the two muscular attendants who held my arms and legs and nose, to make me swallow it.

There were no provisions for even a sponge bath in my cell. I was not supposed to wash myself, but I did.

Directly underneath my cell, on the floor below, another woman, apparently a recent arrival, was locked up. Suffering as I was, without my drugs, and from the inhumane treatment, her condition must have been a thousand times worse.

I never saw her. But I heard her.

Day and night she kept up a constant moaning, as if in the deepest physical agony.

One of my night attendants was fairly kind. I struck up an acquaintance with her and she really wasn't a bad sort at heart, though she was in deadly fear of being caught hobnobbing with a patient, something that was strictly forbidden.

She told me that the poor woman underneath had lost her mind, following the death of her husband, two sons and a daughter, in rapid succession. On top of that she was in the last stages of cancer of the throat. Incurable, she was taken to Patton to die.

My heart went out to the poor sufferer. I almost—but not quite—forgot my own trials and tribulations. No one can forget the drugs, you know. Even the tentacles of the relentless monster stretches out for its victim, sleeping or awake, the dreadful urge, the spirit-crushing yearning, with the physically torturing deprivation cramps always present.

Such was my condition, but in spite of that I could still feel for that other far more unfortunate woman. The days were dry and hot. As I said before, sometimes, in the daytime, the temperature would rise to 118 degrees.

On this particular day, just about the end of my second week there, the woman in the cell below constantly moaned and cried for water.

I could stand it no longer. I went to the water pipe that led down from my toilet. I knelt down on the floor and called her. She must have been lucid at the moment, despite her suffering. She answered me. I told her to take water out of the toilet bowl in her cell; that it was clean, and anything was better than undergoing physical agony.

She said there was no toilet in her cell.

So I, after pondering a moment, tore off a piece from the bottom of my sack-cloth dress, soaked it in the bowl, then squeezed the water out against that lead waterpipe, allowing it to trickle through the floor to the cell below.

And that poor woman stuck her tongue to the pipe, caught those straggling drops of the life-giving fluid as it trickled down, and thus appeased her unendurable and throat-parching thirst. For hours I kept up the procedure and she lapped that water like an animal.

The next morning she died. Died on the floor, without even an attendant present—so I was told by my friendly night nurse—and with her tongue glued to the moist coolness of that slimy, gray water pipe.

Only a few nights later I was up and pacing up and down the narrow confines of my cell. It was extremely chilly—the nights were always cold and the bedding insufficient to keep one warm—and I hadn't been able to fall asleep.

The lights in all the cells were out hours before. But I had been standing in front of my window, gazing at the moonlight and listening to the faint notes of a piano that drifted across the lawn from one of the doctors' cottages.

Something, I don't know what it was, prompted me to stop in front of the door of my cell, stretch up on tiptoe and pull my eyes up level with the bars.

## Chapter Thirty-Three

The corridor outside was dimly lighted. Directly across the way was another cell, with the outer block door partly ajar.

Through the cell door, on through the room, and by the dim light of the moon, I could see a stark form hanging by a twisted sheet, tied high to the bars of the window.

Not a move. Just hanging there. I don't know how I knew. I had never seen a hanged person before. But I knew that she was dead. I knew that at least one hopeless soul had had the sense and the courage to know that there was more mercy beyond. I couldn't call. I couldn't scream.

A few moments later an attendant, on the regular half-hourly trips around, discovered the suicide. And I again took up my tortured position at the peephole, watching them cut her down. I had to look. I couldn't help it.

And I lay awake the rest of the night, trying to summon up my own courage to emulate her example. But I couldn't even do that! I wanted to, but I was afraid!

A few nights later I was again kept awake, this time by a woman moaning and writhing in physical agony on the cot in the very same cell.

When the attendant came around—this one was a particularly brutal one—I asked her what was the matter with the girl across the way. "What ails her?" I demanded.

"Nothing but what they all get," she responded callously. "They sterilized her today. Guess it hurts her a little. But that's just what they all get—and what you'll get, too, if you get to making eyes at the men when you're transferred to one of the cottages."

At that instant the poor creature across the way shrieked in a high-pitched voice that fairly curdled my blood. I begged the attendant to let me go in with her and try to do something to ease her pain.

Instead, she crossed over, unlocked the door and went in herself, cautioning me to get to bed and mind my own business.

"Shut up!" she commanded the screaming unfortunate. And, to my horror—I had climbed back up to my vantage post—she turned the poor, screaming, bandaged thing over onto its stomach and beat her unmercifully on the back with her huge ring of big brass keys.

And on one occasion I saw a young girl, an epileptic, struck in the face with a bunch of keys by a heartless attendant, struck so hard that her cheekbone was laid open, necessitating a visit from a doctor, who had to sew it up.

Under such unspeakable horrible conditions I remained almost three weeks in that receiving ward cell. Every day I would witness some new atrocity, some new act of cruelty that caused me to shudder in pity and disgust.

Then came the time for my transfer. My probationary period was over.

## Chapter Thirty-Four

The principal attendant came around one morning. There was a gleam in her eye, which bespoke of some new indignity to come. I had already learned the signs.

"Well. You're going to work," she announced triumphantly. "You've got to work here. You may be a movie actress, but you're no better than anyone else in this place. You're on the 'polishing' squad from now on."

My probationary period was over, my stay in the receiving or observation ward at an end. I was to become a full-fledged "nut" in the California "Crazy House," that grim little City of the Living Dead—Patton—where the "nuts" are allowed a little freedom, a little exercise, as a reward for carrying on under an almost incredible amount of back-breaking, soul-grinding drudgery.

When the reward is due and payable, the poor tired body is beyond its acceptance.

But I didn't know that then!

I remember how thrilled I was; how elated at being taken from that skimpy little observation ward cell where, within a scant three weeks, I had witnessed more unspeakable sights and had passed through more spirit-crucifying ordeals than the average individual encounters in a lifetime.

I was to go to work—on the "polishing squad."

Even now, more than a year since I left Patton, I shudder whenever I hear the word "polish," so vivid, so terrible are the memories that it recalls.

I was transferred to another building—"cottage," the employees called it—and given my outfit of institutional work clothes. Up until then I had had nothing but that miserably rough, unbleached cotton, flour-sack night-gown with holes for arms and the drawstring around the neck. I even had been barefooted from the moment I was locked up.

The first thing they gave me when I moved into my new quarters was a pair of black cotton stockings and a pair of heavy, brogan-like shoes, with two nails sticking up inside that lacerated my foot.

Incidentally, that foot—my right—became so calloused that, following my release eight months later, I had to undergo an operation.

The next garment handed me gave me quite a laugh. Thank God I've always had a sense of humor and if it hadn't been for this, I don't know how I ever could have stood up under the ordeals and the suffering which I have gone through in more than a decade of drug addiction.

It was a pair of gray woolen drawers of the old-fashioned, open-in-front style. To the bottom of each leg—apparently they had been too short for the previous wearer—had been sewed a section of flour sack, which brought it down as far as my ankles.

## Chapter Thirty-Four

This extension was not a ruffle, yet its circumference was the full size of the flour sack, giving the garment the appearance of such. Perhaps it was added for modesty's sake. Certainly not for beauty or comfort.

Across each leg in indelible blue lettering was the name of the issuing concern—a milling company.

The harsh wool of the main section of the suit irritated my skin—accustomed to the finest silk and lace lingerie—beyond belief.

And the flappy bottoms of the legs caused my stockings to bulge grotesquely. I think it must have greatly resembled that funny little Rose La France of the hideous symmetricals who "stopped the show" on the night of my first appearance on the stage so many years before.

The costume was completed by a gingham dress and a little gray woolen cape. The ensemble was most ludicrous.

My initiation into the mysteries of the "polishing squad" began at once. "Polishers" are employed all day long at the back-breaking work of polishing the floors, all of which, in Patton, are of warped, splintery, soft-wood boards, averaging, I suppose, more than a foot in breadth. They are, however, kept in a high state of polish and slipperiness.

And if one of the patients slips on the wax and breaks an arm or leg, it's just too bad—just further proof of his or her insanity!

Throughout many weary weeks the sorry little brigade of which I was a member formed in a dreary line, each provided with a weighted block, the bottom of which was covered with old Brussels carpet, and which we propelled back and forth across the floors by means of a six-foot handle.

Over us stood the dreaded attendants, two to every squad of twenty patients, always lashing us with their tongues, jibing at us, goading us, and, occasionally, if we weakened, some of them would crack down on our backs and heads with those bludgeonish brass keys.

Even on the coldest day no "polisher" ever worked more than five minutes before the perspiration began oozing from his pores.

How I ever survived that first day as a "polisher" is one of the mysteries I have never been able to solve. I was still weak from the drug-deprivation pains and from the lack of proper food. Yet, hour after hour, I kept up the monotonous drudgery until at the end of the day's toil I was virtually in a daze.

Thinking back, I believe I must have been unconscious during a big part of that first day's labor, or else I could not have lived it through.

There was muttering and groaning on all sides of me. A patient would become recalcitrant, drop her mop handle and try to run away. Instantly the guards were after her. She was shoved back into line, or else, if she showed fight, was dragged away to an especial punishment cell. Most, however, as did I, worked on with dogged endurance.

One thing, above everything else, led me instinctively, to keep on with my labors, regardless of my state of exhaustion and the extent of my mental and physical suffering.

That was the fact that I knew the guards were watching me, waiting for me to rebel, thus giving certain ones the excuse they craved to manhandle me.

Or, better still, that which would furnish their sadistic natures an even greater thrill, the sight of Alma Rubens, the movie star, falling upon my knees with exhaustion, begging and pleading for mercy.

Many, many times have I seen this cruel exhibition. I've seen some of those ignorant attendants actually laugh and grimace with joy while they "lorded" it over their poor, unfortunate victim during such a performance.

Some queer intuition warned me of this condition that first miserable day I worked on the "polishing squad." And, knowing it, I kept at my task long after my arms were as of lead, my shoulders one horrific blaze of tortured nerves and muscles, and my mind paralyzed.

My will was sovereign in its scope! That stubborn trait, inherited from my dear, long-deceased father, would not let me admit defeat at the hands of another person; would not let me grovel and whine at the feet of my persecutors, no matter what mental or physical injury they might inflict.

Ah! If I could only have done likewise with my one and only master— DOPE!

Every morning I was awakened at half-past four. I had to be dressed and ready to begin my duties a half-hour later.

We had either hominy, rice, or beans for breakfast, and always the same gray, muddy drink, which it would be flattery to call coffee.

The food at Patton is distinctly bad.

Perhaps the other inmates had some attention from physicians while they were there; this I cannot say, but for myself, I do know that the only time I saw a doctor in all the eight months that I was in Patton, was the day I was admitted and the day I was discharged—as cured.

The time dragged on, with terrible monotony.

There was no time for me to read in the daytime. I could not talk to any of my poor, dazed companions, and in the evening, as soon as the sun set, I was put into my cell in the pitch dark.

I hit upon the plan of trying to picture a month as one day.

Thirty sunrises, thirty sunsets, thirty periods of darkness—that I told myself would mean to me one day.

I had eight of these strange days to wait, eight months to pray and hope and wonder about my mother, and my husband, and the good friends who lived out in the real world, the world where people laughed and talked and went in and out, like free creatures.

Not one word did I hear from one human soul.

Every Sunday I hoped someone would come to see me—but no one ever came.

I couldn't understand it. My mother, so faithful and true. I couldn't believe that she had deserted me at last.

Of course, I couldn't blame her if she had.

Time and again I had fooled her, betrayed her, insulted and humiliated her. It wouldn't be strange if she had made up her mind never to see me again. But, somehow, it didn't seem like mother to do that, and it wasn't like her. I afterward found that she had been to see me, time and again, but the people in the office told her that it was best for her not to see me. I must take the cure—alone.

## Chapter Thirty-Five

Naturally, after having been deprived of drugs for more than a month, I craved sweets with that abnormal craving which follows the sudden withdrawal of narcotics or strong drink from an addict.

I wanted just a bite of candy in the worst way. Patients in Patton are allowed to spend $2.50 a month for such tidbits—providing they have the money and buy it at the institution commissary.

But I had no money. Not one red cent.

Up until that Sunday I had partially satisfied the craving with the cheap maple syrup used to flavor our breakfast hominy and rice. I had eaten so much of it that I had broken out in a rash. Yet I craved candy. A lollipop would have meant a feast.

And the opportunity to satisfy my yearning came on that Sunday afternoon. I had gone to the writing room. Fullfledged [sic], working "nuts," in Patton, are allowed to write two letters every Sunday, that is, providing you have means of buying the paper for the second. The institution only allows one sheet of paper and one envelope a week.

I had written one letter to my mother, and I went back and asked the "custodian" for material for another, which I intended for Ric—my darling husband.

"You've had yours," the attendant replied. "How do you get that way?"

"Why, I saw a lot of the others writing two," I answered. "I've written mother; now I want to write one to my husband."

"You're out of luck, kid," he laughed. "They pay for their own paper. The State is furnishing yours. I suppose you think the State can give you paper to write a book. Your husband doesn't write you. Why should you write him?"

I had no answer for this, so I went over and sat down.

Just then my confidant—the sympathetic male guard who supervised my duties on workdays, came in. He walked over to me and conversed a little while. Then he enticed me into a little anteroom, off the main writing room, with a little five-cent bag of chocolate drops!

Once inside and alone with him, he withheld them because I wouldn't repay his kindness with a kiss!

Never in my life have I placed love on a monetary basis. My love was never for sale—not even for that beautiful bag of candy which at the time, I suppose, I craved more than anything else in the world.

When the man saw that his plans were gone astray, he adopted other tactics. Boldly he seized me and tried to caress me by force.

I screamed at the top of my voice. He released me and fled from the room.

An instant later, several other attendants, accompanied by a doctor, rushed in, demanding that I name my assailant. Of course, I didn't know his name, and if I had, it wouldn't have made any difference. I simply never was a "squealer."

The doctor, noting my hesitancy, ordered everyone else from the room. Then he questioned me privately, but still I refused to identify the man who had attacked me.

Well, the sequel to the whole incident was that the doctor tried me out of on the same basis, not with the lure of a bag of candy, but by offering me one pitiful little cigarette.

My God! How I wanted that cigarette. But, even that was not sufficient to tempt me. And, that failing, that detestable beast of a doctor threatened me with sterilization.

"Don't try to fool me," he said. "You're just like all the rest. I can make you or break you. I'll say you've been annoying the men and then, they'll operate on you. Now what do you say?"

He stood back and glared at me. And I, frightened to death as I was, glared back at him.

"Go to hell!" I hurled at him.

He tried to stare me down, but he couldn't. And, finally, he strode out, muttering to himself predictions of what was going to happen.

I went back to my cell, disillusioned, afraid, leaping to my feet at every little noise, expecting any moment for the doctors to come in and lead me away for sterilization.

The picture of what had happened to that other poor unfortunate, whom I had seen beaten after the operation, when she was lying on her cot, undergoing the tortures of Hell, haunted me.

Yet, thank God! I was strong enough to stand pat. My love was not for sale—not even for a bag of candy, for a cigarette, or even as a bribe to protect me against sterilization.

Some of you readers may think that this was no real exhibition of will power; that if I'd had any strength of will I never would have been conquered by the drug habit, but, having passed through the experience, I want to say, that never before or since, have I been so near the breaking point.

All my ideals had been shattered, except one. That was the keeping of love on a pure plane. I was a romanticist at heart. I had always lived that way, and I expected to die that way. Love to me still is everything. The only thing that matters, the only thing that cannot be bought or sold.

My fears of the operation, however, never were realized. Instead, for insubordination, I was locked up in a punishment cell for 24 hours.

"You're getting away easy, this time," an attendant, a vitriolic-tongued woman observed. "Hereafter you'd better be careful how you 'sass' your betters."

She stood back, hands on hips, gloating over my misfortune. I could tell by her eyes that she was holding something back; something that was far more terrible than the day and night in solitary confinement.

"Well," I taunted her, "go on with the rest of it. I've got broad shoulders, and I can bear it."

Her eyes narrowed and she stuck out her chin viciously, as she hissed:

"So you're asking for it, huh? Well, how do you like this? You ain't goin' to see your mother for eight months. Not 'til you've finished your time. How does that strike Alma Rubens. The great, beautiful movie star?"

How she rolled those sneering words over her tongue, tasting them and savoring their full flavor, smacking her lips in anticipation of my reaction. Maybe I'd faint, or make a scene. Mentally, I could see her, rolling up her sleeves so she could physically chastise me, in case of the latter.

But I disappointed her. I made no answer. I just sat down on the cot and sat there, staring right through her as if she did not exist. Eventually, she went out.

And I quit counting the days. I knew she had meant what she said; that I wouldn't see my mother, or my husband, as long as I was in Patton.

Fate had been unkind. I had been frustrated on every count, but, damn it, they might beat me, kill me, but they couldn't make me admit I feared them. Nor would I give them the satisfaction of knowing how cruelly they had hurt me.

After a month on the "polishing squad," I was transferred to the "bath gang." That meant that I was stationed in the dark, filthy bathroom, all day long, every day except Sunday.

I bathed patients in a bathtub, an enormous, cracked enamel bathtub, where fifty to a hundred patients bathed every day. Negroes, Mexicans, white persons, all used the same tub. Some were eaten away by ravaging social diseases. Others suffered from great running sores that threatened the health of anyone with whom they came into contact.

Yet I had to bathe them. An attendant ran the water. The patients were lined up, and little Alma did the job!

And, after I had bathed these unfortunate outcasts, I was allowed to take a bath in the same tub—as my reward for good work. In the same cracked, chipped enamel tub, that all the scrubbing in the world never could have made sanitary.

Poor, broken bodies housing poor broken minds. How I pitied those poor victims of heredity and abuse, which I bathed. I felt so sorry for some of them that I even forgot to HATE the job.

Instead, I prayed; prayed as I washed their bodies and their hair, that I would not get the harsh soap in their eyes, and prayed that I would not contract some loathsome disease.

Kicking was a favorite indoor sport of some of the attendants at Patton. Some of their victims were pitifully scarred. One of the poor wretches had a scar on her stomach, inflicted by a brutal attendant, which reminded me of a horse I once saw disemboweled at a Mexican bull fight.

Individual towels were an unknown luxury. A yellowish-gray sheet, in keeping with the general color scheme at the institution, hung from the bathroom wall, and served to dry person after person, regardless of their diseased condition or state of mind.

Continuous baths and immersions were used on patients who became disturbed, apparently with the idea that it quieted the nerves. I believe that this is a treatment generally recognized by the medical profession as a sedative.

From my experience in Patton, however, I'd say the real sedative was the big ring of heavy brass keys, not the baths.

Many times I have seen nervous patients beaten over the head with the keys until blood ran from their scalps. Beaten almost into unconsciousness if they struggled against entering those filthy tubs.

Once I saw a hard-boiled attendant deliberately hold a woman's head under water until her face turned blue, simply because she tried to tell a matron of this particular attendant's former mistreatment.

A patient's tale of brutality doesn't mean anything; they're only another "nut," incapable of realizing or telling the truth. And the heartless attendants cover injuries inflicted on their victims by noting in their record book:

"So-and-so fell today. Struck their head on the cot, inflicting a slight scalp wound."

That's the way they cover up those dreadful beatings with the heavy brass keys. I have witnessed the beating, and later seen the entries.

And, bad as were the days in Patton, the nights were worse.

It was during the nights in that California "Crazy House" that I suffered most. In the daytime I was kept so busy, so occupied with my daily drudgery that I had little time to think either of my unhappy surroundings or of my lack of drugs.

But as soon as the sun had set, and I was locked up in my cell, the real suffering began. The flood-gates of memory were turned loose. All there was to do was to sit on the side of my cot—and think!

I couldn't even read. Even if I had had a book or magazine to peruse, I would have had no opportunity. The moment the sun went down I was in darkness, my cell door was locked, and I would begin to brood.

Of course, if I so chose, I could step over to my barred window and peer out into the moonlight, if there happened to be a moon. The moonlight cast queer shadows on the walls of my cell, trickling through the steel bars of the window and etching the most weird designs.

The moonlight and the steel bars. Symbolic of my state of mind.

Outside the night, warm moonlight, washed with a tropical breeze of romance. The darkened sky, with the myriads of stars peeping out of the blackness. Cool little brooks, singing in ripply ecstasies, on the way to the sea. The sea itself, wild, untrammeled, hurling itself against the bleak cliffs, bursting into pin points of scintillating diamonds. The wind, its fury unleashed and biting, nipping at any and all loose things. And the roads, those white concreted California State roads that lead everywhere—from Patton.

Thinking is what breaks one. I endure the sad thoughts as long as I can, then fall across my cot and try to forget it all. But it is not to be.

As I lie there the sound of music steals to my ears from across the lawn. It is a radio, or a piano, in the cottage of one of the doctors. Much as it augments my troubles, I strain my ears to listen. I wish they would make it louder. They are playing the sad notes of a Chopin nocturne. I am enthralled. I forget my worries. Forget that I am a drug addict, suffering the torturing deprivation pains in Patton.

The music brings back pleasant memories. In my imagination I am quickly transported on the clouds of romance to my home. My beautiful little house in Santa Monica. I am sitting before the mirror of my dressing table in my boudoir.

This holds everything most dear to my heart. What pleasure, what joy I took in purchasing its furnishings. Many of the articles are of special design, manufactured to my order.

The prevailing style is Louis XIV, modified to suit my individual taste. The heavy Oriental rug with its double padding underneath, allowing me to sink in up to my ankles, drowns all harsh footsteps. When I arise of a morning, I stretch my bare toes, like a cat, just for the luxurious feel of its silky texture.

The draperies are in mauve orchid. They too have been especially designed for me. There is my beautiful square mirror, hung in a crystal frame. It shines like a huge diamond, reflecting my own likeness, the Alma Rubens, pretty, clear-eyed, untarnished by contact with the world and the sordid drug habit.

My especially designed bed into the depths of whose scented floss mattress I love to bury myself, next attracts my fancy. Besides it stands my beautiful French cloisonné telephone, the gift of my dearest friend, a famous movie actress.

Many of the dainty silken and lace pillows are the gifts of other friends, costly gifts which I appreciated to the utmost. In my wardrobe are so many costly gowns that I haven't the time to count them.

My dear mother, who has been visiting me, has just kissed me goodbye. She is returning to our ranch house at Madera.

The day itself has been one of joyful happiness and excitement. I have just had my voice tested for the new talkies. They had predicted a great future for me and have already told me I am to have the star part in "Show Boat." I am to play Magnolia. How I shall make her live, that fragrant flower sprung from the fertile fields of a thousand Mississippi floods. The ambition of my lifetime has been attained. I have climbed the ladder from poverty to riches and am now on the topmost rung.

Topping the whole elaborate mental picture is my dearly beloved picture. Ric strides in, his deep, vibrant voice murmuring sweet nothings into my ears. He is in evening dress. We are going out. Out to dinner and a premiere. He is very proud of me. He says that I am quite lovely, charming, in my new evening gown. I am simply flooded with happiness.

The faint notes of a piano creep in through the rose-bowered garden, from the house adjoining my wide and handsomely rolled lawn. I sit there straining my ears to catch the notes, meantime flattering my husband by telling him he looks like a Spanish aristocrat. Tall, dark, and slender, he resembles that type, though I am fully aware that he is a Hebrew.

Then the bubble bursts.

A blood-curdling scream from across the corridor, brings me back to face reality. I drop from Heaven into the fiery abyss, in an instant. I am back in my cell at Patton.

A million little devils leap across the walls, pecking at me with their sharp little three-pronged spears, taunting me, reviling me, hurting me.

"It's nobody's fault but your own," they shriek. "Your fault alone. You had everything. You didn't have brains enough, intelligence enough, to appreciate it. You sold your heritage for a mess of DOPE!"

I know in my heart, however, that they are all wrong. I am in Patton because of unscrupulous doctors, who would send me to Hell, just to get the comparatively paltry sums I paid them for morphine and cocaine.

Never had I set out with the intent to hurt any one. I had had to work so hard, so very, very hard, from the time I was a small child. I had gone to work at five o'clock in the morning, before dawn, crowded in a trolley car between men who had been handling horses, laborers, and Chinese coolies on their way to the wharves.

I had been hungry, so hungry that I had stolen milk bottles from unprotected doorsteps. I had even gone three days at a stretch without anything at all to eat.

And, through years of hard work, and grief, I had finally arrived—by my own efforts—at the top; to the pinnacle of success where I commanded an income of $150,000 a year. And, when I had gotten it I hadn't spent it all on myself.

My greatest pleasure had been to spend it on my mother, in buying nice things for her; things that she had never had before in her whole unhappy existence. I had spent a lot on my husband's family, too. On that pretty, white-haired old Jewish mother, in Brooklyn, whom Ric had failed to tell me about when we were first married. I should have been supremely happy.

Instead, there I was in Patton, the California "Crazy House," an associate of insane people, murderers even, just because a few ethicless physicians had envied my toil-wrung and newly attained riches. Instead of riding on the crest of the wave of happiness, I was sacrificed into a net of evil circumstances, too strongly woven for me to break away.

Search my mind as I would, I could find no reproach for myself. I didn't become a drug addict because I wanted to. I did it because I couldn't help myself. It was an illness, just like diphtheria, whooping cough, scarlet fever, any number of children's diseases from which I had suffered early in my girlhood.

The dope habit was the same thing. I'd caught it, and I must endure it until I was well.

Night after night, I'd like awake, thinking, thinking, thinking. Sometimes my reveries would revolve around my earlier life. When I was still an extra girl. I would live it all over again. Step by step I'd follow my own career.

How happy I was when I "got the leading part" in "Humoresque." That outstanding success, the best picture of the year, was followed, or had followed others, not so magnificent.

There was the "Half Breed," in which I had played opposite Douglas Fairbanks; "The Valley of Silent Men," in which I had co-starred with Lew Cody, who shortly before her death married my dear old friend, Mabel

Normand. Drugs ruined her career too. Then there was "Enemies of Women," where Lionel Barrymore was my lead; "The World and His Wife," with Motagu Love, and "Under the Red Robe," with Robert Mantell.

I'd fall asleep sometimes under the sheer spell of my own self-hypnotism. Then, when I'd awaken, there'd be a dull explosion in my brain. The first rays of God's sun would shine through the steel bars onto the numbers stamped on my pillow.

I would sit up and turn it over. But there they were again. They were stamped on both sides. I had lost my personality. I was nothing but a number; the same as if I had been a criminal, convicted of some hideous crime.

No longer was I Alma Rubens—Mrs. Ricardo Cortez. No, I was simply another "nut," in the "Crazy House," with a number instead of a name.

This insurrectionary reaction to my imprisonment and continued hard labor, became more and more recurrent, by the end of the first four months.

I had become emaciated, just wilted from the lack of love in my environment, like a plant would die without water. Around me was nothing but heartbreak and sorrow.

I felt that I must escape, or die in the attempt; that I'd surely die anyhow, if I remained there another four months. But, figure as I would, day in and day out, I could see no hope of success.

Then came a ray of mental sunshine, in the form of a letter from my darling mother.

"Don't think of trying to escape," she wrote. "They have just passed a new law making anyone who attempts to run away from a State institution liable to five or six years' imprisonment, at hard labor, in San Quentin Penitentiary.

Like a flash, this passage kindled the long suppressed flame in my mind. I determined to make the attempt and, if caught, as I probably would be, I'd be sent to San Quentin, which, despite its hard name, could not be half as bad as Patton.

I mapped out my plan to escape as a general would concentrate on a strategic move for his army. I would either escape, be sent to San Quentin, or die. And I didn't care much which happened to me.

Once my mind was made up to escape, I lay awake all night, scheming, planning, discarding one plan after another which at first seemed plausible, but later developed some insurmountable obstacle. At last I settled on the plan of stealing out, by sheer cunning. I would outwit my captors.

I would become very humble, very docile, so tractable that they would think they had broken my spirit, that which they had tried to do from the very beginning. I placed my scheme into operation at once.

Day after day, through the tiresome routine I went, never grumbling, never "sassing my superiors," bearing their jibes and abuse without a murmur, and eating the unspeakable food without protest.

After all, I was an actress, and if they could get a vicarious thrill out of my humility, I would cater to the whims of my audience and thus, by seemingly falling into accord with their own desires, lull them into a state of false security.

With my new objective—escape—ever in mind, I began to let down the barriers of reserve. I narrated my experiences, both in New York—Broadway to them was another world—and in Hollywood, that Golden City of Make Believe.

They listened, spellbound.

And, all the time I was planning, scheming, mapping out a way to still further deaden their powers of observation, their constant, suspicious supervision.

I knew I was gaining ground. More and more often I was receiving those few poor privileges accorded to the more cowed, the quiet, harmless type of patients from whom no arbitrary actions might be expected.

One of these was an hour of "recreation," under a worm-infested mulberry tree, a hundred yards, or more, from the main structure of the group comprising the institution.

My plans for escape revolved around this pestiferous mulberry tree.

Patients, despite the "recreation" clause of the privilege, were not allowed to move around. They had to sit on the hard benches under the tree, and were not even permitted to converse freely. If anyone so much as dared to stand up and stretch, instantly a guard would come running, with the shout:

"Sit down there, you. And stay down. One more move like that and I'll lock you up again."

Then, the "mutiny" quelled, the blatant guard would return to his group of fellow-workers, sitting around at ease within earshot, gossiping of the good things they had to eat.

Most of this little group that daily gathered under the mulberry tree were sane on all but some one subject, and many were persons of the highest education and refinement, who would have appreciated good food, nice clothes and a little diversion.

My addition to the unhappy little band of "mulberry benchers" was the signal to attract the notice of half a dozen of the various doctors' children, who lived on the grounds. They had heard of me, perhaps had seen Alma Rubens in one of my pictures, and, naturally, their childish curiosity was aroused. They wanted to see what I looked like.

Ordinarily, I would have welcomed their attentions, and did at first, because I could talk with them as much as I liked. The attendants didn't dare forbid this, because the children themselves carried the conversation and they couldn't take a chance of offending the powers-that-be.

Starved as I was for a little human intercourse, even these bratty children were a diversion. I painstakingly answered their questions about Hollywood, about other big motion picture stars I knew, what they looked like, how they acted, and even the guards drank it all in with the greatest interest.

Then one of the boys—I suppose he was about 11—pulled from his pocket a pair of white rats. That broke off our friendship. I let out a shriek of terror and ran as though the devil was after me.

On and on I sped, screaming, and on the verge of fainting. I could hear the children behind me, shouting in glee, and the loud guffaws of my guards, who, apparently thought it was a most excellent show.

Fully 200 yards I was away from them by that time, and as I ran, and got my second wind, I looked back over my shoulder. Not a one had taken a step towards catching me.

I took in the situation at a glance.

Now was my time.

From the beginning of my scheming I had planned my flight to start from beneath that old mulberry tree. I hadn't expected my opportunity to come so soon. And, to tell the truth, I hadn't expected to make a successful getaway.

But that comforting thought of San Quentin, the new law which provided for imprisonment there for any who should attempt to escape from such an institution as Patton, was my main objective.

Even if they caught me I'd be sent to San Quentin.

Like a deer, I sped across the lawn and down a steep embankment. I leaped across a little ravine, climbed a wire fence and dashed into an orange grove, adjoining the Patton grounds.

Then to my ears were wafted faintly, the rumble of excited voices, herding the other patients into formation for return to their cells and of others—the hunters—organizing the pursuit.

I rested a moment, then sprinted up a little slope where, for an instant, I must have been in full view of my keepers, although by now I was half a mile away. Somebody raised an outcry. A dozen other voices took it up, and I spurted ahead.

Down the opposite side of the little ridge, I ran. I was terrified. I tried to go faster, but my feet became entangled in the long, tough fox-grass of the grove, and I fell. I struggled to my feet and went on. I fell again, and got up.

I had forgotten all my carefully mapped out plans.

I didn't want to go to San Quentin. I was a wild thing. A fox. The hunters after me. I could hear the dull baying of the dogs, which they had set on my trail. I was free. Out of Patton. Away from the crazy people. I wanted to remain free.

My breath was coming in chest-wracking sobs. I panted. And as I ran, staggering from near-exhaustion, I prayed that God would help me; that He would enable me to find a hiding place, a place where the poor little fox would be able to hole in, despite the keen noses of the hounds on its trail.

On and on I went, the sounds of the pursuit ever growing closer and closer. My face and hands were torn from the stiff grass and shrubs. They were bleeding. My clothes were almost off. But I didn't give up hope.

I could see through a gap in the trees below me, an open road, with automobiles dotting its white expanse at intervals. If I could only make that, perhaps I could catch on behind a fleeting car and elude my pursuers.

Could I make it? I sprang ahead again, desperately. I leaped another ravine. Through a briar patch, which all but denuded me. My ankle twisted and I fell again. But I scrambled to my feet and kept on.

Then came the end of the flight. I caught my toe under a fallen branch, treacherously buried in the tangled grass, and fell heavily, striking the top of my head against a tree trunk.

I stuck with great force, although it did not knock me unconscious. I could still think clearly enough, but I was half-stunned.

So I tried to crawl, and did, but my progress was pitifully slow. Before I had covered 50 feet, my pursuers were upon me.

Their clarion call of success, their calling off of the hunters, struck my ears like the voices of a thousand wolves. And, like wolves, they descended on me, slapping and smacking my bloody face and twisting my arms behind me.

Ignominiously, I was led back and into the superintendent's office. He ordered my transfer to Ward 5, the next to the worst ward in the place, as punishment.

"But, I thought you'd send me to San Quentin," I gasped, having somewhat recovered by this time. "How about that new law about patients that try to escape? I want to go there."

He smiled.

"Your attempt doesn't count," he said. "You didn't come any way near succeeding. We'll keep you around with us for a while. We all like you so much, you know." And he smiled again.

I was led away to Ward No. 5, where I was placed in a room with another young woman, an epileptic of the semi-violent type, according to the two guards who took me there. They gloated in my misery and laughed at my protests.

## Chapter Thirty-Six

Up until the moment I was thrown into the violent ward with that poor epileptic as my cell-mate, I though [sic] I had seen everything in the way of misfortune that there was possible to be seen—even in Patton. But, I was to learn that my education had only begun.

Many of the patients in No. 5 were criminals. We even had a murderer, or two. Religious maniacs, epileptics, filthy patients, degenerates of every description, and dozens of poor people without any minds whatsoever.

The latter were just as apt as not to strike at their keepers, for any reason, or for no reason at all. They'd be yanked out of bed, dressed by their guards in a way, and dragged to high-backed chairs, grouped in a circle in the huge open ward, where they would sit all day.

If they attempted to get up and walk around, they were roughly seized by members of the "strong arm" squad—ever on duty—and hurled back into their seats.

Sometimes they'd show fight. If they did, they were beaten into submission, then dragged to the ever-yawning immersion tubs with the cruel, hard-canvas covers, where they were kept in the water for sometimes as high as 24 hours at a time.

Seldom did the guards dress their injuries, though their noses might be bleeding, their teeth broken off, their tongues cut, or their scalps bleeding from the blows on the head from the big brass keys. They just had to sit in the tubs and endure their agonies in whatever way they could.

On occasions I have even seen these fiendish guards actually throw a particularly disliked patient into a frenzy, merely so they would have an opportunity to beat them up.

And, then, oftimes, there'd be another entry in the record: "So-and-so, violent today. Fell. Cut nose. Continuous bath until restored."

Within three days of my transfer, I saw a frail young girl, barely 20, and suffering from a religious mania, deliberately thrown into a violent condition because she insisted on dropping to her knees to pray, before getting into bed for the night.

A brutal woman attendant dragged her to her feet, smacked both her cheeks, leaped behind her and pushing her knee into the small of her back, threw her heavily, striking her head on the floor. And, that poor creature, kept on praying:

"Oh, Lord, forgive them, for they know not what they do."

And, with each new exhortation by the poor victim, this female Nero, chortled with glee and beat and kicked her with renewed vigor.

Eventually, the poor, frail little creature, turned on her tormentor. She spat on her, the signal for a blow from the huge bunch of keys that knocked her unconscious. I thought she was dead.

But she wasn't. And, they dragged her to the continuous bath where they kept her all night.

The following morning they brought in two sisters. "Cattleman," I think, was their name. One about 49, the other about 51. Gray-haired, motherly-appearing, but on the verge of imbecility, they were a pitiful sight. One became very ill after her arrival and was taken out, supposedly to a hospital ward to be operated on. I never saw her again.

The other had a craving for ice cream. The temperature that day must have been around 115. It was stifling hot. All day she cried and begged and pleaded for ice cream, but she didn't get it. Along late in the afternoon an attendant, a husky young woman of about 30, seized the poor weak-minded woman by the hair, smashed her in the face with her keys, and dragged her, too, into an immersion tub, where she held her head under water until her face was blue.

Such happenings, which I was powerless to prevent, kept my mind in a constant state of turmoil. I was so nervous that my teeth were chattering almost all the time and my heart would be thrown into palpitation by any unexpected little sound.

The nights were unbearable. The mosquitoes did everything but actually devour me. They bit me, stung me, until my face, neck, hands and feet and arms were a mass of red welts. I took a chance on asking one of the attendants for a fly-swatter.

Her reply was to the effect that no patient was allowed anything with which they might possibly do themselves harm.

Apparently she feared I might attempt to crush my skull with it!

Then, on my third day there, my cellmate had one of her attacks. We had been whispering about some of the horrid things that were going on around us. Without any warning she suddenly stiffened, and pitched backwards, striking with her full weight directly on the back of her head.

The creamy-white froth oozed from her mouth and it seemed that she had ceased breathing. I was paralyzed for a moment, then screamed wildly, beating on the cell door, trying to get away from the fearful scene.

A guard rushed in. She started to hit me with her keys, then saw the prostrate form on the floor and changed her mind. She walked over and pushed her in the ribs with her foot.

"Whatcha screamin' about?" she demanded. "She's got a fit—that's all. Shut up, or I'll crack yuh one with these!" And she again menaced me with those great keys.

I fell into a little heap on the floor. She went out and returned a moment later with a pail of water. Without ado, she swished it into her face, drenched her body, and then picked her up bodily and without further ceremony tossed her onto the bed.

"Quitcher sniveling, now," she grunted at me. "She'll be all right in an hour. G'wan to bed and don't let's hear nothing more from you."

Sure enough, within an hour, my poor cellmate did gradually recover consciousness, although it was fully 24 hours later before she became sufficiently normal to converse with me again. When she did, neither of us mentioned the incident.

I remained in that ward but a short time. Then I "sassed" one of my keepers and was transferred into No. 6, the worst in the place.

In there I might as well have been confined with a brood of pigs. The other patients were all dirty. All day they sat and stared vacantly ahead of them. Some were deformed.

There was little brutality in this ward, however. There was no opposition to the wills of the hard-faced women who were in charge. They could take one or either of the patients and stand them in a corner. They were so stupid, so lacking in intelligence, that they would stand there for hours, without moving, without exhibiting interest in what went on about them.

And, most of them had to be fed. They couldn't even feed themselves. A large portion of their food, of necessity, fell down over their clothing.

Yet I had to eat with these, seated at the same long table, listen to their mouthings, and try to refrain from watching their hideous practices.

Once a day we were herded down a long queue, marched down a long, slippery steel spiral staircase, into an exercise pen. It wasn't a recreation yard. It was actually a pen.

A few weeks of this and I suppose I must have been almost as bad off mentally as were the others. I had long since lost all interest in life. I didn't brood. It was no use. It was too much of an effort, too painful to think. I didn't even long for drugs. My feelings had become so wrecked that I no longer dwelt upon the memory of my mother or my husband. There were no newspapers, no magazines, no books to read, and no one with whom I might talk.

I was just another animated ghost in that grim gray graveyard which is the City of Living Dead—PATTON!

All things must eventually come to an end. And so came the time when the end of my incarceration was in sight. I had been sentenced to Patton Asylum for eight months and they couldn't keep me without a recommitment. To get that I'd have had to have a hearing.

So one day while I was sitting in my cage, wearily doing nothing, who should come along with the asylum superintendent, Dr. Webster, but Jensen, the director of State institutions.

He wiggled his finger at me with a beckon of command.

Broken under the iron glove of discipline, I hastened to comply.

"Do you think you could behave yourself if we transfer you to 15?" he asked through the mesh of the steel fence.

"Well, I think I could," I replied brokenly, yet with a bit of the old fire. "Other people seem to get along all right there. And I don't see any reason why I should not be there. You've got to let me out some time."

"You still need discipline," he retorted. "But I suppose we'll have to take you there. Your time is about up. You're virtually CURED!"

"Yes," I replied, sarcastically. "That's right! I'm cured of the drug habit, I suppose. Also I'm cured of love, of my faith in human nature. I'm cured of happiness, and I'm cured of everything else that makes life worth living. Thank you so much!"

They merely grinned and walked away.

That same afternoon, however, I was sent to Ward No. 15, the best cottage in the grounds. There patients had considerable freedom. There was a broken-down piano that sounded like a zither with the asthma, a radio that reminded me when tuned in of nothing so much as an alley full of tomcats, and, on Sunday, we'd have a little baseball in the afternoon, after being allowed to attend chapel in the morning.

I was in No. 15 a month. Every day I waited and waited for that summoning bell, a summons saying that my mother or Ric had come to see me. Other patients' relatives came regularly, but mine never did. At least I was so informed.

Then one day I was sitting at the dilapidated old piano, trying to pick out a few chords from its wheezy depths, when I heard the glad cry:

"Alma. Whoo-oo-o! Alma, my darling."

It was my mother. She came rushing toward me. I sat there in a stupor. I thought it was just another dream. I couldn't believe it was true.

She took me in her arms. She kissed me. And, eventually, she convinced me that it was true. That my time was up. And that she was taking me home. My God, how can I describe that feeling? I was cured of the drug habit. I was going home with mother, to see Ric.

"Cured?" did I say? "Cured?" Bah! only temporarily cured. I was just a "set-up," a "pushover" for the first unscrupulous doctor that came along, though I didn't meet him for almost eight months.

That wondrous day when I was released from Patton, I suppose was the happiest I shall ever experience. There was only one thing lacking to make it complete. That was the absence—in the East—of my husband, Ricardo Cortez, the only man I ever really loved.

Dear Ric. How I loved him. Even though he had sent me but two crisp notes and a picture post card throughout the eight torturous months I had endured while in "The Crazy House."

My God! How I loved that man.

In my new freedom, I could even overlook his neglect. I needed him so badly. I wanted to see him. I wanted to feel his caresses. I wanted him to kiss me. The taste of his lips would have been as of nectar. I was dying just to stroke his hair, that coal black hair, with its glossy sheen, which is but one of his claims to handsomeness.

But I realized that vagaries of the motion picture business; he couldn't break away even for my homecoming and a celebration of my CURE. So I was happy, extremely happy, the happiest I shall ever be, simply because I was free.

No longer was I a "nut;" no longer a subject of that invisible "something" that makes devils of the majority of the men and women employees of Patton.

No guards. No meshed-steel wires. No abuse. I was Alma Rubens again.

No longer a slave to the use of drugs. I was cured of the use of dope. I was young. In time, I would regain my beauty. Ho, how happy I was because of that.

Once more I was free of that terrible slavery to money-grasping doctors, who'd send your soul to hell for a few paltry dollars wrung from the tear-drops of a thousand broken hearts.

And, above all, the physical relief. Free forever—I thought—of those terrible deprivation pains that made life miserable for one when their drugs ran out. I was happy as a bird.

My first act when I reached home was to rush to my room, where I sat down and wrote a long letter to Ric. I couldn't wait for morning to mail it. No. I marked it air-mail, and sent it by messenger to the main postoffice [sic] so it would get out that night.

That completed, I sat down to supper with mother. And, after supper, I made her take me out.

I didn't want to go any place in particular. No shows. No night clubs. No restaurants. I just wanted to be in the great outside, to feel my new freedom, to know that if I wanted to step in any particular direction, there was no one to stop me.

We went to Los Angeles. I window-shopped until my poor mother was near fainting on her feet. Up one brilliantly lighted street we would wander, stopping in front of every decorated window, gazing at every beautiful object we saw. Then, when we had passed the main business district, we'd cross over, and do the same thing over on the other side of the street.

Finally mother grew so tired that she couldn't walk another step. We climbed into a taxicab and started home. How strange it was for me, who for eight weary months had been accustomed to obey without question any

## Chapter Thirty-Six

command of others, to give directions. On the way home, I ordered the driver to go this way, that way, just feel my restored authority.

I was my own self again. Alma Rubens. Perhaps only a great picture star that was, but anyhow in possession of my full faculties and on the road back. I'd fight my way to the top again; I'd make them restore my standing.

And in this ecstatic state I went to bed. So tired, so excited, so happy that I fell into a sound slumber that carried through until later afternoon the following day; the first untroubled sleep I had had in years.

After that first night I didn't care to go out. I was ashamed. I didn't want to meet my friends. I knew that eventually I must, but I wanted to put it off for a time. I was satisfied to stay in the house, running downstairs every few minutes just for the sake of taking a look at my darling mother and the privilege of being able to run up again without having to ask anyone's permission.

Several days passed thusly. I had received no answer from Ric. I wondered what had happened to my letter; whether he had received it. I worried until I was almost frantic. Surely, I reasoned, if he had received it he would have answered by this time.

I went to the telephone. I called him at his address in New York. They said he had left there but a few minutes before with a "party." He was out having a good time. I knew he could have called me on the telephone but he hadn't. I was disconsolate. I would have called him long before, but I had wanted him to call me. I had undergone torture for days, waiting for him to get my letter, so that he would call.

Then, when he hadn't called, I had waited for his letter. And it hadn't come. Even that setback had not overthrown my good cheer, however.

One day I picked up an old newspaper and learned that Jeanne Eagels was dead, beautiful, talented Jeanne Eagels. I knew her as well as I did Mabel Normand, Julia Bruns, Wally Reid, and others of that brilliant company who went down the dark road of dope ahead of me.

I fell on my knees and thanked God that I was cured, even if I had to be sent to Patton to make the cure complete.

My mother took me to the ranch in Madera and there I lived quietly, resting and sleeping, and building up my health on good home food.

February 19 was my birthday. And I felt that I had indeed been born again, so I made up my mind to go to New York, to get back into my regular routine, see the new pictures, buy some new clothes, make new acquaintances, and gradually work up the courage to look my old friends in the face again.

When I stepped off the train in New York there was my husband waiting for me. Before I had a chance to realize that he was really there—really alive, and as handsome as ever, I was surrounded by a surging crowd.

There was a truck full of roses and orchids—there was a great armful of telegrams—greetings from Broadway and Hollywood stars, messages of faith and affection from old friends, from rich people and poor people, messages from society women, and one pretty, simple, little corsage came from a little dressmaker who had once worked for me. For some strange reason I loved that best of all. I pinned it to my coat and my husband ordered the best of the gifts sent to the hotel.

More flowers, more telegrams, more friends. My heart sang and I was a poor foolish woman in paradise.

The moment I was alone with my husband I knew that everything was over between us. He had nothing to say to me, except what he would have said to any stranger. He was playing at a Broadway theatre, and he asked that I come and sit in a box and see the performance.

The theatre was packed, and when my husband came on the stage, he threw his arms to me and introduced me from the stage saying: "My dear little wife, Alma Rubens, Mrs. Cortez."

We had decided to "put up a front" for the sake of business, but we were never happy together for one minute again.

Within four weeks I signed up for eighteen weeks on the vaudeville circuit. I was paid $1,500 a week.

I have often done imitations of well known actresses, but I never gave any imitation of the way I looked and acted when I was being "cured" at the Patton insane asylum.

My imitations were a great success, but when I got back to New York, flushed with my triumphs, I met another well-known and highly-respected doctor.

And in no time at all he had me trapped into dope—again!

And all that I had hitherto known or imagined about drug orgies and degenerate existence faded into nothingness.

Love cults, devil worship, drug madness—I got to know them all. That was how I stayed "cured."

## CHAPTER THIRTY-SEVEN

Drug orgies, devil worship, Sadism, love cults, all the horror and degradation that the world today calls perversion—I might as well have stayed in Ward Six at Patton, with the poor mindless animals there.

For a week or so I fought against losing what courage I could muster. It was all I could do to play my part at the matinees and evening performances.

I knew I was on the verge of collapse. If I could only get to New York!

There were good doctors there, fine men, honest doctors, who would take pity on me and help me to keep the desperate promise I had made to myself.

The hour that I left the stage after my last engagement, I rushed to New York.

I had heard of a fine physician there, a well-known practitioner, trusted and admired by well-known women in the world of society as well as by many well-known actresses.

I went to see Dr. Exclusive—that wasn't his name, but it will do as well as any other.

The doctor was glad to see me. He knew my name and he knew many of my friends. Some day he would give himself the pleasure of seeing me on the stage.

Too bad that my nerves were misbehaving. Nothing serious about it, of course, but annoying—very, especially to a young woman like me who should be in the best of health and spirits all the time.

He would arrange all that. Oh yes, it was quite simple. So the good, kind, wise doctor gave me a prescription, told me to have it filled at a certain drug store and take it that night.

I did take that medicine that very night and for the first time in weeks I slept like a healthy child, or like a tired farm hand.

I was charmed.

It was going to be all right after all.

Then one morning ... there was no more of the medicine left in my little cabinet.

"I'll get some when I go out," I thought.

But I didn't have the prescription. The doctor thought it was best to get it for me himself after he had been giving it to me for some time.

I called the doctor. A sudden fear possessed me—suppose he was out town! How careless I had been to let the medicine run out.

The maid at the doctor's office said that the doctor had gone with his family for a weekend to a distant resort.

I realized that I would have to wait for his return to get any more "medicine."

I tried to read but the words on the printed page did a crazy dance before my eyes. I went out for a walk, but my knees shook so I had to come back again. I took a hot bath and a glass of hot milk and tried to sleep.

Every nerve in my body was jerking—what could be the matter with me? I felt exactly as I did when I was taking the "cure."

Who was that beautiful woman I had met in the doctor's office one day. She seemed to be so kind, so sympathetic. I found her name in the telephone book and called her. She answered the telephone herself. The moment I spoke she seemed to know what was the matter. She said she would be right over.

In fifteen minutes she arrived. I could hardly totter to the door to admit her.

"Why, my dear," said the beautiful, middle-aged woman in her soft cultivated voice, "Don't be so frightened. All you need is a shot."

"A shot!" I repeated after her. "A shot of what?"

"Why, darling," she said, "a shot of cocaine. Do you mean to say you have run out?"

Ill, shaking, faint, dazed as I was, her words struck on my brain like the shot of a gun.

"Cocaine!" I whispered. "Is that what he was giving me?"

The woman stared at me in bewilderment. "Why, you poor darling," she said, "of course. I thought you knew that. I thought you went there just the same as I did—to buy drugs."

"Are you a drug fiend too?" I shuddered.

The woman smiled a little sadly. "Yes, Alma," she replied very seriously. "Yes, I'm an addict too, but I hope we're not fiends."

I fell back on the bed. I don't know whether I fainted or not, but a little later, as I hazily remember, Mrs. Blank was sitting beside me on the bed drawing a little packet of white powder from her purse. She gave it to me and I snatched it as a drowning man snatches at a straw. I took a little pinch, put it on the base of my thumb, drew it into my nostrils. Soon courage returned.

King Dope was back on his throne....

When she left she handed me another little white package. I took it without a word.

That poor woman was a leading member of New York society. Her hair was gray and she was the mother of a beautiful daughter.

I don't blame her for what she did. She was just trying to help me.

But how about that highly respected, well-known and successful doctor, who had deliberately led me into dope again just to get my money?

## CHAPTER THIRTY-EIGHT

I made up my mind that I owed something to the world—something to other poor girls who might make the same dreadful mistake as I had made.

"I will take the remainder of this coke," I whispered to myself, "and by that time that doctor will be back in town. Then I will go and kill him and kill myself, and leave my confession behind to let the world know what a man like that means to poor, weak, ignorant women who go to him for help.

But when I went to see the doctor on Monday morning and tried to speak to him about what he had done, he laughed and brushed the whole matter aside, as if it was all a rather stupid joke.

And before I had left his office with a fresh supply of dope in my bag, I was persuaded that he was the best and kindest and the most considerate friend I had in the world.

Then he began to raise his prices like all the rest.

He had me "hooked." I was at his mercy, and he made me pay, and pay, and pay, a hundred times over for ever whiff of cocaine he gave me. Finally his prices became so outrageous that I had to leave him, but by that time, my new friend, Mrs. Blank, had left him, too, and she took me a dozen different places where I could get all the dope of every kind I wanted.

Mrs. Blank knew every speakeasy, every drug dealer, every vice den in town. She hated to be alone a minute and she surrounded herself with a group of rich men and women, every one of them either a degenerate in some other way or a dope fiend to the worst degree.

She took me to parties and dope orgies that lasted from one to two hours to three or four days and nights. Not all at once, of course.

I began by going to Mrs. Blank's house to a cocktail party.

Mrs. Blank lived in a magnificent house in Park Avenue. Her party began at four o'clock. I was a little late when I got there, but the party had already begun. Mrs. Blank's gray-haired husband was the host. A rich lawyer was one of the guests, and so was the estranged husband of a Swedish nobleman, a French Count and his fiancé, the widow of a millionaire wholesaler, and a pretty little blonde woman who was the wife of a once famous motion picture director.

The minute I came into the room the host gave me a water goblet full of rye whiskey.

And not five minutes later the lawyer offered me, without a word of apology or explanation, a sniff of cocaine.

"Well, now, dearie," said Mrs. Blank, stepping up to us and taking a sniff herself, "you're one of us. Everything goes in this camp."

She made a sweeping gesture at the tapestried drawing room—one of the most gorgeous rooms I had ever seen, and in Hollywood we know what gorgeous rooms are like.

"We're all sniffers, so you needn't be embarrassed."

That party was comparatively mild. We all drank as fast as we could drink, and we all had three or four sniffs of cocaine, but left before 8 o'clock.

Two of the men I met there tried to persuade me to go to a "big jamboree" to be given in the Park Avenue home of a rich stock broker the next evening.

I said no.

The next morning, that man and two of the other men I met at the party called me up, but I refused their invitations.

For three or four days, I lived in a strange, terrified, haunted haze.

I didn't see anyone. I never left my room. I couldn't bear to look at a human being in the face.

My opportunity to indulge this newborn fancy came almost immediately. "Mr. Dee" called me on the telephone and asked me to be his partner at a "tea dance and party" in the Park Ave. home of Baron and Baroness ———. I accepted.

When we arrived we found that fully a dozen other guests had preceded us. They were sitting around the drawing room, nervous-like, expectant, as though they feared something sad would happen.

The guests were about evenly divided as to sex. The radio was turned on full blast, but no one seemed to have any desire to dance. There was little conversation and an air of glumness prevailed.

I might mention that it is not the custom at dope parties to introduce the guests. If you are acquainted with the others, well, and good, but if they are total strangers, you just accept them at their face value and make no mention of that fact. Nobody seeks an introduction and nobody offers one.

Incidentally, the regular servants are always dismissed for the day when a dope party is to be staged. The host or hostess relies on outside "caterers," who specialize in this form of entertainment.

The "caterer," never under any circumstances called a butler, although he does the actual serving, is called a "chef." I don't know why, but "chef" he is. I know half a dozen of them.

Well, "Mr. Dee" found seats for us and we sat around just as gloomily as the others for a time. I was fidgety as the dickens.

"My heavens," finally exclaimed my escort, in a strained voice. "Who's dead around here? Where's the funeral? I hope it isn't the 'chef.'"

"Oh, Mr. Dee," answered the hostess, almost in tears. "The 'chef' I engaged has failed to put in an appearance. What shall we do?"

There were sighs of disappointment from every side.

"I'll try and see what I can do," he reassured her. He went to the telephone in the hall, called a number and then shook his head disconsolately when there was no answer.

"Let me try the man," volunteered a stocky, past-middle-aged guest, whom I afterward learned was a wealthy and influential banker in New York. "Perhaps I can save the day."

He, too, failed to get a response.

Just when half a dozen eager voices chimed in with suggestions, the day was saved by the arrival of the "chef" already engaged by the Baroness.

He apologized profusely, explaining that he had been detained at another "tea party up the street a little ways."

The Baroness excused herself for a moment and led the "chef" to the serving pantry. I could hear the tinkling of spoon against glass and the rattle of a silver tray.

A little later, the Baroness returned, followed by the "chef," who bore a tray on which rested a solitary goblet, one which must have held at least a quart—half-filled with a colorless liquid.

Starting with a prominent Broadway actress, who sat directly opposite me, the "chef" held out the tray in front of her.

Without hesitation, the woman, whose name has graced the big electrics along the White Way for many years, reached into her purse and pulled out what appeared to be a fountain pen.

Unscrewing the top, she pulled out a little plunger, however, which enlightened me to the fact that the "fountain pen" was really a cleverly contrived hypodermic needle. She dipped it into the liquid and filled it.

The next to be served was the elderly wife of a socially prominent sportsman, and the next the pretty blonde wife of the once famous movie director whom I had seen at my previous "cocktail party."

So on, all around the room, he went, pausing while each woman "loaded her gun." When he came to me—I was the last except for our hostess, the Baroness—I was forced to make the embarrassing confession that I had none.

Instantly, my escort was on his feet and made excuses for me.

"Doggone it. Isn't that a shame, Alma?" he asked. "I know exactly where you left it. I saw you put it on the edge of your dressing table just before you put on your hat."

Then, turning to the Baroness, he explained that he had been late in getting started and that, in the rush, apparently I had forgotten my "gun."

As a matter of fact, it was then for the first time that I realized why each of the other women carried their handbags into the drawing room. I had left mine in the ante-room where I left my coat.

Apparently no one noticed my breach of etiquette however, in as much as the "chef" came to my rescue by pulling from his pocket a most beautifully etched silver instrument, which he handed me with a bow.

When the women were all served, the "chef" made another tour of the room, permitting the men to fill their "guns" from the same huge goblet. The men's needles, like the women's, resembled fountain pens, with the addition of a metal clasp to hold them in their pocket.

Eventually, we all had our "guns" cocked and primed, the men arose to their feet, and our host, the Baron, gave a toast in the same jovial manner which would have characterized a similar gathering in front of an ordinary bar.

The response was a mingled chorus of "Here's how. The same to you. Here's mud in your eye. Bingo. Let's go!"

There was a moment's pause, then:

"Z-z-i-p!" and a prolonged "A-aah!"

The needles were sunk into their veins and you could hear little gasps from a few who, apparently, had struck themselves a trifle too deep.

And, the ceremony completed, each of the party meticulously wiped off their needle with a napkin supplied by the bowing, scraping "chef," and replaced their "guns" in their customary receptacles.

No one seemed at all astonished at the proceedings. They continued to sit and gaze dourly at one another with few attempts to chat or entertain one another. Occasionally one or two couples would venture to dance a few steps, but then they'd stop, as if too weary or too lazy to carry on.

Morphine, a solution of which the goblet had contained, is depressive in its action, and for a time I thought that was about the most dismal party I ever had seen. When the conversation lagged a funeral silence prevailed, broken now and then by a prodigious sigh by one or another.

I was bored stiff, but under the circumstances, and feeling strangely out of place, I could not be rude and make the first move to leave.

As I was to learn, however, the party was just in its infancy.

When I accepted "Mr. Dee's" invitation I thought it was just for a couple of hours, a "tea dance," which I supposed lasted, perhaps, until possibly six o'clock.

Before my education was completed, however, I learned that they could—and most generally did—last anywhere from one to three days.

"Mr. Dee" was the first to suggest injecting a little life into the party.

"I think it's about time we had a little 'sniff' of 'snow,' to warm things up a bit," he said.

"I second the motion," chirruped the pretty little blonde matron who sat next to the Broadway star. "Let's all get hot!"

There was a general chorus of approval, so the "snow" was passed around, each taking a pinch between the thumb and forefinger, which they held until all had been served.

Again the toast, and I "sniffed" as loudly as the others.

Within a very short time I began to feel its effects. I couldn't account for this quick reaction. I thought when I took it that it was cocaine, although I had noticed that the powder appeared a shade whiter than the ordinary "coke" to which I had been accustomed.

I inquired of my escort.

## Chapter Thirty-Eight

"Oh!" was his response. "That wasn't cocaine. That was heroin. It's much stronger and works faster than 'coke.'"

And so, that was my introduction to the use of heroin, a drug which I rarely ever have used, except on the occasions when it was passed around at parties I subsequently attended.

Soon I was feeling a fine "edge." I wanted to dance, and when "Mr. Dee" whirled me around the floor I imagined I was treading on air. In less time than it takes to mention it the others were dancing, too.

From the most gloomy party I had ever seen it was transformed within a few minutes into about the liveliest.

I had a strange impulse to yank off my clothes. I felt that my dress was binding me, retarding my freedom of movement so that I could not dance the way I wanted to.

I never had before experienced such a feeling. I glanced around the room to see if I could notice anything unusual in the appearance of the other couples. The scene was one of mad frenzy. The radio was playing at full volume a catchy jazz air. All were pirouetting crazily around, laughing and singing at the top of their voices.

Then, while I restrained my own mad impulse to cast aside my fetters of convention—my clothing—strange things began to happen.

The lights had been dimmed. Six heroin-maddened couples, an even dozen men and women, the oldest 60, the youngest not more than 25, pirouetted dizzily around that lavishly-fitted drawing room to the strains of the weirdest of weird jazz music drifting in on the radio.

My escort, "Mr. Dee," and myself, were as frantically carrying on as the others, but our hosts, Baron ———, and his beautiful wife stood at the end of the room beaming their approval. Apparently they had not taken as big a "sniff" as the rest of us.

On with the dance!

Even as I whirled around the floor in the arms of my partner, steeling my will against the mad impulse to cast aside my clothes, I couldn't help but transform—mentally, of course—the Baron and his charming wife into a pair of red-hued devils, standing there waiting to catch us near the edge of the crater so they could shove us into the bottomless, fiery pit.

On with the dance!

My train of thoughts was broken by the sight of that pretty little blonde wife of the once famous movie director, hurling aside her shoes. She was dancing in her stocking feet. Her partner, the wealthy, aging, rotund philanthropist, was urging her further...

I watched him help tear off her outer dress. I looked away. I was sickened. I couldn't stand any more.

I looked on my other side. That middle-aged Broadway actress, whose name had been in the bright lights so long, was almost nude, crushed in the arms of her gaily spinning partner, a nouveau-riche writer, who had risen to fame and crashed society on the strength of one successful play.

Even as I followed them with my eyes the red-headed, perspiring playwright threw off his coat, his vest, his shirt, without ever once relinquishing his hold on the buxom actress or missing a step.

I covered my eyes with my hands and then looked in another direction. I was just in time to see the youngest woman in the party, the brunette daughter of a wealthy manufacturer and a bride of little more than a year, throw off most of her clothes, except her lingerie and brassiere.

Her partner was a world-famous Broadwayite, who eloped with the daughter of one of the "400" and thus gained entrée to the golden portals.

His wife, a charming blonde woman under thirty, was tightly clasped in the arms of a dashing, waxen-mustached broker, a member of one of the biggest brokerage houses in Wall St. He was coatless and the beads of perspiration stood out on his forehead from his exertions, but she had not yet reached a disrobed condition.

The elderly, graying-haired wife of the internationally famous sportsman, a woman past 50, her ample bosom heaving rapidly and getting her breath in pitiful little gasps, tottered along in the arms of an equally decrepit Don Juan—another stockbroker—who, it was whispered, had been her illicit sweetheart for a score of years.

They, too, had started to disrobe, and if the sight hadn't been so disgusting it really would have been pitiful.

Only "Mr. Dee," and myself were fully clothed—that is, with the exception of our host and hostess, who had disappeared from their vantage point at the end of the long room.

"Well, Alma," whispered my partner. "What do you think of it? Did you expect to see anything like this?"

And, before I could answer, the piece de resistance of the show, up to that state, was put on.

In came the Baron and his Baroness in sheer, silken pajamas.

Their entrance was the signal for a chorus of acclaim. And, as they joined the mad whirl, the others, ever with the exception of "Mr. Dee" and myself, threw off more garments.

Around and around and around they went, shouting, crying, nearly hysterical in their frenzy.

One by one they were forced to drop to the floor from sheer fatigue. Then they lay where they fell, exhausted, utterly irresponsible and without shame.

And, as the hysteria wore down, in came the "chef," fully attired, with his whitecap and apron, serving another "sniff" of the powdered dynamite which had brought on the mad urge to partake in the shameless orgy.

When he reached me I refused a second helping. All I could think of was that I wanted to get out of there; I wanted to get away someplace where I could wash my eyes, wash away that sordid picture.

My escort so informed our hostess and she, without the slightest hesitation and despite her disrobed state, ran over to me and kissed me. She begged me to stay, but I insisted that I would have to leave.

"That's all right, darling," she assured me. "I know how you feel. I felt the same way once when I visited my first party. But you'll get used to it in time. We all do it. There's something in the drugs that forces you to act this way."

She made a sweeping gesture, indicating the guests, lying half dead on the floor. She looked a little sad, I thought.

Tears crept into her eyes as she followed us to the front door. The others did not even say good-bye when we went out. Just before we stepped outside the Baroness, a lovely woman still in her early 50's, squeezed my hand.

"You'll forgive me, won't you, dear?" she said. "Please don't think too hard of me. And, if you can, get off the racket. Drop it like you would hot lead. If you don't, it'll get you. Then you'll enjoy doing just what you've seen here tonight."

Neither my escort nor myself spoke a word during the taxicab ride to my apartment.

I left him downstairs. I didn't invite him up to my apartment, although it was not yet midnight. And he didn't insist.

I wanted to be rid of him for two reasons. The first was, I was ashamed, and the second, I wanted a "shot" of morphine and didn't want him to know I needed it so badly.

There are many such parties given in New York today.

I don't know about the other cities, but I do know about New York, and London, and Berlin, and Vienna, and Paris.

You meet the strangest people at these parties, men and women well-known in various parts of the world, some of them of secure position, and some of them shabby adventurers, who have climbed up the ladder—of dope!

At one of these parties I met a little Cockney cab driver who could neither read nor write, but he was amusing when he was "snowed under," so he was a regular guest, and we all called him "London" and let it go at that.

I really liked "Mr. Dee," and, if he had been a few years younger I believe I could have fallen in love with him. I nearly did at that, all of which I will explain later.

I went to bed, but it was not to sleep. In spite of an extra large "shot," my nerves were in such a jangle from my experience that I could not rest. I arose, dressed myself, called a cab and went to a speakeasy I knew, where I tried to drown my thoughts in bootleg liquor.

When I left there, after daylight, I was dreadfully tight. I was barely able to get back to my apartment, and hardly had I arrived there when the hotel manager knocked at my door and informed me that I would have to move—and at once.

In spite of my intoxicated condition, his order struck me like a blow between the eyes. I was mortified. It was the first time such a thing had ever happened to me.

I told him I would move and then staggered into bed. I lay there for hours, my mind befuddled, my nerves upset, crying and cursing that day, so long before, when Dr. A., that old university doctor in New York, had started me on the road to ruin by that first deadly injection of morphine.

There was nothing else to do but move. I knew that the hotel manager meant what he said. I also knew that I had been slightly hysterical when I said goodbye to "Mr. Dee" in the lobby the night before, and I fully realized I was "soused to the eye-balls" when I returned that morning.

I felt no hard feelings towards the manager. It was his duty. If some of his other guests had seen me they probably would have moved if I didn't. I couldn't blame them, either. It was my own fault.

I had made my bed and I would have to lie in it.

In my dilemma I thought of "Mr. Dee." I called him on the telephone at his apartment and asked him if he would help me pack my things. I had no maid and I felt utterly incapable of packing my three trunks by myself.

He said he would. He was there within an hour. We sat down and talked things over. During our conversation he told be [sic] that he loved me, that he wanted to marry me, after which we would both go away into the country, where we'd get the best doctors and try to be cured of the drug habit.

Of course, marriage was out of the question. I was still married to Ric, although I no longer felt the slightest love for him. I told "Mr. Dee" so, and explained to him that I would accept his proposition, without marriage. We packed, loaded them into his huge limousine and went to his town house, where we gathered enough of his belongings for a month's stay in the country.

Then we drove to his palatial shore home.

Accustomed as I was to the lavish display in some of the more pretentious homes in Hollywood, the extreme splendor of "Mr. Dee's" country residence completely dazzled me. Rich in furnishings, rugs, tapestries, works of art, library, in and outdoor swimming pools, both inlaid in the most colorful mosaic tile, the gorgeous rose garden, the stables, the kennels, everything about his estate simply petrified me with amazement because of its supreme magnificence.

On the three-hour drive there we had mapped out in greatest detail the way in which we were going to overcome the drug habit; how we would gradually exercise our physical selves into such a state of normal well-being that we could drop its use.

In that wonderful limousine, driving along the beautiful country roads in the sunshine, it had sounded easy. But once we had reached our destination, unpacked and made a tour of the grounds, we both were fatigued and sadly in need of a "shot."

Each of us knew that the other was aware of our mutual plight, yet we sat around and fidgeted for hours, undergoing the tortures of deprivation pains with the accompanying mental anguish, both too stubborn, too reluctant to voice our needs.

I stood it as long as I could, then I excused myself and went to my room, where I prepared an injection of morphine. That over, my nerves calmed down, and I returned to the drawing room half an hour later, feeling greatly relieved, although slightly depressed.

Much to my surprise I noted that "Mr. Dee" too, seemed to be in a much better mental state, and then I knew that he had taken advantage of my absence to do exactly the same thing that I had done. I couldn't help smiling.

"Billy," I said, calling him by his given name for the first time. "Billy, I guess it isn't much use for us to try to reform. I suppose we are doomed to continue. We both hate the drugs, yet we simply must have them. It's no use trying to kid ourselves."

He arose with such an air of unhappiness as I never have before, nor since, seen on a man's face, unless it was on that occasion when I reproached poor old Uncle Tom Hayes for luring me into the hands [of] the doctor who sent me to the psychopathic ward.

"It's a bitter pill to swallow," Billy declared. "Yes, Alma. It's indeed bitter. Here," and he made a sweeping gesture, indicating his sumptuous estate, "here I have almost everything that should make a man happy. And now, with you here, I ought to be doubly happy. But I'm not. I can't be as long as we're both faced with this thing."

I began to weep. He took me into his arms and kissed me.

And, at that instant, his wife, a stately, middle-aged matron, pushed aside the portieres and icily demanded, pointing at poor little me:

"What's the meaning of this? Who is this person?"

My God! I was horrified. I just wanted that floor to open up and let me drop through, drop out of sight forever. That was the first inkling that

I had had that Billy, "Mr. Dee," was married. I was speechless; but he quickly came to the rescue.

"Well, Tilly," he said in supercilious tones, "now that you're here, what are you going to do about it?"

"Do about it!" she repeated haughtily. "Do about it? Why I'm going to name this lady as co-respondent. What do you think of that?"

She paused a moment, and glared at me. I was simply rooted to the spot. Her husband bit his lip in anger. She went on:

"Don't think her identify is unknown to me. Ha! Ha! It's Alma Rubens. The gr-r-r-e-eat movie queen. And I'll also sue her for alienation of affections. What do you think of that?"

She snapped her fingers in a gesture of disdain.

"But, but you can't do that," he replied. "You can't do that. You have no evidence of misconduct. We just got here for a day's visit, that's all. Anyhow," he hesitated a moment and then sort of half smiled. "Anyhow, you've got no witnesses, and our word is as good as yours. So what can you do?"

"Ha! Ha!" she laughed. "So that's the way the wind blows, eh? I have no witnesses, eh? What a clever man my husband turned out to be!"

She reached behind her and again pulled aside the other half of the portiere.

There, grinning in the most exasperating fashion, stood another woman, a prominent member of the "400," and a big, tall, gray-haired man, who, a moment later, was sarcastically introduced as "Mr. S——," one of New York's most famous private detectives specializing in the troubles of society.

"No witnesses, eh? Ha! Ha! Ha! Goodbye, dearie. I'll see you all in court."

And with that she swept out just as regally, as dramatically as she had entered, her two satellites pressing along in the rear of her stately march of triumph.

"Mr. Dee" staggered over to a divan and sank down, chin in the cup of his hands and elbows on knees. He reminded me of Georges Carpentier the night Jack Dempsey—I think it was—knocked him out. "Mr. Dee" was simply knocked out, mentally and physically.

Not any more so than I, however. When I finally snapped out of my trance I was so weak and shaken that I had to force my under jaw closed with my hand. It had dropped in amazement when "Mrs. Dee" entered, and I don't think I closed it throughout the time she was staging her most exquisite little song and dance.

"Mr. Dee" didn't look at me and I didn't look at him again for several minutes. We kept our respective positions, too dumbfounded to say anything.

Then I lost my temper. I had liked him a great deal, so much in fact, that I had cast aside the scruples of a lifetime in order to accompanying [sic] him to his marvelous home. I had done it with my eyes wide open.

He knew—I had also told him—that I was a married woman. I also had informed him that I had never been promiscuous, that I had always been a romanticist; that I'd always placed love on a pedestal and considered it the one thing in the world above price or physical desire.

And he—he had trifled with my affections. He hadn't even told me he was married.

Under no circumstances would I have accompanied him to the country had I been aware of this. I think he knew it, too. That was what made it hurt me so. He had deliberately taken advantage of me; caught me in a weak moment when, exhausted by the liquor and drugs, by my mortification at being ejected from my hotel, and sickened by the remembrance of that last terrible drug orgy which I had attended with him, I was willing, anxious to get away from it all.

I had wanted to get out in God's clean sunshine. In the country, where such things did not exist. And, above all, I had believed his protestations of love, and, believing him, had sacrificed my ideals in the hope that we could mutually work out ways and means to overcome the inroads made on us both by the relentless dope monster.

I launched a tirade of abuse at him. He tried to stop me, but he couldn't. I just raved on and on. I called him everything I could think of and repeated it over and over. I picked up a heavy book end—I remember it was a bronze elephant—and hurled it at his head.

It missed him by an inch and he sprang to his feet, catching me by both wrists and forcing me back onto the divan. He held me there while I continued the verbal castigation. Eventually I collapsed. I think I fainted, but I recovered almost instantly.

I fled to my room, locked the door, and packed a few things in an overnight bag. When I came down the steps, he tried to stop me. I wouldn't listen.

He begged me to let him drive me back to New York. I refused. Then he asked me to let his chauffeur drive me there. That, too, annoyed me and I told him so. I insisted on walking to the railroad station, which was more than a mile from his estate. He tagged along behind me all the way.

I wouldn't let him carry my bag and I wouldn't talk to him. I knew he was greatly distressed, but I didn't give a hang.

That walk almost killed me. I had on new shoes and I don't believe there was a square inch of skin left on my heels. As I strode along that highway, with my bag and with my former suitor following, and me limping from my sore heels, I must have been a site for sore eyes.

But I didn't weaken. I made it all right.

I bought my own ticket to New York and, finding that I had to wait more than an hour for my train, I calmly went into the station's rest room, leaving "Mr. Dee" literally pulling out his whiskers in the waiting room.

I remained in there until I heard the train rumbling into the station and then I dashed out, actually dashed, in spite of my burning feet, and with my little overnight bag bumping against my knee I triumphantly climbed up the steps and went inside the train without once giving the slightest indication that I heard the by-this-time tearful entreaties of my former host.

Once back in New York, I went to a moderate-priced East Side hotel, where I registered and then sent a telegram to "Mr. Dee," requesting him to ship my trunks by express. He sent them down in his car the following day, and, although I saw him twice after that—at dope parties—neither of us spoke.

Just recently, after worrying for weeks over the possibility that his wife would name me co-respondent in her divorce action, I learned that they had made a peaceful settlement, whereby he established a fund providing her with a $20,000 a year income, in return for which she agreed to obtain a Reno decree without bringing me into the picture.

Once settled in my new hotel apartment, I succeeded in making a contact with a Broadway dentist, who was able to produce all the cocaine needed to keep me in a fairly normal state. Incidentally, he took care of me until I left New York, our "arrangement" having carried on longer than any I had had with any previous doctor.

## Chapter Thirty-Nine

I lived in a weird world, people with ghosts.

Parties, parties, parties, orgie [sic], orgie, orgie—a few hours of sanity and then down into the dirt and slime of degradation again.

One night at one of these horrible affairs I saw a white-haired old man with sunken jaws and the dull eyes of a confirmed addict, galvanize suddenly into a semblance of life.

His corpse-like face, flushed with something like honest blood, he leaped to his feet and stood like some hideous caricature of death dragged from the grave, and gazed at a young man and young woman who came into the room so dazed with drugs that the young man could scarcely stagger.

The young man stopped in his tracks.

Then he laughed—a wild, cracked laugh that sounded like the hideous screams of laughter I had heard in the madhouse of Patton.

"Hello, dad," hiccoughed the young man, "you on the dope, too. So that's what's the matter with you, eh, and I thought you were a nice, clean old man, just getting a little groggy with age. Gee, I may have to wait for your coin after all."

The old man turned livid. Then the half-naked girl who was with the young man took him by the arm.

"Aw," she gurgled in her hoarse voice of the streets, "aw—what do we care. Take another sniff and dance it off."

And the old man followed the street girl's advice and took another sniff, and in five minutes' time he was shaking his aged flanks in a goat-like dance, and the pale girl who came in with his son was his partner.

The son danced with me.

He laughed all the time we were dancing.

"Gee," he said, "the old man sure is some stepper, and to think I've been afraid of an old goat like that all my life."

I left that party—I couldn't stand it. Even I, the poor, dazed, broken wreck.

I heard afterwards that the party lasted for three days, and the young man and his father changed partners and everyone seemed quite happy.

I broke the usual rule of the dope world and discovered who the old man was. YOU'D be surprised to hear his name. He has two beautiful granddaughters, not yet five years old, and a proud, heartbroken wife.

When the parties began to grow a little dull, they brought around a big silver bowl of something I thought was cocaine.

It seemed a little whiter than the ordinary "snow" to which I had been accustomed.

"Awfully white tonight, this snow," I said to my escort.

"Say," said the escort, "you're new, aren't you? That isn't coke, that's heroin—watch it work. It will give you a laugh."

And it did give me a laugh, a crazy, wild, mad woman's laugh that rings in my ears to this very day.

The laugh of a lost soul, staggering down to perdition.

Heroin is about five times as strong as cocaine. It works faster, and it lasts longer, and it lashes the nerves into a wild fury of such excitement as none but maniacs know.

For the cocaine user is a maniac while he is using the coke. And he will do anything in the world to get that coke to use.

Home, friends, mother, father, wife, husband, children, honor, self-respect, decency. These are all merely funny words to the habitual coke user.

Every once in awhile I came to, out of this wild whirl which was my life. Sick and trembling and dazed, I would make up my mind to reform—but the coke and heroin and the morphine grinned at me like skeletons, and I grinned back again like the poor crazed fool that I was.

Shortly after my return to New York I received an offer to play the leading role in a state presentation of "Lady Chatterley's Lover," a part which would have meant an ideal one for me, but one which I couldn't carry out because of DOPE!

My heart sang with joy. Why, I wasn't just a poor, dazed nobody after all. I was still Alma Rubens, the actress. I could still "make good."

I took the part home with me and began to study it.

I locked myself in my room in a good hotel and went to work.

No use.

I couldn't remember a sentence of the new part—not one sentence after the other. Dope had taken its toll.

I called in a good physician—a really good physician. The doctor came to see me, gave me one glance, and telephone to my mother in California.

"Your daughter needs you, sorely." That's what the doctor said in his telegram.

Did my mother respond to that cry for help?—Why, she was my mother. Of course she did. She came on the very first train and the first thing she said to me when she arrived was: "Darling, has dope got you again."

I lied to my mother. I told her that I was through with dope once and for all. Oh, how I wished that what I said was true.

My mother nursed me until I got back on my feet—apparently. This took several weeks. I took my drugs all the time, but I took them in moderation. And she never suspected me at all. Or if she did she never said a word about it.

I drank a good deal too. She knew that, and she begged me not to drink. I paid no attention to her, and we quarreled bitterly.

I was turned out of the hotel, and poor mother tried to get me to go to California with her, but I didn't want to go. I told her I was studying my role in "Lady Chatterley's Lover," and that I would straighten up and stop drinking that very day.

I did stop drinking and I did stop dope. I never touched a thing for three days, and by the time I put my mother on the train I was in such agony of pain that I was barely able to crawl.

Poor woman, she was on her way to California.

On her way home to the ranch in the green hills, home to peace, and happiness, and comfort, and I—poor wretch, was back again—on the dope.

## Chapter Forty

I put my mother on the train for California, kissed her good-by [sic], snatched the first taxi I could get, and rushed back to the hotel, weak and

## Chapter Forty

sick, shivering from head to foot, and wracked with hideous pains of the poor wretch who has been too long without the daily "dope."

I was too weak to go out looking for a peddler—I didn't want to see any of my dopey friends—I just wanted to sink out of the world, down and down into the dull stupor of oblivion.

I called up the dentist, who by this time was my best "friend" when it came to supplying me with "dope."

He was always obliging, with cocaine—I don't know whether he used it himself or not, but he always had plenty on hand.

Some incompetent dentists, who have failed to make a place for themselves in their profession, eke out an existence by selling cocaine. They sell it to you cheap at first and gradually they raise the price, till you are spending every penny you can get for the stuff.

Every penny—that's just what I mean!

You let the rent go, you wear your old clothes, you even go without face cream or makeup; you wear stockings with runs in them and put the money for a new pair into—"dope."

I sent for my dentist the minute I got back into the hotel, and it wasn't ten minutes until he was with me, with a big box of the little white powder that was going to pull me out of my depression and give me, for an hour or so, peace of mind and comparative comfort of body.

I took a good big sniff of the stuff, a little too big that time. It sent me completely stark, staring, raving mad!

My dentist stayed with me for fear I would jump out of the window and kill myself. He called a regular doctor and obtained a morphine solution. As soon as I had taken a "shot" of that I sank into a doped stupor.

When I woke I tried to pull myself together. I took the book of my part in "Lady Chatterley's Lover" and tried and tried to learn the lines. No use.

I depressed my heart with morphine then I took cocaine to pull myself up and then I took morphine again to quiet the terrible drum that beat in the place where my poor, exhausted heart was supposed to be.

I tried my best to keep away from the dope parties. I really wanted to learn my part and have a chance to get back.

But I was friendless and alone and terribly blue. And finally I went back to the dope parties again.

There's no use of going into particulars about them—they were the same disgusting, degrading orgies. Over and over again.

That famous Broadway actress—Edna, I shall call her, but that isn't her real name—had guests in her West 57th St. apartment that night, that astonished me beyond measure. Two of them were 15-year-old high school girls from Newark.

The sight of those two poor little girls, who should still have been in pigtails and playing with their rag dolls, "sniffing" cocaine, just about broke my heart.

One of the kids, Alice, who had seen me in the pictures as well as during my stage appearance in New Jersey, appealed to my sympathies. She was the sweetest thing imaginable.

I took her home with me—we left early—and tried in every way to fathom her mind, to coax her into telling me how she had become mixed up in such a dangerous game. Finally, I was successful, and she told me that many of her schoolmates were addicts. Some of them, she said, were even younger.

"I got started on the stuff," she went on with an air of mixed innocence and sophistication, "Through a boy friend. He gave me candy with dope in it and I ate it for weeks before I knew what it really was. He got it from a peddler who always hangs out around the school."

"Some of the kids actually steal money from their parents, or whoever else they can, to pay for their 'snow.' I have tried to do without it, but it seems like it is impossible. I must have a little every day. I guess it's a habit."

"My family is poor. My father has a little store from which he barely earns a living. I can't ask him for money, so I earn it any way I can. Helen, my girl friend, is in the same boat. She must have it too."

"When we can't raise money any other way, we entertain men. It's a terrible thing to do, but we can't help it."

"Some way or other Helen became acquainted with Edna. She thinks it's the smart thing to have a couple of kids like us around and we've been there several times. She's very liberal with money."

"Alice" told her pitiful little story casually, without embarrassment, as though it were nothing outside the ordinary. Apparently, she still believed I was one of the "regulars" at Edna's parties.

And, when I disillusioned her, she broke out crying. She didn't want to go home.

"But, Alma, please," she sobbed. "I haven't got a cent. I've got to raise money tonight so that I can buy some dope tomorrow. Right this minute, I need some. Won't you please help me?"

I was dumfounded. I was so sorry for that poor kid that I didn't know what to do.

"What," I asked her, "do you tell your parents? How do you manage to stay out late? Don't they suspect something; don't they worry about you?"

"Oh," she replied, between sobs, "I call them up and tell them I'm staying at Helen's house. They know Helen and think she's a nice girl. Our parents are not acquainted, so we get away with it."

I comforted her the best way I could. I gave her a little packet of drugs and $25 in cash. Then I took her downstairs and made her get in a taxicab and go home. She wept as though her heart was going to break because I sent her away and for several weeks wrote me daily letters, sometimes two in a day.

The epistles were as heart-breaking as they could be. Couched in the language of the ordinary 15-year-old girl, they were a strange mixture of sophistication and everyday commonplaces.

Accustomed as I had been for years to receive fan letters, I have never had anything to so touch me as have these startling missives from "Alice," none of which, incidentally, I ever answered.

"Dear Alma," one of them, dated "Newark, N. J., Dec. 9, 1930," read: "This is the second time I'm writing to you today. Now, I'll tell you why."

"I've been writing all these weeks sine I've seen you, and, of course, I haven't heard a thing from you since then. It was about a month ago, or a little more, that I sent you a little gift. I was supposed to get a return receipt, which I never got. And since I haven't heard from you, I don't know whether you got it. Now I think it's clear."

"I've just finished mailing you a letter. In this letter I told that I had HEARD SOMETHING which made me feel terrible. In fact, so terrible that I called up the ——— Hotel. I was told that you had checked out a couple of weeks ago, and I was given your new address."

"Gee, Alma, I can tell you I was nearly crazy for worry over you. I thought... Oh! I couldn't imagine what was wrong. I asked the information at the hotel whether your mail was forwarded to you, and the answer was 'Yes.' But I don't know. Gee! When I think of all the crazy things I wrote in letters, and think of someone else reading them..."

"I really don't know what to write now, because I've written most of it in my other letters. OF COURSE I don't know whether you'll get it. If you'll please let me know whether you've received them or not I'll feel so much relieved."

"Alma, have you ever read 'Of Human Bondage,' by Somerset Maughan? [sic] I think it's one of the finest books I've ever read. When I first looked at the book I thought it was that other one with a name similar to this one. Then, I know that Maughan [sic] didn't write 'The House of Bondage'—is that it?"

"Now, I've got two good books here that I'm going to read—'The Fool of the Family,' by Margaret Kennedy, and 'Mosaic,' by G. B. Stern. My brother has 'Monks Are Monks,' by George Jean Nathan. If I ever get a chance I hope to read that, too."

"You know with all the homework I get now I'd never get a chance to read if I didn't stay up until very late. And, oh, my eyes! I took an eye test and it was very disappointing."

"Well, I guess I'll have to close now. I promised Helen that I'd help her with her Latin and she asked just now whether I ever intended to terminate this letter. As I haven't anything more to say, that is a good idea."

"Dear, dear, I must be upset. Could I possibly make more mistakes?"

"Au revoir, Alice."

"P. S. Oh, please, Alma, answer this. I've been waiting weeks and weeks to... Just once."

That's just another example of the far-reaching tentacles of the hydra-headed monster—DOPE! Think of those two poor little girls. Their lives absolutely ruined before they even grow up.

And, if Alice's pitiful little story is to be believed, there are dozens of other children, both boys and girls, in her school, who are in the same plight.

Dope, dope, dope. On every side. And once caught in the net, there is no escape. Why, oh why, don't the authorities do something?

For many days I brooded, not only over my own troubles, but also over that poor little girl's. I firmly resolved to cut out the parties.

But, eventually, I weakened. I simply could not stand to be alone another minute. So, one evening, when the estranged husband of the Swedish noblewoman—the dapper son of the prominent New York society woman whom I met at the same time I became acquainted with "Mr. Dee," called me and invited me "out," I accepted.

There was no dope party that evening. We visited several speakeasies and did quite a bit of drinking. I had formed quite a liking for ale by this time and had found that it interfered less with my drug-taking than anything else. I drank ale all evening.

My escort, however, whom I shall call Don, drank heavily. And, during the course of the evening, he disclosed that he was a drug peddler.

Yes, Don, that black sheep of one of the bluest of blue-blooded New York families, not only was a drug addict himself, but he actually peddles the life-sapping "stuff" to his social intimates in the upper crust of the celebrated "400."

Likewise, Don is a typical gigolo, that queer male, counterpart of the "lily that toils not, neither does it spin," but, nevertheless, lives in the greatest affluence.

I later met one woman, quite an elderly society woman, who regularly paid him $200 a week, simply to take her to a show on Wednesdays and a night club on Saturday nights, in addition to which she paid all expenses.

Don showed me a beautiful sapphire-set ring which she had given him but a few days before and which must have cost upwards of $500. She also bought him neckties, shirts, silk underwear, pajamas and hosiery. I went to his apartment several times and never in my life did I see a man so fully equipped, sartorially.

## Chapter Forty

Through Don I met several others of his ilk, one of whom, Alfred, I employed on several evenings when I felt like going out and had no gentleman friend available. Don never took a penny from me, except in payment of drugs, and we went together quite regularly until we quarreled over his actions at another Park Ave. dope party.

This party was given by a noted financier whom I have mentioned before and was climaxed by a spectacular meeting between our host and his son, who was unaware the party was in progress. It turned out that the son, too, was an addict.

Just try and picture a father and son, the elder gray, paunchy, well past middle-age and scantily attired, the son, a mere stripling of a youth, with his bride-to-be, a charming little musical comedy dancer, clinging to his arm, suddenly confronting each other in the midst of two-score cavorting, heroin-crazed men and women, without either having previously suspected that the other was a confirmed inebriate and a hopeless drug addict...

Then imagine, if you can, what my feelings were when that tragic, that soul-devastating scene, actually was enacted before my startled eyes at Mr. "X's" dope party, the most elaborately staged orgy I had ever attended.

For obvious reasons I will not refer to my host, the world-famous promoter previously mentioned in this holographic biography by name, so he must remain Mr. "X," although he is the most ardent devotee of the occult and the most persistent worshipper at the shrine of Bacchus, in New York.

Wherever you may find the wildest, the most sordid Bacchanalian revel under way, there he will be found in its midst. And, because of his unlimited wealth and fiendish ingenuity in staging bizarre affairs, his invitations are eagerly sought, not only by the debauchees of the celebrate "400," but by many of his business intimates and their women-folk.

Mr. "X's" family, except for his eldest son, who maintained an apartment of his own, had sailed for Bermuda several days before the party and, consequently, he had thrown his entire upper floor Park Avenue apartment wide open for the accommodation of his guests, some 40 odd in all.

Among them were some of the biggest "minds" in New York, including the owner of a big retail establishment, two editors, a high city official, a renowned member of the judiciary and a prominent Washington lawyer-politician.

A third of his spacious private art gallery was cut off with rich, black velvet curtains into a "party room." An altar, perhaps 6 feet square and 3 feet tall, was built against the middle of the north wall. It was covered with a deep, crimson plush. A throne chair of gilded wood, stood on the dais. In it sat a hideous-faced, bronze Chinese idol, fitted, eyes and mouth, with blood-red electric bulbs, giving the impression that they were composed of huge, sparkling rubies.

Over the idol's shoulders was thrown a brilliant purple robe, tinseled with silver, while in its hands, folded in its lap, was a jewel-studded sceptre.

The richest of Far Eastern tapestries adorned the walls of the "party room," and the floor was covered with the most luxurious Chinese carpet, the surface of which was dotted here and there with little islands of the most magnificent leopard and bearskin rugs.

Silk-tapestried settees and divans were arranged, pew-fashion, in a big semi-circle, so that all of those seated, or lounging there-on, had an unobstructed view of the grimacing devil-god on the throne.

Overhead, completing the weird ensemble, was a black and gold silken canopy, sloping upward to its center in huge billowing folds which were held in place by gold-tasselled [sic] cords, the ends of which hung loose.

The moment that "Don" and I entered at the south end of the gallery, the dolorous, symphonic throbs of a Chinese orchestra, hidden in an alcove off from the main "party room," struck our ears.

As we walked down the length of the gallery to the throne room, flanked on either side by a fortune in beautiful paintings, etchings and relics, the ancestral pictures of our host and even the steel-studded knights-in-armor along the route seemed to frown down upon us in ghastly disapproval.

And, for hours after my arrival, after we had been welcomed by our host and had seated ourselves on one of the rich divans, I continued to feel that vague uneasiness that so depressed me upon my entrance. I felt like I was inside a somber, gilt-and-gold sepulcher. Any moment I would not have been surprised to see that hideous Chinese monster of an idol leap to its feet and devour us all in one mighty swallow.

Except for the weird strains of the Oriental orchestra, there was no sound, except now and then a husky whisper exchanged by two or more of the guests. Every one seemed under a stress, waiting; waiting for something.

My companion, in the course of time, whispered that apparently we were in for an opium-smoking party, a suggestion which made me shiver inwardly when I recalled the dreadful nausea that followed my first such venture with Henry Tape, my Chinese boy friend, in Hollywood, almost two years before.

"But," he added in an afterthought, "we won't start to 'hit the pipe,' probably until some time tomorrow. Before that, well have a little shot and a snuff, and maybe a drink or two to warm us up for the party which will begin to get good along about midnight. We won't 'hit the pipe' until we're all worn out."

Mentally, I resolved that I wouldn't be there when "tomorrow" came, but before I could voice my intention of leaving early the "chef" came around with his huge goblet of morphine and lavished it out in the same fashion which had characterized the serving of that indispensable at the party given by Baron and Baroness ———, some weeks earlier.

On this occasion, however, I was prepared. I pulled out my little fountain pen hypodermic, filled it when the "chef" came around, and when the last man had been served, took my "shot," the same as the others.

A half hour later came the heroin. And a little after that the same frenzied dancing, the gradual discarding of clothing that marked the hysteria of the leaping, pirouetting, gyrating, mauling men and women I had seen at that other never-to-be-forgotten "tea-party."

And, I am sorry to say, I so far forgot my inhibitions that I joined in with the mad jamboree. In my exhilarated state, it seemed all right, the thing to do.

Twenty or more heroin-crazed couples, dancing to the rhythmic throb of the pounding cymbals and drums, interspersed with the weird strains of Chinese stringed instruments and the occasional hysterical cries of the women.

God! What a sight! And I was part of it. It's hard for me, in my present normal mood, to believe it; believe that I had so far sunk in this whirlpool of moral degradation.

I was fascinated at the time, however. I entered into the spirit of the orgy with all the zest of a "regular," inspired, as I was, first by one and then a little later by a second "sniff" of the powerful heroin.

"Don" swung me around with the greatest abandon. Occasionally we would fall or bump one of the other couples, but it was all in the game. Sometimes I was hurt, but I didn't protest, and I didn't nurse my injuries.

Then, the only thing that could have stopped us all, unless it was a broken leg, occurred.

Into the dim-lighted room, into the midst of that whirling, frenzied mob, stepped the slender figure of the son of our host.

He was intoxicated. So was his bride-to-be, the pretty musical comedy dancer, who clung to his arm. Back of them stood another youthful couple. They, too, were completely subjugated by drugs and liquor.

Instantly, every one of those mad dancers froze in their tracks. They might as well have been statues in bronze, like that huge glowering idol on its crimson-hued throne. Not a sound could be heard except the muffled breathing of tired men and women. Even the orchestra had ceased playing as if by magic.

Our host stood in the middle of the floor, gazing spell-bound at his son and the three other young people who had stalked in with him like apparitions.

The boy, too, still with the little girl gripping his arm, stood as though in a daze. He broke the ice. He reached up with his free hand and mopped his brow.

"Father!" he gasped, in maudlin tones.

"Bobby!" ejaculated his parent in a horrified, frantically frightened voice.

The little bride-to-be stood there, her face set in an expression of absolute terror. The other pair of youngsters had drawn closer together just behind their companions as though to blot out the sight.

Fully two minutes after that brief exchange, father and son must have stood there looking at each other, with their unattired audience breathless with suspense.

Again the silence was broken by the son.

"Never mind, father," he said. "I know what it's all about. This is a 'coke party.' Let us in on it. 'Tommy' and I have tried it out before. 'Irma' and 'Peggy' can learn. They'll probably have to later on, anyway. It doesn't matter."

His father made no reply. He stood there and looked at his son and shook his head sadly. I wanted to protest, but I couldn't make a sound. I suppose there were others there that were in exactly the same fix.

And then those two little girls, those two pretty "debbies," broke out in hysterical laugh. The sound in that sepulchral chamber was too horrible to describe. They laughed. Then the boys smiled, and, finally, almost everyone tittered, too. I didn't join in. That's about the best I can say for myself. I didn't laugh.

Somebody gave a signal. The music started up, we all resumed the dance and a moment later had a "sniff."

And inside an hour those two boys, one the son of our host, and their two pretty little girl companions had divested themselves of most of their clothes, too, and went thumping and leaping around as madly as the rest of the revelers.

Long before morning, however, an incident took place which all but broke up the party and caused me to cast off "Don" forever and to abruptly depart from that hell after rudely insulting my honor . As a matter of fact, I was ejected.

How I ever endured as long as I did the mad eccentricities of some of Mr. "X's" guests, I do not know. My conscience worked overtime throughout the eight or nine hours I was an integral part of that shameful exhibition of debauchery.

I suppose King Dope was the sole cause. Once in his terrible trip, all inhibitions, all the teachings of a lifetime are cast to the four winds. Nothing else matters; religion, friends, money, all are as nothing when the King and his imps of evil desire beckon.

"Don" and I danced as all of the others did at that hectic gathering.

## Chapter Forty

Two more "sniffs" of the potent heroin and we forgot the heart-breaking reunion between father and son—when each learned the other was an addict—which we had witnessed earlier that night.

Then I grew too tired to continue the mad whirl. I told "Don" that I had to rest. I curled up on one of the divans and watched the others. It seemed to me that it was all a bad dream; that I must wake up and find myself secure in my own hotel apartment; such debauchery simply couldn't exist!

But, ever and anon, I'd glance again at that hideous, grinning red-mouthed, red-eyed Chinese idol on the throne, glowering down upon me, and I'd shiver with fright; I'd realize that it was all too true that I was a part of this inexcusable exhibition. Then, my mind would wander. I'd try to explain away to myself, my inhibitions, and try to justify it all.

Enough "snow," and an addict can justify almost anything. King Dope is always ready to advance a reason, a justifiable reason for any excess for which he is responsible. So, the night wore on.

I must have dozed off for a few minutes. Anyhow, I awoke with a start. I had a feeling that something was unutterably wrong, but I couldn't exactly explain what. Then it came to me. My escort, who had stretched out on a bearskin rug at my feet, had disappeared.

That in itself was no reason for my apprehension. Always of an extremely sensitive nature, I knew there was something else wrong. Something I must do. Some highly important duty that I must perform at once. I arose and glanced over the company.

Many, like myself, who were too exhausted to continue their mad gyrations, had followed my example. They were stretched out on the divans, the settees, on the floor, resting. A few couples, were still dancing.

Then, I heard a giggle in back of me. I turned around. There was "Don," the son of our host and his pretty bride-to-be, the other little "debbie," and her boyfriend, in the corner.

I walked over to see what was going on. I joined the party just in time to see "Don" and the other two boys, release the little bride-to-be.

They had been holding her, holding her hands and feet, and one holding his hand over her mouth and nose, so she couldn't breathe. Then, after almost smothering her, they suddenly released her nose, and as she gasped for air, "Don" held a pinch of the heroin to her nostrils, so that she inhaled it all.

The other girl was sobbing.

Apparently, "Irma," and "Peggy," had refused to join the others, and they were forcing them to do so against their will.

My eyes saw red, redder than those brilliant ruby-eyes of that monstrous idol. I felt a flame that seemed to sear my heart.

I picked up a woman's shoe from the floor—I don't know whose it was—and I struck "Don" as hard as I could with its sharp heel, squarely in the face. I hit him again and again, until he fled. Then I walloped those two boys.

They tried to seize me, but before they could pinion my arms, our host and several male guests rushed over. The two little "debbies" were sobbing their hearts out in each other's arms. I continued to belabor the two boys.

Mr. "X" grabbed my arm. I wheeled, quickly shifted the sharp-heeled shoe to my other hand and hit him a glancing blow on the side of the head that brought the blood. Before I could strike again, half a dozen other men held me so that I could not move.

He turned livid with anger.

One of the men clasped his hand over my mouth. I bit him. He screamed and cursed. Eventually, they overpowered me. They dragged me to a divan and sat on me. I could scarcely get my breath.

Mr. "X," somewhat composed by that time, demanded an explanation. Hysterically, I told him what I had seen.

He frowned at me a moment, then threw up his hands in a gesture that said all too plainly: "Well, what can I do about it?" He ordered me to leave at once.

I was only too willing. And, I firmly resolved that that would be my last party. It wasn't, however. I weakened again later. I got so lonely and so nervous that I simply had to have company and the only company I could have consisted of hopeless addicts like myself.

It was more than a month, however, before I broke my resolution. And, in the interim, I made the acquaintance of several girls, most of whom turned out to be human leeches, and three gigolos, each of whom turned out to be as unscrupulous, as conscienceless as "Don." They were out for the money.

## Chapter Forty-One

Not a plain, honest, decent, hard-working man, and not a single, self-respecting, decent, hard-working girl, or quiet wife and mother or good husband and son did I know in all New York.

I used to know men who worked for a living—lawyers, doctors, clerks in banks, grocery men, and healthy, clean-living young fellows who ran oil stations maybe, and hadn't a cent in the world.

I used to know ambitious young actresses who worked hard and tried to get to the top of the ladder—by hard work.

## Chapter Forty-One

I knew good mothers and faithful wives, rich and poor, but now I knew nobody but derelicts—gigolos and vamps, and their silly, half-crazy victims.

I lived in a world of fraud, cheating, lying, and deceit.

Once when I was a little girl, I stayed in a little country hotel for a day or so, and when I looked into the mirror which hung over the bureau in my bedroom I didn't know whether to scream with laughter or shudder with disgust.

Everything was wrong—my eyes were too high in my face, my mouth was twisted to one side—I looked like some hideous idol carved by some savage hand.

Well, that's the way the world I lived in—the dope world—was.

It didn't just look that way—it was like that—distorted, out of drawing, everything that should have been beautiful was ugly, what should have been strong was weak, and what should have been pure was soiled and degraded.

Adventurers, male and female, old and young—some dressed like the lilies of the field, and some in shabby, outworn clothing.

But almost all the women had been beautiful—once!

And all the younger men were, at first sight, what I suppose most people would call good looking.

I got sick of the sight of good looks.

I got sick of shining hair and manicured nails, square shoulders and wasp waists in beautifully-fitted coats.

There were times when I would have cried for joy to have a decent, hard-working man in overalls for a companion—just to see what a real man looked like once again.

Poor, painted old women, their wrinkled claws, heavy with jewels, and showing their hideous backs and ugly arms as if they were sweet sixteen.

Little, cold-blooded, calculating girls, not over seventeen, and capable of any crime on earth so long as there was money or dope in it.

Doddering old men with check books—always with check books, or they had to dodder alone.

I drifted lower and lower—finally I didn't even have money.

I just had dope.

The first girl I invited to share my apartment, was "Wilhelmina." Our friendship lasted but a few days. She turned out to be one of those women who'll eat your bread and then rifle your purse.

The next was "Kitty," the sloppiest girl I ever knew. That girl, besides being an addict, too lazy to make her own bed, actually had nerve enough to entertain men in my apartment while I was absent. I caught her and kicked her out.

Another week alone and I became acquainted with "Charlotte," a pretty little blonde showgirl who hadn't had a job for four or five weeks. She didn't have a penny, and when I met her, she was on the verge of collapse from the lack of a "shot." I took her home with me and we got along fine together.

"Charlotte" was a peach of a girl. It was too bad that she was on the dope. She was only 20, and had been on Broadway for about three years. She became an addict through an unfortunate love affair with a doctor, who fed it to her for months before she got wise.

When she did learn that he had trapped her, she quarreled with him and consequently he had her thrown out of the apartment which he had maintained for her for more than a year. Before moving in with me, she had rehearsed in the chorus of two shows that failed to materialize, and had been ejected from several rooming houses when she could not pay the rent.

Between "Charlotte" and my return to the study of Christian Science, I all but forgot "dope parties," and, while I did considerable drinking, and regularly used small quantities of cocaine—just enough to keep me normal—I felt that I was in the way of again getting back on my feet.

My physical condition so improved that I again began to study the lines in "Lady Chatterley's Lover," and for a while I had visions of resuming my place in society. At that time, if I had had the slightest encouragement, I would willingly have gone to a sanitarium and tried another "cure."

In the meantime, I had decided to divorce Ric. I had consulted a lawyer, negotiations were begun seeking a property settlement, and my divorce papers were drawn up. Under the California laws, a husband and wife must split 50–50 all properties either or both acquire, subsequent to their marriage.

Daily "Charlotte" made the rounds of the booking offices, seeking a position. I did everything I could to help her, but it seemed as if it was no use. Each evening she would return a little more broken, a little more disheartened than before.

I could sympathize with her because of the lean days I had experienced in Los Angeles before I obtained my first real opportunity to play a part on the silvered screen. I have always maintained this policy. Without throwing bouquets at myself, I can say that I believe I've given more money, given more help, to down-and-out screen aspirants, women and men, than any other of the present-day stars. And, I've never sought any return.

Occasionally, "Charlotte" and I would go out of an evening. We'd go to the movies, the theatre, night clubs, and speakeasies, together, although I always had to do the most of the drinking. It's a pity that she had to fall for the wiles of that ruthless doctor. She would have an ideal wife for some conscientious man.

Things drifted along this way for more than a month. My memory did not improve a great deal—I still had trouble trying to memorize parts—but, physically, I was feeling fine. I took long walks in Central Park and got a little color back into my cheeks.

Then, "Charlotte" had an experience that all but drove her insane. And, if it hadn't been for the fact that I ate something that didn't agree with me and made me ill, I probably would have accompanied her and met a similar fate.

Poor "Charlotte," broke, jobless, unhappy little blonde show girl, had the ill fortune to fall into the clutches of a modern "Dracula."

Surely, I was lucky. I suppose if it hadn't been for my sudden attack of indigestion earlier in the evening, I would have accompanied "Charlotte" to that male vampire's love nest, where she witnessed an exhibition so terrifying that she all but lost her mind.

Never shall I forget that midnight when she staggered out of the elevator in our hotel and collapsed in a heap at the door of our suite. Happily, I heard her body strike against the door as she fell. I had just retired.

I arose and opened the door. Her body tumbled half-way inside. At first I thought she had been drinking, then I knew that she had fainted. I dragged her to the bed and loosened her clothing. I bathed her temples and finally, she recovered.

Following "Charlotte's" nerve-shattering experience in Mr. "T's" mortuary chapel, I thought she was doomed to spend the remainder of her life in an asylum. In broad daylight, sometimes, she would doze off while I sat alongside her bed, then suddenly leap to her feet with a shriek of terror that would all but curdle the blood in my veins. At night she slept fitfully and would moan in her nightmares.

Day by day her condition grew worse, instead of improving, and, eventually, after more than two weeks' treatment by my own doctor—one of the greatest psychiatrists in New York—I was forced to notify her parents of her serious mental condition. Her mind was a blank. Her parents lived in a small Western city and were too poor to come for her. I advanced the money out of my fast dwindling savings to pay her expenses home.

Later I received a letter from her saying that her condition had improved somewhat, but that it would be many months before her family physician would permit her to return to New York.

## Chapter Forty-Two

Upon "Charlotte's" sad home-going, I again renewed my battle to drop my orgy-loving, dope addict society friends. I shut off my telephone and did not answer their letters and telegrams of invitation.

Virtually all my waking hours were spent studying Christian Science and the astrological teachings of Evangeline Adams, from which I seemed to obtain some measure of comfort.

From time to time I would attempt to memorize the lines of my prospective role in "Lady Chatterley's Lover," but with little success. While my mind was clear as to past events and future happenings, still there was something missing that frustrated me again and again.

I was becoming more and more embittered each day on account of my deplorable mental state. With the exorbitant prices I had to pay for my daily drug supply I could see the end of my bank account. And I knew from past experience that the little money I could hope to get from my mother in California would be insufficient to pay my living expenses and drug bills. And drugs cost money.

The only solution of my problem that I could see was to return home, and, if I did that, I knew my family would immediately shut down on money the moment they suspected that I had resumed the habit.

## Chapter Forty-Three

In the midst of one of these periods of blues there came a knock at the door of my suit and I opened it. There stood Mr. "L," notorious Broadway playboy, and his charming young society-girl wife, with whom I had become acquainted at the home of the Baron and Baroness.

"My goodness, Alma," said Aileen, after they had seated themselves. "Where have you been keeping yourself? We called you and called you on the telephone and the information desk said you refused to accept any messages. We were really worried about you."

"Well, I'll tell you the truth," I replied. "I've been keeping away from everybody. I'm trying to cut down on my drug usage. And I cannot say that I have been particularly successful."

"Heaven knows we have tried the same thing," said her husband with a gesture of futility. "Yes, 'Aileen' and I have tried over and over, haven't we, darling?"

An expression of unutterable sadness flittered over the pretty little wife's countenance for a moment. Then she exchanged fond glances with her husband and smiled.

"I guess it's no use. It's disgusting. We're sick of it. We'd do anything to stop it, but we can't. I suppose you're in the same boat, dear. Aren't you?"

What a silly question. They, with a fortune at their command. Would I like to break the habit? My God! Me with hardly a nickel to my name, unable to remember my lines and therefore unable to work, and on the edge of a nervous breakdown from sheer worry and despair, and they asking me if I'd like to stop.

It was too much. I broke into tears.

They comforted me, or at least they tried to, and, the upshot of their visit was I accepted their invitation to a "Harlemania" party that same evening.

The "Harlemania" party was given in one of the most exclusive colored night clubs in the Harlem belt. They had the entire floor above the main club rooms set aside for their guests. They had retained a colored orchestra and some of the best colored performers in the country for our entertainment.

In addition to almost all the so-called elite whom I had met at previous drug parties, there were many more—all socially prominent and nearly all extremely wealthy—whom I had never before met. Surprised as I had been at learning the names of some of the prominent addicts I had already met, I was truly amazed when I learned the identity of some of these.

Two members of one of the foreign diplomatic corps were present, in addition to a former United States Senator and a Congressman from the West. Several other prominent Washingtonians brightened the roster, including one Capitol society woman whose name has never been mentioned in connection with the slightest scandal. Before the night was over she carried on disgracefully.

After the manner of the previous parties—or orgies—I had attended, the first general service was that of morphine, with its usual effect of temporarily throwing a damper on the party. It wasn't long, however, until the heroin was passed around and it became lively enough—too lively, in fact, to suit me, with my habitual prudishness.

As the powerful drug became effective on the gathering the affair developed into an orgy of disgusting character. To the weird jazz of that colored orchestra, punctuated by the dull throb of the monotonous tom-toms, the dance went on.

Our host, as on the previous occasion, spent most of his time in the company of that charming little brunette daughter of a socially prominent manufacturer—the bride of a little more than a year—while "Aileen," again found solace in the arms of Mr. "R," a dapper, waxed-mustached prince of Wall Street, with whom she had disported herself at the home of the Baron and the Baroness.

It has always been a mystery to me how a couple, so obviously in love as "Aileen" and her husband, could tolerate the sight of each other, scantily attired, clutched in the arms of a rival. Not even the dope devil could so dull my jealousy, were the one I loved present.

Incidentally, at none of the orgies which I attended have I seen a quarrel develop between husband and wife. Apparently, King Dope insidiously operates to quell the ordinary reactions of natural emotions.

I had gone to this party without an escort. "Aileen" and her husband had assured me it would be quite proper to do so. And during the course of the entertainment I had suffered no dearth of partners when I chose to dance.

Having taken little part in the "sniffing," naturally I was not so aroused as were most of the others, and, while I cannot say that I really enjoyed the affair, it was something different, a genuine relief from my monotonous solitude and constant brooding that had marked my existence since "Charlotte" went home.

The lack of an escort, however, came near getting me into difficulties. Only by the "skin of my teeth" did I escape spending the remainder of the night in the police station.

Right in the midst of the festivities—about 3 a. m., I should surmise—a fusillade of shots rang out downstairs. Our party of revelers stopped in their tracks, with looks of mingled consternation and fear.

A moment later the colored proprietor of the resort came rushing in, his eyes popping out and gasping for breath from excitement and his exertion in running up the steps.

"Everybody out!" he shouted. "Quick! There's been a shooting and the cops will be here in a minute. Beat it! Quick!"

Instantly our party was in an uproar. The women screamed and the men cursed. Everybody was pulling and tugging at everybody else. Several women fainted. Their escorts picked them up bodily and fled.

Some were assisted out by the colored entertainers and waiters. And in less time than it takes to tell it the room was deserted. I was there alone, standing right in the middle of the dance floor in too much of a mental muddle to move.

The place looked like as if a hurricane had struck it. The fleeing guests had not stopped to don their wraps. The guests had dashed out to taxicabs in various stages of undress.

The sight of the discarded clothing aroused my mental faculties. I remembered my highly prized ermine wrap, which I had worn but three or four times, was in the cloakroom at the head of the stairs.

I started to look for it. Two or three colored employees urged me to leave, but I would not listen.

I forgot all about the shooting and the hasty departure of my fellow-guests that followed it. My sole thoughts were bent on recovering my beautiful ermine wrap. The police might hold me for murder, but that wrap was more important.

Eventually I found the cloakroom. Half the garments inside were thrown to the floor by fleeing merrymakers who, apparently, had seized the first garment they came to in their haste.

I clawed and pawed around until I found my belongings. Then I calmly walked down the steps and started to leave by the main entrance. Just as I was about to step outside there came the shriek of the police sirens.

A colored man seized me by the arm and dragged me back through a narrow hallway into a rear room which had a door leading to an alleyway.

In order to get out I had to step over the body of a man who lay, face up, directly in front of the door.

I caught but a glimpse of his face, but I knew that he was an Italian. Blood trickled from his nostrils and there was a dark spot over one of his temples, no doubt the bullet wound which killed him.

I didn't wait to make inquiries. By that time I was as thoroughly frightened as those who had gone before. So was the colored man, my escort. We could hear the police battering their way in. My escort threw open the rear door and yanked me outside. There was a step outside and we both fell in a tangle.

Up in an instant, however, we dashed back towards the alley. There we fumbled around with a latchkey on the gate, which we could not open.

We could hear other sirens as additional police poured onto the scene. Those first arriving by that time had forced an entrance to the main clubroom and apparently had discovered the body.

The gate wouldn't open. My escort lifted me up in his arms to the top of the high board fence and pushed me over. I dropped in a heap on the outside in the alley. A moment later he landed on all fours beside me.

Not a word passed between us. He seized my hand again and dragged me after him. Down that dark alley, perhaps half a block, we ran. Then we climbed another board fence and went through the basement of a tenement house on the next street. [Editors' note: The following passage is a differing account as it appeared in an alternate source.]

That night Midas and his bride took me to a new type of party. It was a dope party to be sure, but there was something else about it that was absolutely new to me.

A rich friend of the couple had brought the idea home from the dregs of Paris. I will not go into the details of that party.

It was held in a beautiful apartment in the "smart" district of New York. There were about thirty couples present. All in magnificent evening dress—some old, some young, some clever and some dull. Most of them fashionable society people.

Two or three actresses, two lawyers, one well known doctor, and a sort of clownish fellow who talked like the most ignorant Cockney. I had met him at dope parties before. He could hardly write or read, but when he was full of "snow," he was what we call a scream.

This party began like most of the others, with a great glass bowl full of liquid morphine. We all filled our needles, someone made a toast—thrust, shudder, groan—the party had begun.

When we were down in the depths of morphine, sleepy, our senses dulled and life outside that room just a dull ache. The cocaine and heroin were brought around and then the mad, half-naked dancing began.

We were all crazy as bedlam. We screamed and laughed and writhed, and leaped like the figures in a mad man's dream. Then a whisper went around. The treat of the evening was to come. Something new, something wonderful.

I cannot describe the horror of that episode. It is enough to say that at the end of it a young girl lay on the floor where she had been whipped and beaten into a dead faint.

They carried her into another room, and dazed and crazy as I was I followed her. She was sobbing and shaking from head to foot. I knelt down beside her.

"Its all over now, my dear," I said. "You will soon be better. Come, I will take you home and get a doctor for you."

The poor wretch gave a crooked smile. "Don't worry," she said. "I'll get five hundred dollars for this night's work."

And sure enough, the host of the occasion came into the room and handed the poor, degraded wretch five crisp, brand new, one hundred dollar bills.

Her partner, a man dressed as a slave, carried her downstairs to a taxi.

I went home deathly ill. I heard afterwards that the party lasted two days and nights.

I was sickened, disgusted, horrified—but I was a dope slave.

So I went on to more parties and more parties, hoping every time that my last shot would be the end of life for me.

But I lived on, and on—and on.

One night we had a Harlem party, about thirty of us. In the midst of our insane revels, there was a pounding on one of the locked doors. The negro orchestra players clutched their instruments and vanished like ghosts.

"Run," yelled the giant negro who ran the place. "Beat it. It's the cops!"

And beat it we did.

My three thousand dollar ermine wrap was under a pile of coats and dresses where I had thrown it when the "snow" began to work. I clawed and pawed through sable, chinchilla, ermine, through velvet, satin and lace, and found my coat, but this had taken me three of four minutes, and all the guests but me had disappeared.

A little slender brown man clutched me by the arm. "Come on," he whispered. "I'll get you out of this."

## Chapter Forty-Four

We walked over to Lenox Avenue and I stood in a darkened doorway while he hailed a cab for me. I got inside and eventually, just about half dead and half alive, I reached my hotel.

I was a deplorable sight. My clothes were torn and disheveled from my sparring match with the high board fence. Somewhere in the flight I must have brushed up against a grease barrel, for my beautiful ermine wrap was smeared on one side with what appeared to be axle grease.

My stockings had huge runs in them. I had lost my purse and one of my slippers. And so I stalked in through the lobby of my moderate-priced yet conservative hotel with one shoe on, one shoe off. The doorman and the elevator operator grinned with amusement.

I froze them both with a haughty movie stare. Nothing was ever said about my disheveled appearance, although I later was forced to move when a woman who occupied an adjoining suite complained to the manager about a verbal battle I had with my current girl friend, "Annetta," another addict, who had moved in with me.

"Annetta" accompanied me to my next dope party, given by that unhappy, kindly old matron, who first initiated me into the mysteries of New York society's hectic life.

At this party all the guests wore pajamas furnished by our host and hostess. There were 16 present besides herself and her husband, one of the closest friends of a former President.

I came near running out on this party before it actually got under way. Much to my chagrin, the first person I bumped into after I entered the drawing room was my old friend, Mr. "Dee," whose wife had spied on us at his beautiful country home. And at that time I fully expected to be named co-respondent in her divorce suit. We passed each other up as though we were strangers.

A few minutes later, however, when I learned that this party was one of those "catch-as-catch can" affairs, where you draw your partners for the evening by chance, I was right on the point of backing out and going home.

I had a hunch that I was going to draw Mr. "Dee" for a partner, and I would rather have died than suffer such a blow to my dignity, especially after his aloofness.

I so informed my hostess and, of course, under the circumstances, I had to explain the whole affair. She sympathized with me and said that if I did draw him she'd arrange it some way so that I could trade partners.

The pajamas were the medium of the drawing. There were 18 sets of the most beautiful silk pajamas I ever saw. Of these there were nine different colors and designs.

They were on a table in a little ante-room. The lights were turned out in there, and one by one each of the guests went in alone and selected a pair without seeing them.

As soon as they had chosen their set—in the dark—they were escorted by the host or hostess to a dressing room where they put them on. Our host and the hostess graciously took the two sets that were left.

Then, at a given signal, everybody emerged into the drawing room, and those that had pajamas alike were "partners." I dreaded that ordeal in the worst way. As I said before I just "knew" I was going to be paired off with Mr. "Dee."

When I did make my entrance, however, I was pleasantly surprised. Mr. "Dee" already had a partner. Then who should come rushing over to me but "Aileen's" husband. He had pajamas exactly like mine, cerise with blue polka-dots. He was as happy as a lark.

Strange as it may seem, his wife, once again was paired off with Mr. "R.," dapper Wall Street broker, who seemed to have a monopoly on her company.

Throughout the evening there was much good-natured bantering about this, almost everybody, including "Aileen's" husband, accusing them of having worked some kind of trick on us all in order to be together.

I had a terrible time with her husband. He was unusually exhilarated after he'd had a couple of heroin inhalations. Inclined as I always have been to prudishness, he certainly made things miserable for me the rest of the night.

"Annetta" and our host were having a wild time. Our hostess was paired off with a playwright, the friend of "Edna," and many years her junior, a fact which he did not relish and made little pretense of hiding.

He was boorish in his actions, but poor Mrs. —— never let on. She just went on in her kindly old way and was too gracious to quarrel.

The party broke up long before daylight. Our host took "Annetta" and me home in his limousine, and we had several drinks of gin, the favorite alcoholic [sic] of almost all addicts.

We were all quite "pipped" when we reached my hotel shortly after dawn.

"Annetta," upon reaching the hotel lobby, insisted on accompanying our host into the privacy of a telephone booth, where they carried on an animated conversation for several minutes, much to the delight of the elevator boy.

## Chapter Forty-Four

And I sat like a dummy on the red plush settee directly in front of the elevator. I didn't suspect it then, but I suppose that was when they did their planning of "Annetta's" new apartment.

Anyhow, they kept me waiting so long that I became impatient and went up to our suite alone and when she came in a few minutes later I was loaded for bear. Half intoxicated as we both were, we didn't realize how early in the morning it was, and consequently our quarrel must have been heard by everyone in the hotel.

Needless to say we both had to move. I took another apartment in a West 57th Street hostelry, where I was joined a couple of days later by "Tommy," another show girl, and, incidentally, one of the sweetest girls I ever met.

She was not an addict, however, and she remained with me but a week. While she made no protest, I knew that my habit depressed her and, following my return from a two-day opium party in Mr. "R's" West 55th Street apartment, she moved out on the pretext that she was taking another apartment with her mother.

I didn't blame her. Haggard and worn out as I was by this exotic party, I must have been a sight.

Mr. "R's" glamorous Oriental party had the most tragic sequel of any I ever attended. One of the girls present, a Titian-haired beauty in her early twenties, and the life of the party throughout the two-day orgy, actually went straight home and leaped to her death from a 12th story window, although I didn't learn about it until almost a week afterwards.

The victim, who had appeared in several Broadway shows and had also filled minor roles in the movies, was the daughter of socially prominent parents, sufficiently wealthy to maintain an elaborate establishment on upper Fifth Ave.

Through their political influence they all but hushed the tragedy, only a few inconspicuous paragraphs appearing in the newspapers, and those few accounts stated that she had accidentally fallen to her death.

I know, and so does every one else present at the party, that she was a suicide.

"Frances"—that wasn't her real name, but it will suffice—started to take morphine following a fall from a horse in Central Park. She was ill quite a long time and when she was able to be up and around she had a quarrel with her sweetheart, a prominent society youth, over some trivial matter.

They broke and, according to the tale I heard, he made several ineffectual attempts to patch up their difficulties, but she was too stubborn to give in, though she dearly loved him. She kept waiting for him to make just one more advance toward a reconciliation, and, when he didn't, she deliberately started out to ruin her life.

From morphine she graduated to the use of cocaine, and then heroin, later becoming infatuated with the gorgeous dreams invoked by smoking the insidious poppy.

Mr. "R's" Oriental party marked my second unsuccessful attempt to "hit the pipe." And, as happened upon the first occasion, in Los Angeles, during my friend friendship with Henry Tape, the Chinese, I became deathly ill.

"Frances," whom I had met for the first time on the evening before—this was the second day of the orgy—came into the bathroom and sympathized with me. Both our partners were already soundly slumbering in the rich, plush-draped couches which Mr. "R" had provided for his guests.

I noticed that she was very nervous. She hopped around as if operated by some kind of clockwork. She said she couldn't remain quiet long enough to smoke a pill. She said she had tried to and that, despite the fact she had grown more or less accustomed to the practice, it had sickened her and she was force to seek elsewhere for a thrill. She explained that even veteran users of opium sometimes are temporarily afflicted that way.

"It's no go for me tonight," she said, following me back to the drawing room. "Usually I like it, but tonight I simply can't stand the smell of it."

I thoroughly agreed with her. I had tried "smoking a pill" earlier. One of Mr. "R's" attendants had heated up the waxy little pellet over an alcohol lamp and squeezed it into the pipe, but at the first whiff of the sickly-sweet odor, I became nauseated and thrust it aside.

We sat and talked awhile, but conforming to the custom at such orgies we discussed other topics.

We had a "sniff" of heroin a little later and "Frances" became so agitated we ventured out alone on a tour of investigation.

We wandered through the apartment to a bedroom and tried to lie down. "Frances" became more nervous. Eventually, I took a packet of morphine from my pocket and fixed her up a "shot," which soon relieved her condition.

It was almost dawn of the second day when we were awakened by several of the others who had started out seeking us.

They chided us good-naturedly, that is as good-naturedly as their respective hangovers would permit them, and we arose and dressed. I felt terribly depressed. So did "Frances." We used a little more heroin, however, and it spurred us on.

A little later—it was Monday morning and some of the male guests had to attend to business—the party broke up. I said goodbye to "Frances" on the sidewalk, where we each took a cab.

An hour later, she was dead.

Dope killed her! Nothing else. King Dope, the insatiable devil, gets them all! He'll get me too! I know it! But I can't help it. It may be today. It may be tomorrow. There's nothing I can do about it. I've gone so far that there is no going back. I know the end is near.

It won't be long now until I see poor "Frances" again. I'll wait for death to overtake me, though. I'll never kill myself. And, I hope, when we do meet on the other side, it will be more pleasant.

Strange as it may seem, I have had no return of the yearning for excitement and large gatherings. I have reached the stage where I actually enjoy solitude. Of course, Ruth Palmer is living with me now, and we get along amiably together.

Our natures are almost alike. She likes to drink a little, talk a little, and then have lots of time to herself. So do I. And I believe we have cemented a friendship that will last to the end.

As I write this, I fully realize that it is impossible for me to break off the use of drugs. I know that it is just a question of months, perhaps only weeks, until I leave to join the ranks of those other unhappy movie stars, Olive Thomas, Wally Reid, Barbara La Marr, Mabel Normand and others, who were murdered by old King Dope!

Only last night I had the queerest dream. I dreamed that I was sitting talking to Julia Bruns, that marvelous brunette stage beauty who passed into the Great Beyond three years ago this coming Christmas Eve.

Dream, did I say? Dream? I'm not so sure about that. Perhaps the ghost of poor Julia Bruns did visit me in my sleep last night. I have just enough of that queer Irish superstition in me to believe that such visitation is possible. I have always believed in premonitions. So has my mother.

Anyhow, whether or not Julia's spirit actually warned me, makes no difference. She delivered me a most vital message, indeed!

"Alma," she said, poising herself on the edge of my bed. "Alma, you're going to die. You haven't got long to wait. Your time is about up. The dope is going to kill you just the same as it killed me!"

"You'd better leave at once for California so you can see your mother and sister once more before you go. If you don't—well, you know what happened to me!"

I awoke with a start. I leaped up from bed and turned on the light, expecting to find Julia sitting there. My body was in a cold sweat. The only sound was the peaceful, gentle snores of my roommate, Ruth Palmer, lying in the nearby twin bed.

Involuntarily I screamed, arousing her. She propped herself up on one elbow, rubbing her eyes sleepily. She was surprised to find me awake. She noticed my agitation.

She got up and patted me on the shoulders.

"What's the matter, honey?" she inquired. "Did you have a nightmare?"

"No," I replied solemnly. "No. It couldn't have been a nightmare. Julia Bruns' ghost was just here and told me I was going to die."

I sank down on the floor with my head against the bed and began to weep.

Ruth continued her ministrations, but they didn't help me in the least. I knew what I knew, and I knew that I had seen Julia. And I was convinced that her prophecy would come true.

Eventually I cried myself to sleep.

Today the feeling is just as strong. I know that soon I'll meet poor Julia. It is a most bitter sensation, this feeling that death is so near at hand. Ruth has gone out. I get up and walk to my closet. Beautiful lingerie. Beautiful gowns. Gowns which I bought with the money earned on my vaudeville tour. I look out the window overlooking Central Park. I can see happy little children darting about in their play, their mothers or nurse-maids watching nearby.

They're happy. Everybody's happy, it seems. I am not. I am the most unhappy person in the world.

I take just a little pinch of cocaine to relieve my depression. I walk over to a hat-box lying in the corner, its lid awry. I take out a handful of letters. Fan letters. I open one at random.

"Times Square Post Office, Box 17, New York City," it is headed, with the salutation, "Dear Miss Rubens."

It is a typical fan letter. The tears spring to my eyes as I continue:

"You were glorious! I have just come from the theatre and I am almost speechless with admiration! Your beauty and charm are indeed breath-taking. And your eyes wring one's heart. I have never seen sadder or more beautiful ones. Your voice is utterly charming and quite unforgettable."

"It is wonderful to see you at last in person and find you as lovely as I have pictured. You see, I have been your sincere fan ever since I first saw you on the silver screen, and I always will be!"

"What a wonderful person you are! And how richly you deserve your success! Everyone seems to adore you. And no wonder! I've wished to meet you for such a long time that, if I'd drop back-stage some night after the performance, would you allow me to speak with you for just a tiny moment? I would consider it a great honor!"

"Ever your sincerest fan, Adele L. Simonds."

Apparently that was written while I was playing at the Palace. I read the next one, dated Norwood, Cincinnati, Ohio, June 17, 1930.

"My Dear Alma," it reads. "We were so thrilled to see you looking so well and giving us such a big treat as you did yesterday afternoon."

"My son, a college man, said your presence brought back to him all the memories of you when you starred in 'Show Boat,' that wonderful photoplay."

"We wanted to rush back-stage and welcome you, but am sure that wouldn't have been just the right thing. So, I am writing you instead. We will always come to the theatre to see you. Extending to you all the health, success and prosperity in the world, I bet to remain one of your motion picture loving public. Lovingly, Mrs. May I. McGrath, 2403 Park Ave., South Norwood, Ohio."

My poor, poor picture—"Show Boat." The picture that my husband, Ric, would not let me complete, rushing me off to the sanitarium for a drug cure, instead. My tears began to flow. Then, I read another:

"Dear Miss Rubens," it begins. "Kindly send me an autographed photo of yourself. Thanking you very much and taking this opportunity to express my appreciation of your splendid work in 'Show Boat.' I am, Sincerely yours, (Miss) L. E. Herrick, Euclid Beach Park, Box 774, Cleveland, Ohio."

Still another from a very, very dear friend.

"1730 Broadway, Nov. 5, 1930. My Dear Alma," it begins. "Hope you have recovered from 'With Privileges.' I haven't yet."

"Paterson was too much for me. Shall be grateful if you will let me have one of the stills with you at the door which you caused to be made for my sake, I know. Or let me know who in the dickens made them so I may get a copy. McHugh promised me faithfully he'd save me one. I won't go near the office. I'm fed up... Love to your mother and yourself and hope the new play is a winner. Lovingly, Marie Hunt."

Darling Marie. She's a peach. If she could only know what I am undergoing. She mentioned my "new play." My new play, indeed. "Lady Chatterley's Lover," the lines of which I could not memorize and in which, therefore, I shall never star.

Maybe I'll be dead by the time it appears on Broadway. Who knows, except God, and Julia, and I?

Usually, I am not so morbid. It's very hard for me, however, to write these, my innermost feelings.

A year ago, shortly after my release from Patton, the California "crazy house," a delegation from the Federated Women's Club called at our ranch near Madera, where I had flown to seclusion. They wanted me to deliver some informal lectures on my experiences as a drug addict.

I was conscious that their motive was a high one. They wanted to use me as a "drawing card" to warn the younger generation against the pitfall of the drug demon who wrecked my life.

I wanted to help them, but, at that time, I simply couldn't. My cuts were, then, too deep and unhealed, the scars too fresh and vivid.

Now, however, things are different. I have been motivated by two things into setting forth my experiences, and revealing the deepest secrets of my soul, as I have. The first is, I hope that reading them may guide some—even one—poor unfortunate away from the dark cavern where King Dope has set his trap. The other reason is to earn money. I have hopes of selling this chronicle.

Except for the money my mother has invested for me and which she will not turn over to me for fear I'll squander it—as no doubt I would—I am absolutely broke.

I have thrown thousands and thousands of my hard-earned dollars into the maws of those human vultures, the unscrupulous doctors and physicians who deliberately wreck a soul for money. But I am not crying over spilt milk.

They're not really to blame. My own weakness is responsible for my plight. Had I the will power six months ago to force myself to again undergo the mental and physical tortures of a "cure," perhaps I might have been saved.

But it's too late now. Nothing can save me. I don't relish the idea of going home, without money and broken in health, to face my relatives with the admission that I was too weak to stand the gaff.

I love Broadway, that beautiful thoroughfare of a million lights and two million broken hearts. I'd like to stay in New York for Christmas. I'd like to visit the shops and spend thousands of dollars in buying gorgeous presents for all my relatives and friends. But, I fear, it cannot be. I have to pause a moment, because of the tears.

I pray:

> "Beloved Father, Mother, God,
> Give me wisdom to meet all problems
> That have come to me today
> Give me understanding
> To Rebuke Error,
> And so speak the truth.
> Oh, Lord, give me just one mind,
> One consciousness,
> And make me love my neighbor as myself!"

I see a great light. I love New York, but I simply must go home. Home to California—and mother! If I don't?

Well. I don't want to die alone, broke, friendless, in a shabby Harlem tenement, as did my dear friend, Julia Bruns, three years ago this Christmas Eve.

So tomorrow I leave New York forever. Ruth Palmer is going with me. Her mother lives in San Jose. Ruth, too, is in ill health.

Yes. We're both going home for Christmas!

# PART III.
# Filmography

## Banzai

CAST: Sherman Bainbridge, William H. Clifford, Alma Rubens**, Richard Stanton.
CREDITS: Directed by Charles Giblyn. Written by William H. Clifford. Key-Bee Pictures. Short. August 1, 1913.

## Narcotic Spectre

CAST: Charles Ray, Alma Rubens**, Gladys Brockwell, Arthur L. Jarrett.
CREDITS: Directed by Scott Sidney. Written by William H. Clifford. Mutual Film Corp. Short. January 9, 1914.

## The Gangsters and the Girl

CAST: Charles Ray (Detective John Stone), Alma Rubens (Molly), Arthur L. Jarratt (Jim Tracy), Elizabeth Burbridge (pickpocket), Thomas H. Ince, Margaret Thompson (uncredited).
CREDITS: Presented by Thomas H. Ince. Directed by Scott Sidney. Kay-Bee Pictures. Short. August 7, 1914.

## The Birth of a Nation

CAST: Henry Walthall (Colonel Ben Cameron), Miriam Cooper (Margaret Cameron), Mae Marsh (Flora Cameron), Josephine Crowell (Mrs. Cameron), Spottiswoode Aitken (Dr. Cameron), J. A. Beringer (Wade Cameron), Maxfield Stanley (Duke Cameron), Jennie Lee (Mammy), Ralph Lewis (Hon. Austin Stoneman), Lillian Gish (Elsie Stoneman), Elmer Clifton (Phil Stoneman), Robert Harron (Tod Stoneman), Wallace Reid (Jeff), Mary Alden (Lydia Brown), George Siegmann (Silas Lynch), Walter Long (Gus), Joseph Henabery (Abraham Lincoln), Raoul Walsh (John Wilkes Booth), Donald Crisp (General U. S. Grant), Howard Gaye (General Robert E. Lee), Sam de Grasse (Charles Sumner), William DeVaull (Nelse), William

*Alma Rubens used alternate spellings of her name in several early films.
**Though credited in some period sources, her appearance remains unconfirmed.

Freeman (Jake), Thomas Wilson (Stoneman's servant), Fred Burns, Allan Sears, Elmo Lincoln, Alma Rubens (uncredited).
CREDITS: Presented by David Wark Griffith. Produced by David Wark Griffith. Directed by David Wark Griffith. Assistant directors Thomas E. O'Brien and George Andre Beranger. Scenario by David Wark Griffith and Frank E. Woods. Based on *The Clansman: An Historical Romance of the Ku Klux Klan* by Thomas Dixon (New York, 1905) and his play of the same name (New York, January 8, 1906). Cinematography by G. W. Bitzer. Costumes by Goldstein Co., Los Angeles. Musical accompaniment composed by Joseph Carl Breil.
David W. Griffith Corp. Distributed by Epoch Producing Corp. Twelve reels. February 8, 1915.

## *The Lorelei Madonna*

CAST: Alma Rubens, Juan de la Cruz, George Kuakel, Marcia Moore, George Stanley, Edgar Martin Teller.
CREDITS: Scenario by L. Case Russell. Produced by Rollin S. Sturgeon.
Western Vitagraph Studios. Three reels. July 20, 1915.

## *Peer Gynt*

CAST: Cyril Maude (Peer Gynt), Myrtle Stedman (Solveig), Fanny Y. Stockbridge (Ase), Mary Reubens (Anitra), Mary Ruby (Ingrid), Winifred Bryson (Annabel Lee), Evelyn Duncan (Virginia Thorne), Kitty Stevens (Notanah), Herbert Standing (St. Peter), Charles Ruggles (the button molder), William Desmond (the parson), Juan de la Cruz (Robert), Alma Rubens (uncredited).**
CREDITS: Directed by Oscar Apfel. Scenario by Oscar Apfel. Based on the play by Henrik Ibsen. Musical accompaniment composed by George W. Beynon.
Oliver Morosco Photoplay Company. Distributed by Famous Players-Lasky Corp.; Paramount Pictures. August 31, 1915.

## *Reggie Mixes In*

CAST: Douglas Fairbanks (Reggie Van Deuzen), Bessie Love (Agnes), Joseph Singleton (Old Pickleface), W. A. Lowery (Tony), Wilbur Higby (Gallagher), Frank Bennett (Sammy, the dude), A. D. Sears (Sylvester Ringrose), Lillian Langdon (Reggie's aunt Susan), Alma Reubens* (Lemona Reighley), Alberta Lee (Agnes' mother), Tom Wilson (the bouncer).
CREDITS: Directed by W. Christy Cabanne. Story by Roy Somerville. Cinematography by William E. Fildew.
*Note:* This film is also known as *Facing the Music*.
Fine Arts Film Co. Distributed by Triangle Film Corp. Five reels. June 11, 1916.

## *The Mystery of the Leaping Fish*

CAST: Douglas Fairbanks (Coke Ennyday), Bessie Love (the little fish blower), Alma Rubens (his female accomplice), A. D. Sears (gent rolling in wealth), Charles Stevens (Japanese accomplice), Tom Wilson (Police Chief I. M. Keene).

CREDITS: Supervised by David Wark Griffith. Directed by Christy Cabanne and John Emerson. Written by Tod Browning and David Wark Griffith (as Granville Warwick). Titles by Anita Loos. Cinematography by John W. Leezer.
Keystone Film Co.; Triangle Film Corp. June 11, 1916.

## The Half-Breed

CAST: Douglas Fairbanks (Lo Dorman), Alma Reuben* (Teresa), Sam De Grasse (Sheriff Dunn), Tom Wilson (Curson), Frank Brownlee (Winslow Wynn), Jewel Carmen (Nellie), George Beranger (Jack Brace).

A portrait from the early to mid–1910s.

CREDITS: Directed by Allan Dwan. Based on Bret Harte's novel *In the Carquinez Woods*, published in 1883.
*Note:* The working title for this film was *In the Carquinez Woods*. Some reviews refer to the film's title as *The Halfbreed*.
Fine Arts Film Co. Distributed by Triangle Film Corp. Five reels. July 30, 1916.

## Judith of the Cumberlands

CAST: Helen Holmes (Judith Barrier), Leo D. Maloney (Creed Bonbright), Paul C. Hurst (Blatchley Turrentine), Thomas G. Lingham (Uncle Jepthah Turrentine), William Brunton (Pony Card), Clara Mosher (Nancy Card), Harry Lloyd (Andy Turrentine), Sam Morje (Jeff Turrentine), G. H. Wischussen (The marshal), Alma Rubens (uncredited).**
CREDITS: Directed by J. P. McGowan. Cinematography by S. A. Sues.
Signal Film Corp. Distributed by Mutual Film Corp.; A Mutual Star Production. Five reels. July 31, 1916.

## Intolerance

CAST—All Ages: Lillian Gish (The woman who rocks the cradle).
CAST—Judean Story: Lillian Langdon (Mary, the Mother), Olga Grey (Mary Magdalene), Baron Von Ritzau, Count Von Stroheim (First Pharisees), Bessie Love (The Bride of Cana), George Walsh (Bridegroom of Cana), Howard Gaye (Christ), William Brown (The Bridge's Father).
CAST—Medieval French Story: Margery Wilson (Brown Eyes), Spottiswoode Aitken

(Her Father), Ruth Handforth (Her Mother), Eugene Pallette (Prosper Latour), A. D. Sears (The Foreign Mercenary), Frank Bennett (Charles IX, King of France), Maxfield Stanley (Duc D'Anjou), Josephine Crowell (Catherine de Medici), Georgia Pearce (Marguerite de Valois), W. E. Lawrence (Henry of Navarre), Joseph Henabery (Admiral Coligny), Louis Romaine (Catholic Priest), Morris Levy (Duc de Guise), Howard Gaye (Cardinal Lorraine), Raymond Wells, George James, Louis Ritz, John Bragdon (Counsellors of the King).

CAST—Babylonian Story: Constance Talmadge (The Mountain Girl), Elmer Clifton (The Rhapsode), Alfred Paget (The Prince Belshazzar), Seena Owen (The Princess Beloved, Attarea), Loyola O'Connor (The High Priest of Bel), George Siegmann (Cyrus), Elmo Lincoln (The Mighty Man of Valor), Robert Lawler (Babylonian Judge), Grace Wilson (First Dancer of Tammuz), Lotta Clifton (Second Dancer of Tammuz), George Beranger (Second Priest of Bel), Ah Singh (First Priest of Nergel), Ranji Singh (Second Priest of Nergel), James Curley (Charioteer of Cyrus), Ed Burns (Charioteer of the Priest of Bel), Kate Bruce (Babylonian Mother), Pauline Stark, Mildred Harris (Favorites of the Harem), Winnifred Westover (Favorite of Egibi), Martin Landry (Auctioneer), Howard Scott (Babylonian Dandy), Arthur Meyer (Brother of the Girl), Alma Rubens, Ruth Darling, Margaret Mooney (Girls of the Marriage Market), Charles Eagle Eye (Barbarian Chieftain), William Dark Cloud (Ethiopian Chieftain), Charles Van Cortland (Gobryas, Lieutenant of Cyrus), Jack Cosgrove (Chief Eunuch), Ethel Terry (Slave Girl).

CAST—Modern Story: Mae Marsh (The Dear One), Fred Turner (Her Father), Robert Harron (The Boy), Sam de Grasse (Jenkins), Clyde Hopkins (His Secretary), Vera Lewis (Mary T. Jenkins), Mary Alden (Society Social Worker), Luray Huntley, Lucille Brown, Eleanor Washington, Pearl Elmore, Mrs. Arthur Mackley (Self-styled Uplifters), Miriam Cooper (A Friendless One), Walter Long (The Musketeer of the Slums), Tom Wilson (The Kindly Policeman), Ralph Lewis (The Governor), A. W. McClure (Father Farley), Edward Dillon (Chief Detective), Lloyd Ingraham (Judge of the Court), William Brown (Warden), Max Davidson (Kindly Neighbor), Alberta Lee (His Wife), Frank Brownlee (The Brother of the Girl), Barney Bernard (Attorney for the Boy), Marguerite Marsh (Guest at Ball), Tod Browning (Owner of Racing Car), Kate Bruce (The City Mother).

CREDITS: Directed by D. W. Griffith. Assistant directors George Siegmann and W. S. Van Dyke. Scenario by D. W. Griffith. Titles by Anita Loos. Cinematography by G. W. Bitzer and Karl Brown. Sets built by Frank "Huck" Wortman. Musical accompaniment arranged by Joseph Carl Breil. Technologist R. E. Wales.

Note: This film was copyrighted under the complete titles *Intolerance, Love's Struggle Throughout the Ages* and *Intolerance, a Sun-play of the Ages.*

D. W. Griffith & Wark Producing Corp. Distributed by Wark Producing Corp. 13–14 reels. June 24, 1916.

## *The Children Pay*

CAST: Lillian Gish (Millicent), Violet Wilkie (Jean, her sister), Keith Armour (Horace Craig), Ralph Lewis (Theodore Ainsley, the girls' father), Loyola O'Connor (Elinor Ainsley, their mother), Alma Reubens* (Editha, their stepmother), Jennie Lee (Susan, their governess), Robert Lohmeyer (Signor Zucca), Carl Stockdale (Judge Mason), Tom Wilson (Officer).

CREDITS: Directed by Lloyd Ingraham. Scenario by Frank E. Woods.

Fine Arts Film Co. Distributed by Triangle Film Corp. Five reels. November 26, 1916.

Alma in a scene from *The Americano* (1917).

## Truthful Tulliver

CAST: William S. Hart ("Truthful" Tulliver), Nina Byron (Daisy Burton), Milton Ross ("Deacon" Doyle), Alma Reubens* (Grace Burton), Norbert A. Myles (York Cantrell), Walter Perry ("Silver Lode" Thompson).
CREDITS: Directed by William S. Hart. Supervised by Thomas H. Ince. Scenario by J. G. Hawks. Cinematography by Joe August.
New York Motion Picture Corp.; Kay-Bee. Distributed by Triangle Distributing Corp. Five reels. January 7, 1917.

## The Americano

CAST: Douglas Fairbanks (Blaze Derringer), Alma Reubens* (Juana de Castalar), Spottiswood Aitken (Presidente Hernando de Castalar), Carl Stockdale (Salza Espada), Tote Du Crow (Alberto de Castille), Charlie Stevens (Colonel Gargaras), Lillian Langdon (Señora de Castille), Tom Wilson ("Whitey").
CREDITS: Directed by John Emerson. Scenario by Anita Loos and John Emerson. Titles by Anita Loos. Cinematography by Victor Fleming. Based on the novel *Blaze Derringer* by Eugene P. Lyle (New York, 1910).
Fine Arts Film Co. Distributed by Triangle Distributing Corp. Five reels. January 28, 1917.

## A Woman's Awakening

CAST: Seena Owen (Paula Letchworth), Kate Bruce (Paula's mother), A. D. Sears (Allen Cotter), Spottiswoode Aitken (Judge Cotter), Charles Gerard (Lawrence Topham), Alma Rueben* (Cousin Kate), Jennie Lee (Mammy).
CREDITS: Directed by Chester Withey. Scenario by Frank E. Woods. Cinematography by David Abel.
Fine Arts Film Co. Distributed by Triangle Distributing Corp. Five reels. March 25, 1917.

## An Old Fashioned Boy

CAST: Charles Ray (David Warrington), Ethel Shannon (Betty Graves), Alfred Allen (Doctor Graves), Wade Boteler (Herbert), Grace Morse (Sybil), Gloria Joy (Violet), Frankie Lee (Herbie), Hal Cooley (Ferdie), Virgina Brown (The baby), Alma Rubens (uncredited).**
CREDITS: Supervised by Thomas H. Ince. Directed by Jerome Storm. Scenario by Agnes Christine Johnston. Story by Agnes Christine Johnston. Cinematography by Chester Lyons.
Note: This film is also known as An Old Fashioned Young Man.
Fine Arts Film Co. Distributed by Triangle Distributing Corp. Five reels. April 15, 1917.

## Master of His Home

CAST: William Desmond (Carson Stewart), Alma Ruben* (Millicent Drake), Joseph J. Dowling (Bill Boggs), Eleanor Hancock (Mrs. Drake), Robert McKim (Van Tyle), Susie Light Moon (Squaw Mamma), Will H. Bray (Mr. Drake).
CREDITS: Directed by Walter Edwards. Story by R. Cecil Smith.
Triangle Film Corp. Distributed by Triangle Film Corp. Five reels. August, 1917.

**A signed portrait from the 1920s.**

## The Firefly of Tough Luck

CAST: Alma Rueben* (Firefly), Charles Gunn (Danny Ward) Walt Whitman ("Tough Luck" Baxter), Darrel Foss (Bert Wilcox), Jack Curtis (Happy Jack Clarke), Aaron Edwards (Silent Dan), Laura Sears.
CREDITS: Directed by E. Mason Hopper. Story by J. G. Hawks. Cinematography by Charles Stumar.
Triangle Film Corp. Distributed by Triangle Film Corp. Five reels, 4911 feet. October 21, 1917.

## The Cold Deck

CAST: William S. Hart ("Level" Leigh), Mildred Harris (Alice Leigh), Edwin N. Wallock ("Black Jack"), Sylvia Bremer (Rose Larkin), Charles O. Rush (Ace Hutton), Alma Rubens (Coralie), Joe Knight (Vigilante chief).
CREDITS: Presented by Thomas H. Ince. Directed by William S. Hart. Scenario by J. G. Hawks. Story by J. G. Hawks. Cinematography by Joe August. Art direction by G. Harold Percival and Robert Brunton.
New York Motion Picture Corp.; Kay-Bee; Triangle Film Corp. Distributed by State Rights; S. A. Lynch Enterprises, Inc. Seven reels. November, 1917.

## The Regenerates

CAST: Alma Rubens (Catherine Ten Eyck), Walt Whitman (Mynderse Van Dyun), Darrel Foss (Pell Van Dyun), John Lince (Owen Duffy), Allan Sears (Paul La Farge), Louis Durnham (William Slade), William Brady (James Forbes), Pauline Stark (Nora Duffy).
CREDITS: Directed by E. Mason Hopper. Assistant director Alfred L. Werker. Scenario by Catherine Carr. Cinematography Charles Stumar.
Note: The original title of this film was *Blue Blood*.
Triangle Film Corp. Distributed by Triangle Distributing Corp. Five reels. November 25, 1917.

## The Gown of Destiny

CAST: Alma Rubens (Natalie Drew), Herrera Tejedde (Andre Leriche), Allan Sears (Neil Cunningham), Lillian West (Mrs. Reyton), J. Barney Sherry (Mr. Reyton), Pietro Buzzi (Lucien Leriche), Frederick Vroom (Sir John Cunningham), Bliss Chevalier (Mme. Felice), Kathleen Emerson, Dorothy Marshall.
CREDITS: Directed by Lynn F. Reynolds. Scenario by Lynn F. Reynolds. Cinematography by John Brown and William A. Reinhardt.
Triangle Film Corp. Distributed by Triangle Distributing Corp. Five reels. December 30, 1917.

## I Love You

CAST: Alma Rubens (Felice), John Lince (Ravello), Francis McDonald (Jules Mardon), Wheeler Oakman (Armand de Gautier), Frederick Vroom (Prince del Chinay), Lillian Langdon (Princess del Chinay), Peaches Jackson (boy).

A trade advertisement for Alma's 1918 film *I Love You*.

CREDITS: Directed by Walter Edwards. Story by Catherine Carr. Cinematography by Gus C. Peterson.
*Note:* The film was re-edited and re-released by Tri-Stone Pictures in 1923.
Triangle Film Corp. Distributed by Triangle Distributing Corp. Seven reels. January 13, 1918.

## The Answer

CAST: Alma Rubens (Lorraine Van Allen), Joe King (John Warfield), Francis McDonald (Guido Garcia), Claire Anderson (Goldie Shepard), Charles Dorian (Robert Warfield), Jean Hersholt (Shepard).
CREDITS: Directed by E. Mason Hopper. Scenario by E. Magnus Ingleton. Cinematography by Anton Nagy.
Triangle Film Corp. Distributed by Triangle Distributing Corp. Seven reels. March 17, 1918.

## The Love Brokers

CAST: Alma Rubens (Charlotte Carter), Texas Guinan (Olga Grey), Joseph Bennett (Peter Ladislaw), Lee Hill (Gerard Townshend), Betty Pearce (Madge L'Estrange), George Pearce (Dr. Catherwood).
CREDITS: Directed by E. Mason Hopper. Scenario by Charles J. Wilson. Story by W. Carey Wonderley. Cinematography by Jack MacKenzie.
Note: The working title of this film was Another Foolish Virgin.
Triangle Film Corp. Distributed by Triangle Distributing Corp. Five reels. March 31, 1918.

## Madame Sphinx

CAST: Alma Rubens (Celeste), Wallace McDonald (Andre Du Bois), Gene Burr (Raoul Laverne), Frank MacQuarrie (Henri Du Bois), William Dyer (Guissert), Dick Rosson (Dessin), Betty Pearce (Lys), Wilbur Highby (Chambre), Arthur Millett (Beauchard), John Lince (Louis).

A movie slide used to promote Alma's film *Madam Sphinx* (1918).

CREDITS: Directed by Thomas N. Heffron. Scenario by Lanier Bartlett. Story by Raymond L. Schrock. Cinematography by C. H. Wales.
Triangle Film Corp. Distributed by Triangle Distributing Corp. Five reels. June 9, 1918.

## The Painted Lily

CAST: Alma Rubens (Mary Fanjoy), William V. Mong (Daniel Fanjoy), Jack Richardson (Cecil Grey), Dorothy Hagar (Jeanette Wayne), Francis McDonald (Tom Burton), Alberta Lee (Mrs. Wayne), Gene Burr (London Louie).
CREDITS: Directed by Thomas N. Heffron. Scenario by Cinema Exchange. Story by Catherine Carr. Cinematography by C. H. Wales.
Note: MPN lists Claire Anderson rather than Dorothy Hagar in the role of Jeanette Wayne.
Triangle Film Corp. Distributed by Triangle Distributing Corp. Five reels. June 30, 1918.

## False Ambition

CAST: Alma Rubens (Judith/Zariska), Peggy Pearce (Felicity), Alberta Lee (Anna), Edward Peil (David Strong), Walt Whitman (Mark Strong), Iris Ashton (Mrs. Dorian), Myrtle Rishell (Mrs. Pemberton), Lillian Langdon (Mrs. Van Dixon), Lee Phelps (Peter Van Dixon), Ward Caulfield (John Van Dixon), Lee Hill (Paul Vincent), Alice Crawford (Lucy Vernon).
CREDITS: Directed by Gilbert P. Hamilton. Scenario by E. Magnus Ingleton. Story by E. Magnus Ingleton. Cinematography by Jack McKenzie.
Note: The film was titled *A Woman of Mystery* until just before its release.
Triangle Film Corp. Distributed by Triangle Distributing Corp. Five reels. July 21, 1918.

## The Ghost Flower

CAST: Alma Rubens (Giulia), Charles West (La Farge), Francis McDonald (Tony Cafarelli), Dick Rosson (Paola), Emory Johnson (Duke De Chaumont), Naida Lessing (La Serena), Tote Ducrow (Ercolano).
CREDITS: Directed by Frank Borzage. Scenario by Catherine Carr. Story by Madeline Matzen. Cinematography by Jack McKenzie. Assistant to the director Amy E. Sacker.
Triangle Film Corp. Distributed by Triangle Distributing Corp. Five reels. August 18, 1918.

## Restless Souls

CAST: Alma Rubens (Marion Gregory), Katherine Adams (Judith Wingate), Jack Conway (Hugh Gregory), Harvey Clark (Chester Wingate), J. Barney Sherry (Dr. Robert Calvert), Eugene Burr (Oliver Sloan).
CREDITS: Directed by William C. Dowlan. Cinematography by Steve Norton. Based on the short story "Restless Souls" by Cosmo Hamilton.
Triangle Film Corp. Distributed by Triangle Distributing Corp. Six reels. February 2, 1919.

A promotional advertisement for Alma's 1919 Triangle Films release *Restless Souls*.

## Diane of the Green Van

CAST: Alma Rubens (Diane Westfall), Nigel Barrie (Philip Poynter), Lamar Johnstone (Carl Granberry), Josephine Crowell (Aunt Agatha), Harry von Meter (Baron Tregar), Wedgwood Nowell (Prince Ronador), Ed Brady (Themar), Alfred Hollingsworth (Mic-co), Irene Rich (Keela), Sydney Hayes.

CREDITS: Presented by F. Laws Hutton. Directed by Wallace Worsley. Scenario by Thomas J. Geraghty. Cinematography by Robert Newhard.

Winsome Stars Corp. Distributed by Robertson-Cole Co. through Exhibitors Mutual Distributing Corp. Five reels, 4800 feet. April 6, 1919.

## A Man's Country

CAST: Alma Rubens (Kate Carewe), Albert Roscoe (Ralph Bowen), Lon Chaney ("Three Card" Duncan), Joseph Dowling (Marshall Leland), Edna May Wilson (Ruth Kemp), Alfred Hollingsworth (Oliver Kemp), Phil Gastrock (Connell).

CREDITS: Directed by Henry Kolker. Scenario by E. Richard Schayer. Story by John Lynch. Cinematography by Robert Newhard.

Winsome Stars Corp. Distributed by Robertson-Cole Co. through Exhibitors Mutual Distributing Corp. Five reels. July 13, 1919.

## The World and His Wife

CAST: Montague Love (Don Julian), Alma Rubens (Teodora), Gaston Glass (Ernesto), Pedro de Cordoba (Don Severo), Charles Gerard (Don Alvarez), Mrs. Allan Walker (Marie), Byron Russell (Captain Wickersham), Peter Barbier (Don Julian's friend), Leon Gendron, Vincent Macchia (Don Alvarez's friends), James Savold (Ernesto's father), Margaret Dale (Mercedes), Ray Allen (Ernesto's mother).

CREDITS: Directed by Robert G. Vignola. Scenario by Frances Marion. Cinematography by Al Liguori. Settings designed by Joseph Urban. Based on the play *El Gran galeoto* by José Echegaray Y Eizaguirre (Madrid, March 1881).

*Note:* Charles Frederic Nirdlinger wrote an English adaptation of the stage play, which had its premiere in New York on November 3, 1908; the film was based on Nirdlinger's adaptation. M-G-M Pictures produced a film entitled *Lovers?* based on the same source, which was directed by John M. Stahl and starred Ramon Novarro and Alice Terry.

Cosmopolitan Productions. Distributed by Famous Players-Lasky Corp.; Paramount-Artcraft Pictures. Six reels, 6702 feet. July 25, 1920.

## Humoresque

CAST: Gaston Glass (Leon Kantor, adult), Vera Gordon (Mama Kantor), Alma Rubens (Gina Berg), Dore Davidson (Abraham Kantor), Bobby Connelly (Leon Kantor, boy), Helen Connelly (Esther Kantor, girl), Ann Wallick (Esther Kantor, adult), Sidney Carlyle (Mannie Kantor), Joseph Cooper (Isadore Kantor, boy), Maurice Levigne (Isadore Kantor, adult), Alfred Goldberg (Rudolph Kantor, boy), Edward Stanton (Rudolph Kantor, adult), Louis Stearns (Sol Ginsberg), Maurice Peckre (Boris Kantor), Ruth Sabin (Mrs. Isadore Kantor), Frank Mitchell (Baby Kantor), Miriam Battista (Minnie Ginsberg).

CREDITS: Directed by Frank Borzage. Scenario by Francis Marion. Cinematography by Gilbert Warrenton. Based on the Fannie Hurst short story "Humoresque" by *Cosmopolitan Magazine* (March 1919).

*Note:* Warner Bros. loosely remade *Humoresque* in 1947 with John Garfield and Joan Crawford in the lead roles. Clifford Odets and Zachary Gold re-adapted Hurst's story, and Jean Negulesco directed it.

An industry trade publication ad for *The World and His Wife* (1920).

Cosmopolitan Productions; International Film Service Co. Distributed by Famous Players-Lasky Corp.; Paramount-Artcraft Pictures. Six reels, 5987 feet. September 19, 1920.

## The Fall of Babylon

CAST: Tully Marshall (The High Priest of Bel), Constance Talmadge (The Mountain Girl), Elmer Clifton (The Rhapsode), Alfred Paget (Prince Belshazzar), Carl Stockdale (Nabonidus, King of Babylonia), Seena Owen (Attarea, Favorite of

Belshazzar), Loyola O'Connor (Attarea's Slave), George Siegmann (Cyrus), Elmo Lincoln (The Mighty Man of Valor), James Curley (Charioteer of Cyrus), Kate Bruce (Babylonian Mother), Howard Scott (Babylonian Dandy), Alma Rubens, Ruth Darling, Margaret Mooney (Girls of the Marriage Market), George Fawcett (Babylonian Judge), Mildred Harris, Pauline Stark (Favorites of the Harem), Winnifred Westover (Favorite of Egibi).
CREDITS: Presented by D. W. Griffith. Supervised by D. W. Griffith. Directed by D. W. Griffith. Scenario by D. W. Griffith. Story by D. W. Griffith. Cinematography by G. W. Bitzer.
Note: This film is an amplification of the Babylonian episode of *Intolerance* and used discarded footage from the original film.
D. W. Griffith. Distributed by D. W. Griffith Service. Seven reels. July 21, 1919.

## Thoughtless Women

CAST: Alma Rubens (Annie Marnet), Merceita Esmond (Mrs. Marnet), E. Holland (Mr. Marnet), Robert Williams (The son), Mathilde Brundage (The mother), Gladys Valerie (The sister), Lumsden Hare (John Hewitt, the banker), Mabel Bardine (Lady Vere-de-Vere).
CREDITS: Presented by Daniel Carson Goodman. Directed by Daniel Carson Goodman. Scenario by Daniel Carson Goodman. Distributed by Pioneer Film Corp.; Daniel Carson Goodman. Six reels. November, 1920.

## Find the Woman

CAST: Alma Rubens (Sophie Carey), Eileen Huban (Clancy Deane), Harrison Ford (Philip Vandevent), George MacQuarrie (Judge Walbrough), Norman Kerry (Marc Weber), Ethel Duray (Fab Weber), Arthur Donaldson (Morris Beiner), Henry Sedley (Don Carey), Sydney Deane (Sofford), Emily Fitzroy (Mrs. Napoli).
CREDITS: Directed by Tom Terriss. Written by Doty Hobart. Cinematography by Ira H. Morgan. Artistic direction by Joseph Urban.

A trade publication ad for *Thoughtless Women*, one of Alma's starring performances for Pioneer Film Corporation.

Cosmopolitan Productions. Distributed by Famous-Players Lasky Corp.; Paramount Pictures. April 2, 1922.

## The Valley of Silent Men

CAST: Alma Rubens (Marette Radison, a Canadian girl), Lew Cody (Cpl. James Kent of the Royal Northwest Mounted), Joseph King ("Buck" O'Connor), Mario Majeroni (Pierre Radison, the father), George Nash (Inspector Kedsty, of the Mounted), J. W. Johnston (Jacques Radison, the brother).
CREDITS: Directed by Frank Borzage. Scenario by John Lynch. Cinematography by Chester Lyons. Production Manager John Lynch.
Cosmopolitan Productions. Distributed by Paramount Pictures. Seven reels, 6500 feet. Silent, B&W. September 10, 1922.

## The Enemies of Women

Alma in a scene from 1922's *Find the Woman*.

CAST: Lionel Barrymore (Prince Lubimoff), Alma Rubens (Alicia), Pedro De Cordoba (Atilio Castro), Gareth Hughes (Spadoni), Gladys Hulette (Vittoria), William Thompson (Colonel Marcos), William Collier Jr. (Gaston), Mario Majeroni (Duke de Delille), Betty Bouton (Alicia's maid), Madame Jean Brindeau (Madame Spadoni), Ivan Linow (terrorist), Paul Panzer (Cossack).
CREDITS: Directed by Alan Crosland. Scenario by John Lynch. Cinematography by Ira Morgan. Sets designed by Joseph Urban. Production manager John Lynch. Costumes by Gretl Urban.
Cosmopolitan Productions. Distributed by Goldwyn Distributing Corp. Eleven reels, 10,501 feet. Silent, B&W, 35mm. April 15, 1923.

## Under the Red Robe

CAST: Robert B. Mantell (Cardinal Richelieu), John Charles Thomas (Gil de Bérault), Alma Rubens (Renee de Cocheforet), Otto Kruger (Henri de Cocheforet), William H. Powell (Duke of Orléans), Ian MacLaren (King Louis XIII), Genevieve Hamper

(Duchess de Chevreuse), Mary MacLaren (Anne of Austria), Rose Coghlan (Marie de Medici), Gustav von Seyffertitz (Clom), Sidney Herbert (Father Joseph), Arthur Houseman (Captain La Rolle), Paul Panzer (lieutenant in the French Army), Charles Judels (Antoine), George Nash (Jules; innkeeper), Evelyn Gosnell (Madame de Cocheforet).
CREDITS: Directed by Alan Crosland. Scenario by Bayard Veiller. Cinematography by Harold Wenstrom and Gilbert Warrenton. Sets designed by Joseph Urban. Musical score by William Frederick Peters. Costumes by Gretl Urban. Art titles by Oscar C. Buchheister Art Title Co.
Cosmopolitan Corp. Distributed by Goldwyn-Cosmopolitan Distributing Corp. Ten reels, 9062 feet (also 12,000 feet). Silent, B&W. November 24, 1923.

## *Week End Husbands*

CAST: H. J. Herbert (William Randall), Alma Rubens (Barbara Belden), Montague Love (Thomas Mowry), Maurice Costello (John Keane), Sally Cruze (Mrs. Dawn), Charles Byer (Robert Stover), Paul Panzer (Monsieur La Rue), Margaret Dale (Mrs. Sarah Belden).
CREDITS: Directed by E. H. Griffith. Story and scenario by Daniel Carson Goodman.
Daniel Carson Goodman Corp. Distributed by Equity Pictures. Seven reels, 6500 feet. Silent, B&W, 35mm. February 10, 1924.

## *The Rejected Woman*

CAST: Alma Rubens (Diane Du Prez), Bela Lugosi (Jean Gagnon), George MacQuarrie (Samuel Du Prez), Conrad Nagel (John Leslie), Frederick Burton (Leyton Carter), Antonio D'Algy (Craig Burnett), Aubrey Smith (Peter Leslie), Wyndham Standing (James Dunbar), Juliette La Violette (Aunt Rose), Leonora Hughes (Lucille Van Tuyl).
CREDITS: Directed by Albert Parker. Story/adaptation by John Lynch. Cinematography by Roy Hunt. Art direction by Clark Robinson.
Distinctive Pictures. Distributed by Goldwyn-Cosmopolitan Distrib-

Though taken much earlier, this photograph was circulated in newspapers like the *New York Herald Tribune* at the time of Alma's death.

uting Corp. Eight reels, 7761 feet. Silent, B&W, 35mm. May 4, 1924.

## *Cytherea*

CAST: Irene Rich (Fanny Randon), Lewis Stone (Lee Randon), Norman Kerry (Peyton Morris), Betty Bouton (Claire Morris), Alma Rubens (Savina Grove), Charles Wellesley (William Grove), Constance Bennett (Annette Sherman), Peaches Jackson (Randon Child), Mickey Moore (Randon Child), Hugh Saxon (Randon Butler), Lee Hill (Grove Butler), Lydia Yeamans Titus (Laundress), Brandon Hurst (Daniel Randon), J. C. Fowler (uncredited).
CREDITS: Presented by Samuel Goldwyn. Produced by Samuel Goldwyn. Directed by George Fitzmaurice. Adapted by Frances Marion. Based on the novel *Cytherea, Goddess of Love* by Joseph Hergesheimer. Cinematography by Arthur C. Miller. Edited by Stuart Heisler. Technical direction by Ben Carré.
*Note:* This film is also known as *The Forbidden Way*.
Madison Productions. Distributed by Associated First National Pictures. B&W/color (2-strip Technicolor), silent. May 4, 1924.

Alma as seen in the Standard Casting Directory while under the management of William Cohill in the 1920s.

## *The Price She Paid*

CAST: Alma Rubens (Mildred Gower), Frank Mayo (Dr. Donald Keith), Eugenie Besserer (Mrs. Elton Gower), William Welsh (Gen. Lemuel Sidall), Lloyd Whitlock (Jack Prescott), Otto Hoffman (Seth Kehr), Edwards Davis (Attorney Ellison), Wilfred Lucas (James Presbury), Ed Brady (deputy sheriff), Freeman Wood (Stanley Baird).
CREDITS: Directed by Henry MacRae.
Columbia Pictures. Distributed by C. B. C. Film Sales. Six reels, 5957 feet. Silent, B&W, 35mm. April 1 or September 15, 1924

Alma endorsing Tuxedo Tobacco in a 1926 advertisement.

## *Gerald Cranston's Lady*

CAST: James Kirkwood (Gerald Cranston), Alma Rubens (Hermione, Lady Gerald Cranston), Walter McGrail (Gordon Ibbotsleigh), J. Farrell MacDonald (Rennie), Lucien Littlefield (Stanley Tilotson), Spottiswoode Aitken (Ephraim Brewster), Templar Saxe (Lord Rawley), Richard Headrick (Arthur), Marguerite De La Motte (Angela), Eric Mayne (Sir James Guthrie), Lydie Knott (Cranston's mother).

CREDITS: Presented by William Fox. Directed by Emmett J. Flynn. Scenario by Edmund Goulding.
Fox Film Corp. Seven reels, 6674 feet. Silent, B&W, 35mm. October 19, 1924.

## Is Love Everything?

CAST: Alma Rubens (Virginia Carter), Frank Mayo (Robert Whitney), H. B. Warner (Jordan Southwick), Walter McGrail (Boyd Carter), Lilyan Tashman (Edythe Stanley), Marie Schaefer (Mrs. Carter), Irene Howley (Mrs. Rowland).
CREDITS: Presented by Murray W. Garsson. Directed by William Christy Cabanne. Cinematography by Walter Arthur and Philip Armand. Edited by William B. Laud. Garsson Enterprises. Distributed by Associated Exhibitors. Six reels, 5221 feet. Silent, B&W, 35mm. November 30, 1924.

## The Dancers

CAST: George O'Brien (Tony), Alma Rubens (Maxine), Madge Bellamy (Una), Templar Saxe (Fothering), Joan Standing (Pringle), Alice Hollister (Mrs. Mayne), Freeman Wood (Evan Caruthers), Walter McGrail (The Argentine), Noble Johnson (Ponfilo), Tippy Grey (Captain Bassil).
CREDITS: Presented by William Fox. Directed by Emmett J. Flynn. Scenario by Edmund Goulding. Cinematography by Ernest G. Palmer and Paul Ivano.
Fox Film Corp. Seven reels, 6583 feet. Silent, B&W, 35mm. January 4, 1925.

## She Wolves

CAST: Alma Rubens (Germaine D'Artois), Jack Mulhall (Lucien D'Artois), Bertram Grassby (André Delandal), Harry Myers (Henri de Latour), Judy King (Fox Trot), Fred Walton (valet), Diana Miller (Céleste), Josef Swickard (De Goncourt), Helen Dunbar (Madame De Goncourt), Charles Clary (D'Artois).
CREDITS: Presented by William Fox. Directed by Maurice Elvey. Scenario by Dorothy Yost.
Fox Film Corp. Six reels,

An ethereal portrait of Alma glancing heavenward.

5783 feet. Silent, B&W, 35mm. April 26, 1925.

## A Woman's Faith

CAST: Alma Rubens (Neree Caron), Percy Marmont (Donovan Steele), Jean Hersholt (Cluny), ZaSu Pitts (Blanche), Hughie Mack (Francois), Cesare Gravina (Odilion Turcott), William H. Turner (Xavier Caron), Andre Beranger (Leandre Turcott), Rosa Rosanova (Delima Turcott).

CREDITS: Directed by Edward Laemmle. Adaptation by E. T. Lowe, Jr., and C. R. Wallace. Cinematography by John Stumar.

Universal Pictures. Seven reels, 6023 feet. Silent, B&W, 35mm. May 17, 1925.

## Fine Clothes

CAST: Lewis Stone (Earl of Denham), Percy Marmont (Peter Hungerford), Alma Rubens (Paula), Raymond Griffith (Oscar), Eileen Percy (Adele), William V. Mong (Philip), John Merkyl (receiver), Otis Harlan (Alfred).

CREDITS: Presented by Louis B. Mayer. Directed

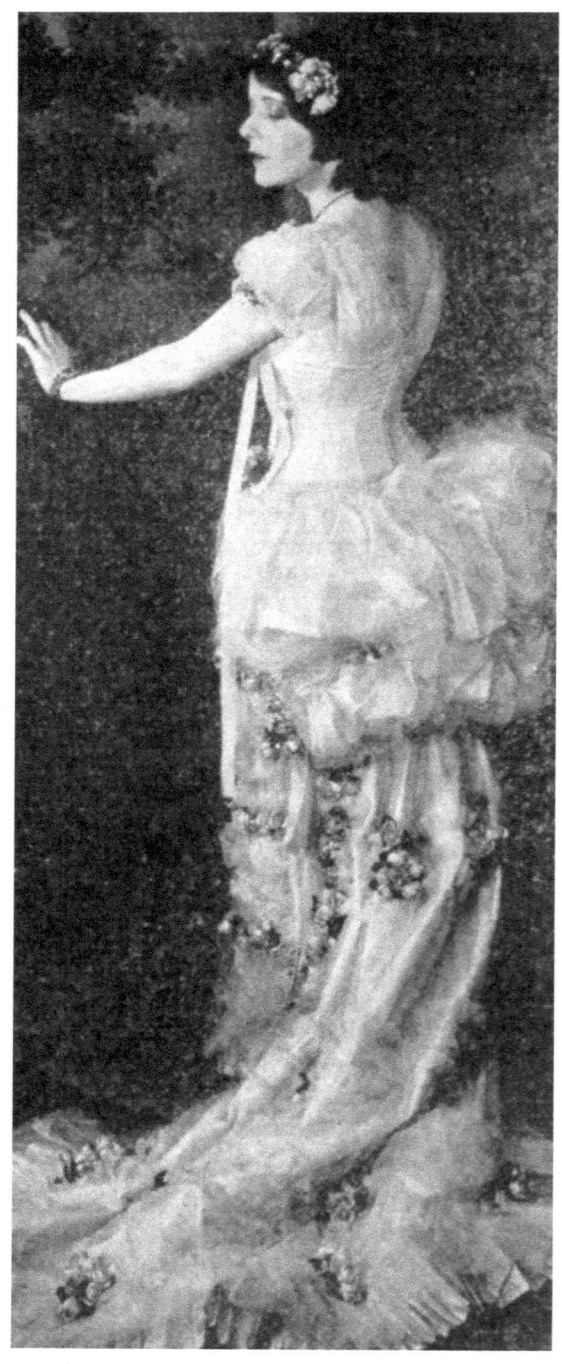

**Alma as Lady Isabel in a still from 1925's *East Lynne*.**

by John M. Stahl. Adaptation by Benjamin Glazer. Cinematography by Ernest Palmer. Art direction by Cedric Gibbons. Editing by Margaret Booth and Robert Kern. Assistant director Sidney Algier.

Louis B. Mayer Productions. Distributed by First National Pictures. Eight reels, 6971 feet. Silent, B&W, 35mm. August 9, 1925.

## The Winding Stair

CAST: Alma Rubens (Marguerite), Edmund Lowe (Paul), Warner Oland (Petras), Mahlon Hamilton (Gerard), Emily Fitzroy (Madame Muller), Chester Conklin (Onery), Frank Leigh (Andrea).

CREDITS: Presented by William Fox. Directed by John Griffith Wray. Scenario by Julian La Mothe. Cinematography by Karl Struss.

Fox Film Corp. Six reels, 6100 feet. Silent, B&W, 35mm. October 25, 1925.

## East Lynne

CAST: Alma Rubens (Lady Isabel), Edmund Lowe (Archibald Carlyle), Lou Tellegen (Sir Francis Levison), Frank Keenan (Chief Justice Hare), Marjorie Daw (Barbara Hare), Leslie Fenton (Richard Hare), Belle Bennett (Afy Hallijohn), Paul Panzer (Mr. Hallijohn), Lydia Knott (Mrs. Hare), Harry Seymour (Mr. Dill), Richard Headrick (Willie Carlyle), Virginia Marshall (Little Isabel), Martha Mattox (Cornelia Carlyle), Eric Mayne (Earl of Mount-Severn).

CREDITS: Presented by William Fox. Directed by Emmett Flynn. Adaptation by Lenore J. Coffee and Emmett Flynn. Cinematography by Ernest G. Palmer.

Fox Film Corp. Nine reels, 8975 feet. Silent, B&W, 35mm. November 23, 1925.

## The Gilded Butterfly

CAST: Alma Rubens (Linda Haverhill), Bert Lytell (Brian Anestry), Huntley Gordon (John Converse), Frank Keenan (Jim Haverhill), Herbert Rawlinson (Courtney Roth), Vera Lewis (Mrs. Ralston), Arthur Hoyt (Mr. Ralson), Carolynne Snowden (Negro maid).

CREDITS: Presented by William Fox. Directed by John Griffith Wray. Scenario by Bradley King. Story by Evelyn Campbell. Cinematography by Frank Good. Assistant director Buddy Erickson.

Fox Film Corp. Six reels, 6202 feet. Silent, B&W, 35mm. January 3, 1926.

## Siberia

CAST: Alma Rubens (Sonia Vronsky), Edmund Lowe (Leonid Petroff), Lou Tellegen (Egor Kaplan), Tom Santschi (Alexis Vetkin), Paul Panzer (commandant), Vadim Uraneff (Kyrill [Cyril] Vronsky), Lilyan Tashman (beautiful blonde), Helen D'Algy (beautiful brunette), James Marcus (Andrei Vronsky), Daniel Makarenko (governor), Harry Gripp (Ivan the Nameless), Samuel Blum (Feodor).

CREDITS: Presented by William Fox. Directed by Victor Schertzinger. Scenario by Eve

A dramatic moment from *Siberia* (1926).

Unsell. Adaptation by Nicholas A. Dunaew. Cinematography by Glen MacWilliams and Robert Martin. Assistant director William Tummel.

Fox Film Corp. Seven reels, 6950 feet. Silent, B&W, 35mm. March 28, 1926.

## "Marriage License?"

CAST: Alma Rubens (Wanda Heriot), Walter McGrail (Marcus Heriot), Richard Walling (Robin), Walter Pidgeon (Paul), Charles Lane (Sir John), Emily Fitzroy (Lady Heriot), Langhorne Burton (Cheriton), Edgar Norton (Beadon), George Cowl (Amercrombie), Lon Poff (footman).

CREDITS: Presented by William Fox. Directed by Frank Borzage. Scenario by Bradley King. Titles by Elizabeth Pickett. Cinematography by Ernest Palmer.

*Note:* Working title was *The Pelican*.
Fox Film Corp. Eight reels, 7168 feet. Silent, B&W, 35mm. September 5, 1926.

## One Increasing Purpose

CAST: Edmund Lowe (Slim Paris), Lila Lee (Elizabeth Glade), Holmes Herbert (Charles Paris), May Allison (Linda Travers Paris), Huntley Gordon (Andrew Paris), Lawford Davidson (Dr. Byrne), Emily Fitzroy (Mrs. Andiron), George Irving (Mr. Glade), Josef Swickard (Old Gand), Jane Novak (Alice Paris), Nicholas Soussanin (Jule), Frank Elliott, Tom Maguire (Blinky), Gwynneth Bristowe (Mrs. Yeoman), Fisher White (Mr. Yeoman), Pat Somerset, Alma Rubens (uncredited).**
CREDITS: Presented by William Fox. Directed by Harry Beaumont. Assistant director James Dunne. Written by Bradley King. Based on the novel by A. S. M. Hutchinson. Cinematography by Rudolph Bergquist.
Fox Film Corp. Distributed by Fox Film Corp. B&W, silent. January 2, 1927.

## Heart of Salome

CAST: Alma Rubens (Helene), Walter Pidgeon (Monte Carroll), Holmes Herbert (Sir Humphrey), Robert Agnew (Redfern), Erin La Bissoniere (Helen's maid), Walter Dugan (Chauffer), Barry Norton (Henri Bezanne), Virginia Madison (Madame Bezanne).
CREDITS: Presented by William Fox. Directed by Victor Schertzinger. Assistant director William Tummel. Scenario by Randall H. Faye. Based on *The Heart of Salome* (Boston, c1925), by Allen Raymond. Cinematography by Glen MacWilliams. Edited by Margaret V. Clancey. Costume design by Kathleen Kay.
Fox Film Corp. B&W, 35mm, six reels, 5615 feet, silent. May 8, 1927.

## The Masks of the Devil

CAST: John Gilbert (Baron Reiner), Alma Rubens (Countess Zellner), Theodore Roberts (Count Palester), Frank Reicher (Count Zellner), Eva von Berne (Virginia), Ralph Forbes (Manfred), Ethel Wales (Virginia's Aunt), Polly Ann Young (dancer).
CREDITS: Directed by Victor Sjöström (as Victor Seastrom). Assistant director Harold S. Bucquet. Content by Frances Marion. Titles by Marian Ainslee and Ruth Cummings. Adaptation by Svend Gade. Based on *Die Masken Erwin Reiners* by Jakob Wassermann.
Cinematography by Oliver Marsh. Edited by Conrad A. Nervig. Sets by Cedric Gibbons. Costume design by Adrian. Song "Live and Love" by William Axt and David Mendoza.
Metro-Goldwyn-Mayer Pictures. Distributed by Metro-Goldwyn-Mayer Pictures. B&W, 35mm, eight reels, 5575 feet, silent/mono (Western Electric Sound System). November 17, 1928.

## She Goes to War

CAST: Eleanor Boardman (Joan), John Holland (Tom Pike), Edmund Burns (Reggie), Alma Rubens (Rosie), Al St. John (Bill), Glen Walters (Katie), Margaret Seddon

**A contemplative pose as photographed by Nickolas Muray.**

(Tom's mother), Yola d'Avril (Yvette), Evelyn Hall (Joan's aunt), Agostino Borgato (Major), Dina Smirnova (Joan's maid), Yvonne Starke (Major's wife), Edward Chandler (Top sergeant), Gretchen Hartman (knitting lady), Eulalie Jensen (Matron of Canteen), Ann Warrington (lady hostess), Florence Wix (knitting lady), Captain H. M. Zier (Major).

## PART III. Filmography

A scene from Alma's last film, 1929's *Showboat*.

CREDITS: Associate produced by Edward Halperin and Victor Halperin. Directed by Henry King. Scenario by Howard Estabrook. Titles by John Monk Saunders. Adaptation by Fred De Gresac. Based on *She Goes to War, and Other Stories* by Rupert Hughes (New York, c1929). Cinematography by John P. Fulton and Tony Gaudio. Art direction by Al D'Agostino and Robert M. Haas. Edited by Lloyd Nosler. Songs "Joan" and "There Is a Happy Land" by Harry Akst.
Inspiration Pictures. Distributed by United Artists. B&W, silent/mono (Western Electric Sound System), 87 minutes. B&W, 35mm, ten reels, 9550 feet. June 8, 1929.

## *Show Boat*

CAST—Prologue: Otis Harlan, Helen Morgan, Jules Bledsoe, Aunt Jemima, The Plantation Singers, Carl Laemmle, Florenz Ziegfeld.
CAST: Laura La Plante (Magnolia Hawks), Joseph Schildkraut (Gaylord Ravenal), Otis Harlan (Capt. Andy Hawks/Master of Ceremonies in prologue), Emily Fitzroy (Parthenia Ann Hawks), Alma Rubens (Julie), Elise Bartlett (Elly), Jack McDonald (Windy), Jane La Verne (Magnolia, as a child), Neely Edwards (Schultzy), Theodore Lorch (Frank), Stepin Fetchit (Joe), Gertrude Howard (Queenie), Ralph Yearsley (the killer), George Chesebro (Steve), Harry Holden (Means), Max Asher (utility man), Jim Coleman (stagehand), Carl Herlinger (wheelsman), Matthew 'Stymie' Beard (child, uncredited), Claude Collins (uncredited).
CREDITS: Presented by Carl Laemmle. Directed by Harry Pollard. Additional direction by Arch Heath. Editorial supervision by Edward J. Montaigne. Scenario by Charles Kenyon. Dialogue by Harry Pollard and Tom Reed. Based on the novel *Show Boat* (New York, 1926) by Edna Ferber. Cinematography by Gilbert Warrenton. Special

**A smiling Alma at the peak of her career.**

effects photography by Frank H. Booth. Edited by Edward J. Montagne, Maurice Pivar, and Daniel Mandell. Song "Look Down That Lonesome Road" by Gene Austin and Nathaniel Shilkret. Song "Here Comes That Show Boat" by Joseph Cherniavsky and Clarence J. Marks. Song "Ol' Man River" by Joseph Cherniavsky, Oscar Hammerstein II, and Jerome Kern. Recording engineered by C. Roy Hunter.

Art direction by Charles D. Hall. Costume design by Johanna Mathieson. Make-up by Jane Rene. Synchronisation by Joseph Cherniavsky.
Universal Pictures. Distributed by Universal Pictures. B&W, silent/mono (Western Electric Sound System), 147 minutes. B&W, 35mm, twelve reels, 11,650 feet. July 28, 1929.

# Appendix.
# Advertisements for Alma's Newspaper Autobiography

### "Why I Remain a Dope Fiend: The Most Amazing Confession Ever Told! Alma Rubens' Own Story, Written Personally by the Once Great Movie Star Who Was Ruined by Drugs."*

A Genuine, Authentic Story—Every Word Supported by Affidavits and Written Evidence. Not a So-Called 'Exposé' but Wholly and Solely THE TRUTH.

The lights of Broadway blazed with huge electric signs a few years ago announcing "ALMA RUBENS, AMERICA'S NEWEST STAR, in Fannie Hurst's 'HUMORESQUE.'"

Today, the front pages of the newspapers blaze forth the police news: "ALMA RUBENS, Dope Fiend, ARRESTED AS DOPE SMUGGLER."

Within that short space of a few years lies the greatest, most intimate and startling story of the rise and fall of a great screen star, ALMA RUBENS. It is a *true* story—far more interesting and amazing than any fiction you have ever read.

It is a story written by Alma Rubens herself. She tells of her struggle from the depths of poverty to the heights of stardom. The intimate details of Hollywood loves and marriages are intermingled with the greatest names that glorify the silver screen.

*An advertisement printed in the *New York Daily Mirror*, 9 January 1931, page 10.

A heart-rending story of Alma Rubens, great movie star at the top of the ladder looking down—and toppling over.

And then come unscrupulous doctors, nurses, narcotic agents. A hectic life amidst the night clubs of Broadway. Dope and more dope.

Society of Park Avenue enters and gobbles up Alma Rubens. Dope orgies follow and she finds herself hopelessly in the clutches of mankind's worst enemy—DOPE.

Eight months in a sanitarium. Alma Rubens sees what happens in a Dope Sanitarium. Inmates die horrible deaths. She herself suffers torture. All the details are told by her. But she lives and is discharged as "cured."

Alma Rubens stages a great comeback. Seventeen weeks in vaudeville. A happy girl. Then she meets a doctor. And dope against enters her life. Perhaps forevermore. Who knows?

Last Monday, Alma Rubens was arrested in San Diego. This story, however, was written weeks ago when everybody believed Alma Rubens had fought successfully to save herself. When Miss Rubens wrote the story she did not ask for pity. And you will not condemn her. Powerful forces were against her from birth. She did not willfully become a dope fiend. She did not purposely desert her movie career.

She had her struggles. Men followed her. Men sought her. Perhaps you think she was weak. Perhaps! But read her story. Put yourself in her place. Consider the men and women she met. Ponder over the handicaps she encountered.

Only thirty years old. Married three times to great names.

You must read the story. This is no cheap, tawdry sensationalism— it is stark, naked truth. The story will reveal to fathers and mothers the pitfalls which await their children. It will warn others of the dangers that beset success. It will teach others to be wary of the fiends that lurk in the shadows, ready to pounce upon their victims. This stirring document flashes the flood-light of publicity upon those human rats who viciously ensnare and bleed their prey from the first insidious dose of dope to the pitiful addict's grave.

DON'T MISS this autobiography... It is beyond all doubt the most dramatic, tragic story ever published. The first episode begins Tuesday, January 13th, in the DAILY MIRROR. Chapter by chapter, this great story will unfold. The gamut of human emotions will be stripped naked and exposed to the eyes and minds of every thinking man and woman.

## "Dope and Tears in Alma Rubens' Own Story."*

Alma Rubens Bares Her Soul—Starting in this issue of the Mirror, Alma Rubens tells the story of her life, which began stormily at the "turn of the century" in San Francisco, in a two-story frame house, numbered 13. You'll be moved when she tells of her early religious devotion; of how she stole the holy water; of her wish to be a nun, and later an actress; and of her desire for forbidden things, which might explain her dope crazing and her downfall!

*An advertisement printed in the *New York Daily Mirror*, 13 January 1931, page 1.

# Notes to Part I

## Introduction

1. Lamb, Grace. "Youth Speaking." *Motion Picture* Aug. 1920: 63.
2. Service, Faith. "Divine Discontent." *Motion Picture Classic* Oct. 1923: 22.
3. MacDonald, Margaret I. "A Man's Country." *Moving Picture World* 12 July 1919: 277.
4. Weitzel, Edward. "Critical Reviews and Comments: *Restless Souls*." *Moving Picture World* 1 Jan. 1919.
5. Service, p. 76.

## Life and Love

1. "Alma Rubens, Film Actress, Dies on Coast." *New York Herald Tribune* 23 Jan. 1931.
2. Throughout the chapter, the spelling of Alma's mother's name will appear as "Teresa," as it did on many formal documents and in numerous press clippings. However, in some documents and newspaper articles her name was spelled "Theresa."
3. This information stems from Alma Rubens's death certificate, released by the Registrar-Recorded of Los Angeles County, California. [Unfortunately, Alma's birth certificate seems lost, perhaps due to the San Francisco earthquake and resultant fires, or perhaps because one was never even recorded. Among the reasons to believe the 1897 birth year would be the 1910 U.S. Census, where John B. "Reuben" and family have a daughter age named "Alma G" listed at 13 years old.]
4. Collins, Frederick L. "Four Women Who Suffered." *Good Housekeeping* July 1932: 193.
5. "Alma Rubens, Film Actress, Dies on Coast." *New York Herald Tribune* 23 Jan. 1931.
6. Calhoun, Dorothy. "She Fought the Good Fight." *Motion Picture* May 1931: 30.
7. California Marriage License and Certificate Extract. Los Angeles County, Book #301, Page #99. [Farnum used his real name, William Franklyn Smith, on the marriage license. His last name "Smith" is the source of some modern publications which refer to Alma by the same last name.]
8. "Farnum Marries Rubens." *Motion Picture News* 10 Aug. 1918: 864.
9. Alma Smith vs. William Smith. Complaint–Divorce. Superior Court of the State of California, in and for the County of Los Angeles. 15 Aug. 1918.
10. Ibid.
11. Service, p. 22.
12. Ibid., p. 84.
13. "Flashes from the Eastern Stars." *Motion Picture Classic* February 1924: 56.
14. Alma G. Goodman vs. Daniel C. Goodman. Complaint–Divorce. Superior Court of the State of California in and for the County of Los Angeles. 3 Jan. 1924.
15. Ibid.
16. "Rubens Suit for Divorce Successful." *Los Angeles Times* 29 Jan. 1925.
17. Ibid.
18. "Film Star Repudiates Separation." *Los Angeles Times* 17 Sept. 1924: A1.
19. "Alma Rubens Asks Divorce." *Los Angeles Times* 11 Jan. 1925: 4.
20. "Alma Rubens an Heiress." *New York Times* 14 May 1925: 14.
21. "Alma Rubens, Film Actress, Dies on Coast." *New York Herald Tribune* 23 Jan. 1931.
22. "Film Pair United in Marriage." *Los Angeles Times* 31 Jan. 1926: 12.
23. A brief mention of their marriage plans

in the September 15, 1925 issue of *New York Times* claimed their forthcoming wedding would be on May 15, 1926.
24. "Alma Rubens to Marry Cortez." *New York Times* 15 Sept. 1925: 29.
25. "Film Pair United in Marriage," p. 12.
26. "Are They Married?" *Lincoln Star* (Nebraska) 14 Feb. 1926.
27. "Bigamy Quiz in Wedding of Actress." *Los Angeles Times* 2 Feb. 1926.
28. "Screen Pair Wedded All Over Again." *Los Angeles Times* 9 Feb. 1926: 8.
29. "Divorce of Screen Pair Under Way [sic]." *Los Angeles Times* 23 Sept. 1930
30. "Alma Rubens Asks Divorce." *Chronicle Telegram* (Elyria, Ohio) 23 Sept. 1930.

## Films and Acting

1. At times she has been credited as appearing in a 1913 film called *Banzai*, but this is unconfirmed and seems unlikely given the date when she first moved to Los Angeles.
2. "The Lorelei Madonna." *Moving Picture World* 17 July 1915: 538.
3. "The Lorelei Madonna." *Moving Picture World* 10 July 1915: 319.
4. "*Peer Gynt* with Cyril Maude in Films." *Moving Picture World* 10 July 1915: 310. [Whether or not Alma actually appeared in the film is difficult to determine.]
5. "Triangle Film Incorporated." *Moving Picture World* 31 July 1915.
6. A brief review of *A Model's Adventure* appears in *Moving Picture World* 4 Dec. 1915: 1852.
7. Montanye, Lillian. "Alma Rubens Comes Out of the West." *Motion Picture Magazine* March 1920: 36–37.
8. Cooper, Oscar. "*The Half-Breed*." *Motion Picture News* 22 July 1916: 452.
9. Howe, Herbert. "Meet the Duchess!" *Photoplay* July 1923: 39.
10. Weitzel, Edward. "Triangles." *Moving Picture World* 1 Dec. 1917: 1337.
11. "Triangle Forges Further Ahead." *Motion Picture News* 5 Jan. 1918: 95.
12. "Alma Rubens and Harry Mestayer Lead Triangle Aug. 1." *Moving Picture World* 24 Aug. 1918: 1138.
13. McElravy, Robert C. "*The Ghost Flower*." *Moving Picture World*: 31 Aug. 1918: 1302.
14. "*The Ghost Flower*." *Motion Picture News* 24 Aug. 1918: 1213.
15. Two-page advertisement. *Motion Picture News* 5 Apr. 1919.
16. MacDonald, Margaret I. "*Diane of the Green Van*." *Moving Picture World* 19 April 1919: 429.
17. Reid, Lawrence. "*A Man's Country*." *Motion Picture News* 12 July 1919: 603.
18. Montanye, p. 37.
19. MacDonald, Margaret L. "*Humoresque*." *Moving Picture World* 15 May 1920.
20. As an example, see "Three Interviews" in *Motion Picture Magazine* of September 1925, page 86.
21. "The Screen." Rev. of *Humoresque*. *New York Times* 31 May 1920.
22. "The Screen." Rev. of *The World and His Wife*. *New York Times* 19 July 1920: 16.
23. Weitzel, Edward. "*The World and His Wife*." *Moving Picture World* 31 July 1920: 638.
24. "From Poem, to Play, to Film." *Motion Picture News* 3 July 1920: 247.
25. Reid, Lawrence. "*Thoughtless Women*." *Motion Picture News* 27 Nov. 1920: 4157.
26. Robb, Jessie. "*Thoughtless Women*." *Moving Picture World* 1 Jan. 1921: 97.
27. "Expect Record Bookings on Pioneer Release." *Motion Picture News* 4 Dec. 1920: 4281.
28. Lamb, p. 103.
29. "*The Valley of Silent Men*." *Photoplay*. Nov. 1922: 66.
30. "The Screen: Men, Money, and Madness." Rev. of *Enemies of Women*. 1 Apr. 1923: 5.
31. "The Screen: The Carmine Cassock [sic]." Rev. of *Under the Red Robe*. *New York Times* 13 Nov. 1923: 25.
32. Rev. of *Under the Red Robe*. *Motion Picture Classic* Feb. 1924.
33. Lamb, p. 103.
34. "The Screen: Love After Forty." Rev. of *Cytheria*. *New York Times* 26 May 1924: 21.
35. Kennedy, Thomas. "*Cytherea*." *Motion Picture News* 3 May 1924.
36. "To Feature Alma Rubens." *Film Daily* 3 Feb. 1925: 2.
37. "Three Interviews." *Motion Picture*. Sept. 1925: 86.
38. "*East Lynn*." *Film Daily* 1 Nov. 1925: 5.
39. "*Fine Clothes*." *Motion Picture News* 15 Aug. 1925.
40. "*Fine Clothes*." *Moving Picture World* 15 Aug 1925.
41. Hall, Mordaunt. "The Screen." Rev. of *Fine Clothes*. *New York Times* 20 Oct. 1925: 28.
42. Undated fan magazine notice in the Alma Rubens file at the Margaret Herrick Library.
43. Hall, Mordaunt. "The Screen." Rev. of *The Heart of Salome*. *New York Times* 6 June 1927: 27.
44. "Actress in Court Fight with Agent." *Los Angeles Times* 19 Apr. 1927: A15.
45. Beauchamp, Cari. *Without Lying Down: Frances Marion and the Powerful Women of Early Hollywood*. New York: Scribner, 1997: 223.
46. Service, p. 84.

## Drugs and Death

1. Lamb, p. 103.
2. "Alma Rubens to Go to State Institution."

New York Times 27 Feb. 1929: 16. [Along with Alma's own behavior, the press also reported on the arrest of her janitor. The Los Angeles Times of December 15, 1928 ran a story about him "prowling under the bedroom window of [Alma's] home." They did not do a follow-up story, but did write on November 22, 1928 the first of a series of articles on Alma's maid, Edna Clayton. Apparently Clayton was driving Alma's car when it collided with another vehicle. Clayton and the passengers of the other vehicle got into a fight in which Clayton hit them. She was arrested, and Alma—emphatically denying any involvement—posted bail. The Los Angeles Times of April 23, 1929 wrote that at trial Clayton was found guilty.]
3. "Alma Rubens, Film Actress, Dies on Coast." New York Herald Tribune 23 Jan. 1931.
4. "Alma Rubens in Wild St. Scene," p. 8.
5. "Judge Raps Actress on Tardiness." Los Angeles Times 9 Jan. 1929: A9.
6. "Alma Rubens Put in a Sanitarium." New York Times 26 Jan. 1929: 3.
7. Ibid., p. 3.
8. The article "Alma Rubens in Wild St. Scene." [Edwardsville Intelligencer (Edwardsville, Illinois) 28 Jan. 1929.] speaks about an aunt of Alma's named "A. Driscoll" that she stayed with her for a time in 1928.
9. "Alma Rubens Put in a Sanitarium," p. 3.
10. "Miss Rubens Shown to be a Drug Addict." New York Times 17 Feb. 1929.
11. Ibid.
12. "Alma Rubens Recovering." New York Times 18 Feb. 1929: 4.
13. "Alma Rubens Re-enters Sanitarium." New York Times 19 Feb. 1929: 9.
14. "Alma Rubens Reported Sinking." New York Times 26 Feb. 1929: 10.
15. "Alma Rubens to Go to State Institution, p. 16.
16. "Victim of Drug Makes Life Fight." Los Angeles Times 26 Feb. 1929: A1.
17. Collins, p. 194.
18. Ibid., p. 194.
19. "Alma Rubens Shows Gain." New York Times 5 Mar. 1929: 22.
20. "Indicted in Rubens Case." New York Times 16 Mar. 1929: 7.
21. "Alma Rubens' Name Injected into Fields' Medical Fight." Los Angeles Times 21 Sept. 1939: 16.
22. "Alma Rubens Leaves Hospital." New York Times 17 Apr. 1929: 56.
23. "Alma Rubens in Asylum." New York Times 17 May 1929: 29.
24. Ibid., p. 29.
25. "Rubens Ring Prompts Quiz." Los Angeles Times 18 Apr. 1929: A17..
26. "Questions Alma Rubens." New York Times 25 May 1929: 2.

27. "Alma Rubens Recovers." New York Times 16 Nov. 1929: 24.
28. "Alma Rubens Released." New York Times 22 Dec. 1929: sec. 2, p. 2.
29. Ibid., sec. 2, p. 2. [Los Angeles Times of December 22, 1929 also reported on this story, but in their version it was not a ranch belonging to Alma's mother that would the site of the convalescence, but instead it would be Alma's "sister's ranch."]
30. Ibid., sec. 2, p. 2.
31. Collins, p. 193.
32. "Alma Rubens Coming Here." New York Times 10 Feb. 1930: 19.
33. Ibid., p. 19.
34. Information culled from the "Route Department" section of Billboard for March 15, 1930 (p. 55), April 12, 1930 (p. 57), and April 26, 1930 (p. 55).
35. Information culled from the "Route Department" section of Billboard for May 3, 1930 (p. 53), May 10, 1930 (p. 51), May 17, 1930 (p. 51), and May 24, 1930 (p. 51).
36. "New Acts Reviewed in New York: Alma Rubens." Billboard 31 May, 1930: 14.
37. "Vaudeville Reviews: E. F. Albee, Cincinnati." Billboard 21 June 1930: 16.
38. Montanye, p. 37.
39. "Theater News." New York Herald Tribune 13 Oct. 1931.
40. Mefford, Arthur. "Physician Blamed for Her Plight." New York Daily Mirror 6 Jan 1931: 3.
41. Mefford, Arthur. "Alma 'Feeling' Death, Feared End Like Julia's." New York Daily Mirror 23 Jan 1931: 3.
42. "Cortez Aids Defense in Libel Suit." Los Angeles Times 24 June 1932: A3.
43. "Milestones." Time 2 Feb. 1931: 18.
44. Mefford, "Alma 'Feeling' Death," p. 10.
45. Ibid, p. 10.
46. Mefford, Arthur. "Arrest of Alma Rubens Starts Big Dope Round-Up." New York Daily Mirror 7 Jan. 1931: 3.
47. "Alma Rubens, Film Actress, Dies on Coast." New York Herald Tribune 23 Jan. 1931.
48. "Alma Rubens Dies; Former Film Star." New York Times 22 Jan. 1931: 23.
49. Alma Rubens death certificate, released by the Registrar-Recorded of Los Angeles County, California.
50. "Miss Rubens Dies from Pneumonia." Los Angeles Times 22 Jan. 1931: A1.
51. Calhoun, Dorothy. "She Fought the Good Fight." Motion Picture. May 1931: 30.
52. "Film World Pays Tribute to Alma Rubens in Death." New York Daily Mirror 23 Jan. 1931: 3.
53. "Tribute Paid to Alma Rubens." Los Angeles Times 25 Jan. 1931: A1.
54. "Alma Rubens, Film Actress, Dies on Coast."

55. Calhoun, p. 30.
56. "Shade of Alma Rubens Rises in Federal Court." *Los Angeles Times* 23 July 1931: 8.
57. "Alma Rubens' Name Injected into Fields' Medical Fight," p. 16.
58. Photo in the Alma Rubens file at the Margaret Herrick Library. Academy of Motion Picture Arts and Sciences. Beverly Hills, California.

## A Note on the Memoir

1. Reel, Rob. "Rob Is Glad He Lives in America after *Siberia*." *Chicago American* 6 Apr. 1926.
2. Calhoun, Dorothy. "She Fought the Good Fight." *Motion Picture*. May 1931: 117.
3. "Alma Rubens Libel Suit Settled." Unidentified clipping dated February 3, 1932, found in the Alma Rubens file at the Margaret Herrick Library. Motion Picture Academy of Arts and Sciences. Beverly Hills, California. [An article in the *Los Angeles Times* of August 6, 1931 claimed that the basis of the libel charges were *Photoplay*'s claims that Teresa intentionally kept Ricardo Cortez from learning of Alma's decreasing health so that no divorce could occur before her death. *Photoplay* had also written about Teresa's "pathetic" attempts to bolster attendance at Alma's funeral. Later, the August 2, 1932 *Los Angeles Times* reported that Teresa's libel suit had ended in a hung jury.]
4. Teresa died in 1940 in San Joaquin County, California.
5. Some issues and/or pages of the *New York Daily Mirror* are absent from microfilm during the period in which Alma's autobiography was published. Hence, we utilized a second newspaper that serialized it, the *Seattle Post-Intelligencer*, in order to supplement missing sections of the text. Their version, which seems more complete overall compared to existing issues of the *Daily Mirror*, sometimes condensed chapters and even rewrote some sections, perhaps for reasons of space. Our presentation then represents a careful synthesis of both newspaper runs, using the *Post-Intelligencer*'s chapter numbering system (which is the more complete), while still privileging as much as possible the text in the *Daily Mirror*, given that it was the original source. The authors have taken extreme care in amalgamating the source material.

# Index

Numbers in **_bold italics_** indicate pages with photographs.

Acosta, Jorge 11
Actor's Equity Association 75
Adams, Evangeline 186
Adams, Katherine 208
"Aileen" 186, 187, 188, 192
Aitken, Spottiswoode 199, 201, 203, 204, 216
Aitken, Thomas 9
"Alexander's Ragtime Band" 58
"Alfred" 177
"Alice" 173, 174, 175, 176
*Aloma of the South Seas* (1926) 88
*The Americano* (1917) 10, **_203_**
Anderson, G.M. "Bronco Billy" 54, 55, 56, 57, 58, 60, 61, 66
Anger, Kenneth 2, 36
*Anna Karenina* 90
"Annetta" 191, 192, 193
*Another Foolish Virgin* see *The Love-Brokers*
*The Answer* (1918) 12, 207
Apfel, Oscar 200
Arbuckle, Fatty 2
Associated Exhibitors 217
Associated First National Pictures 215
Avezzanae, Prince 11
Ayres, Agnes 87

Bainbridge, Sherman 199
"Ballad of Reading Gaol" 131
*Banzai* (1913) 199
Bara, Theda 83
Barker, Reginald 11
Barnett, Zoe 60, 61
Barnum, P.T. 56
"The Baron" 160, 161, 163, 164, 179, 186, 187
"The Baroness" 160, 161, 163, 164, 165, 179, 186, 187

Barrie, Nigel 209
Barrymore, John 46
Barrymore, Lionel 18, 146, 213
Beaumont, Harry 221
Bellamy, Madge 11, 22, 217
The Belmont (New York) 31
Bennett, Constance 21, 215
Biggers, Earl Derr 12
*The Billboard* 30
"Billy" see "Mr. Dee"
*The Birth of a Nation* (1915) 199
*Blaze Derringer* 203
Bledsoe, Jules 223
*Blue Blood* see *The Regenerates*
Boardman, Eleanor 25, 221
"Bobby" 180
Borzage, Frank 12, 15, 17, 23, 208, 210, 213, 220
Broder, Edith 31
Browning, Tod 201, 202
Bruns, Julia 109, 155, 195, 196, 197, 198

C.B.C. Film Sales 215
Cabanne, Christy 37, 74, 200, 201, 217
California State Asylum for the Insane see Patton State Hospital
Carewe, Edwin 108
Carewe, Rita 108, 110
Carpentier, Georges 168
Catlett, Walter 60
Cavany, Christy see Cabanne, Christy
Chaney, Lon 14, 210
Chaplin, Charlie 73, 76
"Charlotte" 184, 185, 188
*The Children Play* (1916) 10, 202
Chopin, Frederic 143

235

Church Around the Corner (Los Angeles) 79
Citron, Dr. L. Jesse 26, 28, 36
*The Clansman: An Historical Romance of the Ku Klux Klan* 200
Cody, Lew 145, 213
Cohill, William 215
*The Cold Deck* (1917) 10, 205
The Coliseum (New York) 30
Columbia Pictures 215
Commodore Hotel (New York) 83, 85
Compton Sanitarium (South Gate, CA) 94, 95
*Confessions of an English Opium Eater* 51
Conway, Jack **24**
Cooper, Miriam 199, 202
Cortez, Ricardo "Ric" 6, **7**, 8, **11**, 27, 32, 36, 40, 87–99, 101, 103, 104, 107, 108, 113, 121, 122, 123, 131, 138, 139, 141, 144, 145, 146, 153, 154, 155, 156, 166, 184, 197
*Cosmopolitan Magazine* 210
Cosmopolitan Productions 5, 15, 16, 17, 18, 84, 85, 87, 210, 211, 213, 214
Costello, Maurice 21, 46, 214
Crawford, Joan 210
Criterion Theatre (New York) 15
Crosland, Alan 18, 213, 214
Crowell, Josephine 199
*Cytherea* (1924) 21, 87, 215
*Cytherea, Goddess of Love* 215

*The Dancers* (1925) 22, 217
*Daily Mirror* see *New York Daily Mirror*
Dalton, Dorothy 81
Darling, Love 76
Darling, Ruth 9, 202, 212
Davenport, Dorothy 122, 123
David W. Griffith Corp. 200
Davies, Marion **11**, 15
De Grasse, Sam 201, 202
de la Cruz, Juan 200
DeMille, Cecil B. 81
Dempsey, Jack 168
De Quincey, Thomas 51, 122
Desmond, William 10, 81, 200, 204
*Diane of the Green Van* (1919) 14, 209, 210
Distinctive Pictures 214
Dixon, Thomas 200
"Dr. A." 86, 166
"Dr. B." 86
"Dr. C." 92, 93, 94, 96, 97, 98, 99, 100, 101, 102, 103, 104, 105, 106, 107
"Dr. D." 98
"Dr. E." 105
"Dr. Exclusive" 157, 158, 159
"Dr. F." 116, 117, 118
"Dr. P." 106, 107, 110, 111, 112
Dodge, Dr. "Old Doc" Washington 39, 42
"Don" 176–182
Dowlan, William C. 208
*Dracula* 21, 51, 185
Driscoll, Genevieve see Rubens, Alma
Dwan, Allan 9, 77, 201

Eagels, Jeanne 155
*East Lynne* (1925) 23, **218**, 219
Echegaray, José 210
"Edna" 161, 163, 164, 173, 174, 192
Edward Small Agency 24
Edwards, Walter 204, 206
Eliot, George 51
Elvey, Maurice 217
Emerson, John 10, 75, 201, 203
*Enemies of Women* (1923) 17, 18, 85, 146, 213
Epoch Producing Corp. 200
Equity Pictures 214
Exhibitors Mutual Distributing Corp. 210

*Facing the Music* see *Reggie Mixes In*
Fairbanks, Douglas 9, 10, 11, 76, 77, 78, 145, 200, 201, 203
*The Fall of Babylon* (1919) 211, 212
*False Ambition* (1918) 12, 208
Famous Players-Lasky Corp. 89, 90, 200, 210, 211, 213
Farnum, Franklyn 3, 4, 78, 79, 80
*Fashions for Men* 23
Federated Women's Club 197
Ferber, Edna 223
Ferguson, Elsie 20
Fetchit, Stepin 223
Fields, W.C. 36
58th Street Theater (New York) 30
*Film Daily* 23
*Find the Woman* (1922) 212, **213**
Fine Arts Film Co. 74, 75, 76, 77, 200, 201, 202, 203, 204
*Fine Clothes* (1925) 23, 218, 219
*The Firefly of Tough Luck* (1917) 10, 205
First National Pictures 21, 87, 219
*The First Year* 22
Fitzmaurice, George 87, 215
Fleming, Victor 77, 203
Flynn, Emmett J. **11**, 22, 23, 217, 219
Foo, Henry see Tape, Henry
*The Fool of the Family* 175
*The Forbidden Way* see *Cytherea*
The Fordham (New York) 30
Forest Lawn Cemetery (Glendale, CA) 36
Fox, Finis 108
Fox, William 217, 219, 220, 221
Fox Film Corp. 22, 23, 217, 219, 220, 221
"Frances" 193–195
Frisco, Joe 88
Fulton, Maude 56
Futurism 18

*The Gangsters and the Girl* (1914) 8, 199
Garbo, Greta 6, 23
Gardella, Tess "Aunt Jemima" 223
Garfield, John 210
Garsson, Murray W. 217
Garsson Enterprises 217
Gates, Crane, and Earl Funeral Home 36
*Gerald Cranston's Lady* (1924) 22, 216, 217

Index 237

*The Ghost Flower* (1918) 12, 208
Giblyn, Charles 199
Gilbert, John 24, 221
*The Gilded Butterfly* (1926) 23, 219
*The Girl at the Gate* 56, 58, 59, 68
Gish, Lillian 10, 76, 199, 201, 202
Glass, Gaston 15, 85, 210
Golden-Smith, John 22
Goldwyn, Samuel 215
Goldwyn-Cosmopolitan Distributing Corp. 214
Goldwyn Distributing Corp. 213
*Good Housekeeping* 27
Goodman, Dr. Daniel Carson **4**, 5, 6, 7, **10**, 16, 20, 81, 82, 83, 84, 85, 86, 87, 89, 212, 214
Gordon, Vera 15, 16, 210
*The Gown of Destiny* (1918) 12, 205
*El Gran galeoto* 210
Grauman, Sid 46, 47, 48, 58
Grauman's Theatre 45, 46
Gray, Gilda 88
Griffith, D.W. 9, 14, 74, 75, 76, 200, 201, 202, 212
Griffith, David Wark *see* Griffith, D.W.
Griffith, E.H. 20, 214
Guinan, Texas 12, 78, 207
Gunn, Charles 205

*The Half-Breed* (1916) 10, 76, 77, 78, 145, 201
Halperin, Edward 223
Halperin, Victor 223
Hamilton, Cosmo 208
Hamilton, Gilbert P. 208
Hammerstein, Arthur 81
Hammerstein, Oscar, II 224
Hansen, Juanita 3, 53
Harlan, Otis 223
Harris, Mildred 11, 75, 205
Harris, Sam 30
Harrison Narcotics Tax Act 28
Hart, Phil 67
Hart, William S. 10, 11, 77, 78, 203, 205
Harte, Bret 201
Hayes, Michael 6
Hayes, Uncle Tom 124, 125, 167
Hearst, William Randolph 5, 15, 18
*The Heart of Salome* (1927) **22**, 23, 221
Heffron, Thomas N. 208
"Helen" 174, 175, 176
*Helen of Troy* 90
"Henry" 71, 72
Herbert, H.J. 214
Herbert, Holmes 24, 25, 221
Hergesheimer, Joseph 215
Herrick, L.E. 197
Hersholt, Jean 23, 218
Hesser, Edwin Bower **10**
Hill, E.C. **11**
Hill, Jack **11**
*Hollywood Babylon* 2, 36

Hollywood Boulevard 25
Hollywood Hospital 26, 94, 95
Hollywood Walk of Fame ix, 25
Holmes, Helen 201
Hopper, E. Mason 205, 207
*The House of Bondage* 175
Huban, Eileen 212
Hughes, Rupert 223
*Humoresque* (1920) 15, 16, 31, 50, 85, 145, 210, 211, 227
Hunt, Marie 197
Hurst, Fannie 210, 227
Hutchinson, A.S.M. 221
Hutton, F. Laws 210

*I Love You* (1918) 12, 205, **206**
Ibsen, Henrik 200
*In the Carquinez Woods* 201
Ince, Thomas 5, 9, 14, 78, 199, 203, 204, 205
Ingraham, Lloyd 202
Inspiration Pictures 223
International Film Service Co. 211
*Intolerance* (1916) 9, 14, 201, 202, 212
"Irma" 180, 181
*Is Love Everything?* (1924) 217

"Jack, the Giant Killer" 117
Jackson, Ben **11**
Jemima, Aunt *see* Gardella, Tess "Aunt Jemima"
Jensen 152, 153
Jensen, Early 28
"Jimmy" 71, 72
John Swett Grammar School (San Francisco) 42
Johnson, Arthur 45
Jones, Buck **11**
Joyce, Thomas F. 27, 28, 113
*Judith of the Cumberlands* (1916) 201
Juno, Beverly 76

Kalem 9
Kay-Bee Pictures 199, 203, 205
Kennedy, Margaret 175
Kern, Jerome 224
Kerry, Norman 21, 80, 212, 215
Keystone Film Co. 201
King, Henry 24, 25, 223
King, Joe 207, 213
King George Roof (Santa Monica) 80
Kirkwood, James 22, 216
Kittrelle, Richard 6
"Kitty" 183
Kolker, Henry 210
Kranz, Jacob *see* Cortez, Ricardo
Kyne, Nellie 45

*Lady Chatterley's Lover* 172, 173, 184, 186, 197
Laemmle, Carl 223
Laemmle, Edward 218
La France, Rose *see* Rubens, Alma

# Index

La Marr, Barbara 195
Lane, Charles 220
La Plante, Laura 25, 223
Large, Bruce 28, 62, 63, 66
Large, Hazel 35, 41, 42, 62, 63, 65, 66, 195
Lee, Lila 221
Lee, Rowland V. **11**
*Lightnin'* 22
Lince, John 205
Lind, Jenny 58
Little Church of the Flowers (Glendale, CA) **35**, 36
"London" 165
Loos, Anita 10, 75, 201, 202, 203
*The Lorelei Madonna* (1915) 8, **9**, 66, 67, 200
*Los Angeles Times* 6, 27, 35
Louis B. Mayer Productions 23, 219
Love, Bessie 9, 76, 200, 201
Love, Motagu 146, 210, 214
*The Love Brokers* (1918) 12, 207
*Lovers?* (1927) 210
Lowe, Edmund **11**, 23, 219, 221
Lugosi, Bela 21, 214
Lyle, Eugene P. 203
Lynch, John 14, 17
Lytell, Bert 23, 219

"M." 96, 97
MacRae, Henry 215
"Madame Beaucaire" 70, 71, 72, 74
*Madame Sphinx* (1918) 12, **207**, 208
Madison Productions 215
Maloney, Leo D. 201
*Manhattan Madness* (1916) 77
*A Man's Country* (1919) 14, 15, 210
Mantell, Robert 146, 213
"Marie" 69, 70, 71, 72, 73, 74
Marion, Frances 15, 16, 24, 210, 215
*The Mark of Zorro* (1920) 77
Marmont, Percy 23, 218
"Marriage License?" (1926) 23, 220, 221
Marsh, Mae 75, 199, 202
Marshall, Tully 211
Masen, LeRoy 108
*The Masks of the Devil* (1928) 24, 221
*Master of His Home* (1917) 10, 204
Maude, Cyril 200
Maughan, Somerset 175
Mayer, Louis B. 218
Mayo, Frank **17**, 215, 217
McCohn, Judge 113
McDonald, Wallace 207
McGowan, J.P. 201
McGrail, Walter 23, 216, 217, 220
McGrath, May I. 197
"McHugh" 197
Meyer, Dr. Emil W. 25
MGM Pictures 24, 210, 221
"Midas" *see* "Mr. L"
Minter, Mary Miles 74
"Mr. Dee" 160–170, 176, 191, 192

"Mr. L" 186–188, 192
"Mr. R" 187, 192–194
"Mr. S—" 168
"Mr. T" 185
"Mr. X" 177, 178, 179, 180, 181, 182
Mizner, Wilson 111, 112
*The Model's Adventure* (1916) 9
Molnar, Ferenc 23
*Monks Are Monks* 175
Mooney, Margaret 9, 202, 212
Moore, Colleen 76
Morgan, Helen 223
Morosco, Oliver 9
*Mosaic* 175
*Motion Picture Classic* 1, 18
*Motion Picture Magazine* 1, 9, **15**, 16
*Motion Picture News* 10, 12, 14, 16, 23
Mountain View Cemetery (Fresno, CA) 36
*Moving Picture World* 8, 9, 14, 15, 23
"Mrs. Blank" 158, 159
"Mrs. Dee" 168
Mulhall, Jack 23, 217
Muray, Nickolas 222
"Murray" 68
Mutual Film Corp. 199, 201
Myers, Carmel 76
Myers, Dr. Emil 112
*The Mystery of the Leaping Fish* (1916) 9, 200

*The Narcotic Spectre* (1914) 8, 199
Nathan, George Jean 175
Nazimova, Alla 20
Negulesco, Jean 210
*New York Daily Mirror* **31**, 32, 33, 37, 227, 228, 229
*New York Herald Tribune* 34, 214
New York Motion Picture Corp. 203, 205
*New York Times* 15, 16, 18, 21, 22, 23, 24, 25, 26, 28
Nirdlinger, Charles Frederic 210
Normand, Mabel 68, 69, 73, 74, 146, 155, 195
Novarro, Ramon 210

O'Brien, George 22, 217
*Of Human Bondage* 175
Oland, Warner 23
*An Old Fashioned Boy* (1917) 204
*An Old Fashioned Young Man* see *An Old Fashioned Boy*
Oliver Morosco Photoplay Company 200
*One Increasing Purpose* (1927) 221
Owen, Seena 204

*The Painted Lily* (1918) 12, 208
Palmer, Ruth 32, 33, 34, 36, 195, 196, 198
Paramount-Artcraft Pictures 210, 211
Paramount Pictures 200, 213
Parker, Albert 214
Parsons, Louella O. **11**
"Paterson" 197

Index 239

Pathé 81, 83, 84
Patton State Hospital (Patton, CA) 28, 93, 114, 122–153, 155, 156, 170, 197
Paul, Maury 11
Pavlova, Anna 51
Pearce, Peggy 208
*Peer Gynt* (1915) 9, 200
"Peggy" 180, 181
*The Pelican* see *"Marriage License?"*
Pflueger, Dr. Charles 34, 35
*Photoplay* 11, 17, 37
Photoplay Publishing Company 37
Pickford, Jack 81
Pickford, Mary 20
Pidgeon, Walter 23, 220, 221
Pioneer Film Corp. 212
Pitts, ZaSu 23, 218
Plantation Singers 223
Poe, Edgar Allan 122
Pollard, Harry 223
Pretty, Grace 76
*The Price She Paid* (1924) 215
Purviance, Edna 73

Rambeau, Marjorie 109
Ray, Charles 8, 81, 199, 204
Raymond, Allen 221
*Real Detective* **33**, 37
*The Regenerates* (1917) 11, 12, 205
The Regent (Patterson, NJ) 30
*Reggie Mixes In* (1916) 9, 200
Reid, Wallace 2, 3, 54, 92, 108, 122, 155, 195, 199
Reid, Wally see Reid, Wallace
*The Rejected Woman* (1924) 21, 214, 215
*Restless Souls* (1919) 14, **24**, 208, **209**
Reuben, Alma see Rubens, Alma
Reubens, Alma Genevieve see Rubens, Alma
Reubens, Hazel see Large, Hazel
Reubens, John B. 3, 4, 36, 40, 41, 42, 45, 46, 47, 48, 54, 58, 62, 64, 76, 79, 80, 81, 82, 138
Reubens, Teresa 3, 4, **5**, 6, 26, 27, 28, 32, 34, 35, 36, 37, 39, 40, 41, 42, 44, 45, 47, 48, 50, 54, 58, 59, 62, 64, 78, 79, 80, 82, 84, 85, 87, 89, 91, 92, 93, 95, 96, 97, 98, 101, 103, 104, 105, 106, 107, 108, 110, 111, 113, 114, 118, 119, 120, 121, 122, 123, 131, 138, 139, 141, 144, 145, 146, 153, 154, 155, 172, 186, 195, 198
Reubens, Theresa Hayes see Reubens, Teresa
Reynolds, Lynn F. 205
"Ric" see Cortez, Ricardo "Ric"
Rich, Irene 21, 215
Robertson-Cole Co. 210
Rock, William 56, 57, 66
Roscoe, Albert 210
Ruben, Alma see Rubens, Alma
Rubens, Alma **2**, **5**, **7**, **9**, **10**, **11**, **12**, **13**, **14**, **15**, **17**, **18**, **19**, **20**, **21**, **22**, **23**, **24**, **26**, **27**, **29**, **31**, **32**, **34**, **35**, **201**, **203**, **204**, **206**, **207**, **209**, **211**, **213**, **214**, **215**, **216**, **217**, **218**, **220**, **222**, **223**, **224**; acting career 3, 4, 8–25, 30, 31, 32; 51, 54–69, 74, 75, 76, 77, 78, 81, 83, 84, 85, 97, 102, 145, 156, 172, 184, 196, 197, 199–229; Australian inheritance 6; Beverly Juno pseudonym 76; birth 3, 39, 40; death and funeral 34, 35, 36; drug use 2, 3, 24–34, 36, 38, 43, 51, 62, 86–99, 103–117, 121, 122, 127, 138, 139, 143, 144, 145, 153–198, 227, 228, 229; early life 3, 4, 39–54; Genevieve Driscoll pseudonym 26; Grace Howard pseudonym 42; institutionalized care 25, 26, 27, 30; marriage to Daniel Carson Goodman 5, 6, 81, 82, 83, 84, 85, 86, 89; marriage to Franklyn Farnum 4, 78, 79, 30, 81; marriage to Ricardo Cortez 6, 7, 8, **26**, **27**, 32, 40, 87–99, 101, 102, 103, 104, 107, 108, 113, 121, 122, 123, 131, 138, 139, 141, 144, 145, 146, 153, 154, 155, 156, 166, 184, 197; Rose La France pseudonym 42, 43, 45, 46, 47, 56, 58, 60, 61, 62, 65, 66, 67, 75, 76, 137; sanitariums 25–28, 94, 95, 100, 101, 102, 103, 104, 105, 112–153, 155, 156, 170, 184, 197, 228; Winsome Stars 14, 15, 210
Rueben, Alma see Rubens, Alma
Ruggles, Charles 200
Russianism 18

S. A. Lynch Enterprises Inc. 205
Sacred Heart Church (San Francisco) 42
Sacred Heart Convent (San Francisco) 3, 54
San Francisco earthquake 42
San Quentin Penitentiary 146, 148, 149
San Remo Hotel (New York) 86
Sands, Edward 73
Sands, George 51
Santa Monica Hospital 28
Schertzinger, Victor 219
Schmidt, Margaret 39, 40
Seastrom, Victor see Sjöström, Victor
Selovus, Annette 69
Sennett, Mack 9, 68, 69
*She Goes to War* (1929) 25, 221, 222, 223
*She Goes to War, and Other Stories* 223
*She Wolves* (1925) 23, 217
Shertzinger, Victor **11**, 221
Ship Café (Santa Monica) 80
Shoelwer, Mrs. W.H. 108
*Show Boat* (1929) 25, 97, 98, 144, 197, **223**, 224
*Siberia* (1926) 23, 36, 219, **220**
Sidney, Scott 8, 199
Signal Film Corp. 201
Simonds, Adele L. 196
Sjöström, Victor 24, 221
*Soldiers of Misfortune* 68
Somerville, Roy 200
Southern California State Hospital for the Insane see Patton State Hospital
Spadra State Hospital for Drug Addicts (California) 27, 28, 112, 113, 114, 115, 121, 128
Stahl, John M. 210, 219

Standard Casting Directory 215
Stark, Pauline 76
Stern, G.B. 175
Stoker, Bram 51, 122
Stone, Lewis 21, 23, 215, 218
Storm, Jerome 204
Straight Arrow 36
Strand Theater **16**
Sturgeon, Roland *see* Sturgeon, Rollin S.
Sturgeon, Rollin S. 8, 66, 67, 200
Swanson, Gloria 81
Sweet, Blanche 54

Talmadge, Constance 202, 211
Talmadge, Norma 46
Tape, Henry 109, 121, 122, 178, 194
Taylor, William Desmond 2, 73, 74
Tec-Art Studio 108
Tellegen, Lou 23, 219
Terriss, Tom 212
Terry, Alice 210
*This Bright World Again* 37, 39–198
Thomas, Olive 2, 81, 108, 195
*Thoughtless Women* (1920) 16, 83, 84, **212**
"Tilly" *see* "Mrs. Dee"
"Tommy" 180, 193
"Tony" 63, 64, 65, 66
*Torrent* (1926) 6, 23
Tri-Stone Pictures 206
Triangle Film Corporation 4, 9, 10, 11, 12, 14, 25, 78, 81, 200, 201, 202, 203, 204, 205, 206, 207, 208
*Truthful Tulliver* (1917) 10, 78, 203
Tuxedo Tobacco 216

Uhl, Elizabeth 108, 110
*Under the Red Robe* (1923) 18, 20, 146, 213
United Artists 223
Universal Pictures 25, 218, 224
Urban, Joseph 18

*The Valley of Silent Men* (1922) 17, 145, 213
Veiller, Bayard 18

Vignola, Robert G. 210
*Virgin Soil* 84
Vitagraph 8, **9**, 66
von Stroheim, Count Erich 201

Walsh, Raoul 199
Walthall, Henry 199
Wark Producing Corp. 202
Warner Bros. 210
Warren, Helen 76
Warwick Hotel 27
Webster, Dr. 149, 152
*Week End Husbands* (1924) 20, 214
Welty, Ruth 31
West, Charles 208
Western Electric Sound System 221, 223, 224
Western Vitagraph Studios 200
Westover, Winifred 77, 78
*The Wheel* 22
White, Pearl 53
Wilde, Oscar 131
"Wilhelmina" 183
*The Winding Stair* (1925) 23, 219
Winsome Stars 14, 15, 210
*With Privileges* 31, 197
Withey, Chester 204
*A Woman of Mystery* see *False Ambition*
*A Woman's Awakening* (1917) 10, 204
*A Woman's Faith* (1925) 23, 218
Wood, Mrs. Henry 23
*The World and His Wife* (1920) **16**, 146, 210, **211**
Worsley, Wallace 14, 210
Wray, John Griffith 219
Writer's Club 30
Wurtzel, Sol M. **11**

Young, Governor Clement Calhoun 112

Ziegfeld, Florenz 223
*Zit's Weekly* 84
Zittel, C.F. "Zit" 84, 85

www.ingramcontent.com/pod-product-compliance
Ingram Content Group UK Ltd.
Pitfield, Milton Keynes, MK11 3LW, UK
UKHW041938140426
5217IPUK00014B/544